"This is a serious, well-thought-through and thoroughly documented book. Tian Dayton is a clinician with a broad view, and the book reflects this great sweep in which she is able to place a number of approaches in the context of healing."

—Zerka T. Moreno, T.E.P.
cocreator of the field of psychodrama

"In *Trauma and Addiction: Ending the Cycle of Pain Through Emotional Literacy,* Tian Dayton does a masterful job of weaving solid scientific findings with her professional and personal experience into a thoughtful analysis of traumatic experience, secrecy and addictive behaviors. Her book should be read by anyone who suffers from an abusive past or is seeking a way to deal with ongoing trauma or substance abuse. Dayton is a superb writer who understands the intricacies of emotional turmoil and the roads to healing."

—James W. Pennebaker, Ph.D.
professor of psychology, The University of Texas at Austin
author of *Opening Up: The Healing Power of Confiding in Others*

"With great skill, insight and compassion, Tian Dayton's new book builds a much-needed bridge connecting addictions to trauma theory. It is a major contribution to addictions, mental-health and psychodrama literature. All helping professionals, especially psychotherapists and addictions counselors, will find new ways of thinking and practical approaches valuable to their work. Tian Dayton is an experienced therapist who has written an immensely readable and compassionate book, whether the reader is a consumer, practitioner or student."

—Jane Middelton-Moz
licensed psychologist and author of *Children of Trauma*

TRAUMA AND ADDICTION

ENDING THE CYCLE OF PAIN THROUGH EMOTIONAL LITERACY

Tian Dayton, Ph.D.

Health Communications, Inc.
Deerfield Beach, Florida

www.hci-online.com

Library of Congress Cataloging-in-Publication Data

Dayton, Tian, date.
    Trauma and addiction : ending the cycle of pain through emotional
literacy / Tian Dayton.
        p.   cm.
    Includes bibliographical references and index.
    ISBN 1-55874-751-6 (trade paper)
    1. Psychic trauma. 2. Self-destructive behavior. 3. Substance
abuse. I. Title.

RC552.T7 D39 2000
616.86—dc 21

                                                        00-023354

Publisher: Health Communications, Inc.
                3201 S.W. 15th Street
                Deerfield Beach, FL 33442-8190

Book cover design by Lisa Camp
Inside book design by Dawn Grove

To Mom
with love and gratitude for
"keeping the show on the road."
To Brandt, Alex and Marina for healing my heart.
And to my beloved father
sober somewhere in heaven.

If *you don't heal the wounds of your*
childhood, you bleed into the future.

Oprah Winfrey

Contents

List of Figures xi
Acknowledgments . . . . ,. . xiii
Introduction xv

1. The Connection Between Trauma
   and Addiction 1

2. Emotions and Emotional Literacy 25

3. How Trauma and Addiction Undermine
   Healthy Styles of Relating in Families and
   Intimate Relationships 57

4. Trauma in the Body and in the Brain:
   The Body-Mind Connection 97

5. Personality Characteristics of Adult
   Children of Trauma and Addiction:
   What Happened to Me? 123

6. Why Am I Stuck in This Loop? 159

7. Why Isn't My Life Working the Way I
   Want It To? 175

8. Letter Writing as a Healing Tool: John's Story . . .193

9. Two Different Worlds:
   The Social Atom as a Healing Tool 207

10. Journaling as a Healing Tool 221

11. Photographs as a Healing Tool: Eva's Story 249

12. Psychodrama as a Healing Tool 263

13. The Character Component—Intangible Aspects
    of Recovery: Resilience, Mental Set
    and Integration 287

14. Treatment 311

15. An Ounce of Prevention:
    A Case for Emotional Literacy 331

Appendix 341
Glossary of Psychodramatic Terms 373
Bibliography 379
Index 389

List of Figures

Response of Heart Rate
to Talk of Significant Life Experiences 16

The Wheel of Trauma and Addiction 19

Trauma Self-Test 157–158

Black Hole Feedback Loop 162

Atom I: Before Trauma 211

Atom II: After Trauma Sudden Death 212

Atom III: How I'd Like It 213

Sample Atoms 215–219

Food History Form 281–286

Sample Genograms 358, 362

Sample Time Lines 365, 366

Trauma Resolution Model for the
Creative Arts Therapies 371

Acknowledgments ──────────

All books are a journey, on which you travel with many people. In the introduction and throughout the book, I acknowledge the research and theory of those who impact these pages: Bessel Van der Kolk, James Pennebaker, Candice Pert, Judith Herman, Henry Krystal, Jean Baker-Miller, Jonathan Bowlby and many others. Their brilliant and inspiring work has opened the doors for continued exploration on the subjects contained in these chapters, and without them this book would not be.

The other group of people to whom I wish to bow in reverence are my clients, trainees and students. They are my constant inspiration—no therapist who is not in awe of the human mind and spirit could remain in this line of work. I am constantly moved through being with them as they open their hearts and share the deepest parts of themselves with each other, me and now you, the reader. This book is a community of voices. As we say in program, "Even though you don't know all of us, you will come to love us in a very special way; the same way we already love you." To you, the reader, and to those who have shared their stories, these words describe the very special bond that develops among those who walk the path of healing together.

A manuscript is a little bit like a snowball tumbling down a hill: It gets larger as it travels and many hands touch it. Matthew Diener and Lisa Drucker at Health Communications, Inc., are people in the publishing world who feel genuinely committed to producing books that help people in real ways. They wrapped their minds around this subject matter and skillfully guided this material through the inevitable bumps and narrow passages along the way. Thank you also to Susan Tobias at Health Communications, Inc., for painstakingly attending to the details and tying up the loose ends that are part of developing a manuscript.

Next, I want to thank Kathleen Fox, who was willing to sink her talented teeth into this manuscript along with her intelligent eye at a very crucial point. Working with her was a complete joy and a pleasure. A special thank you to Phoebe Atkinson for assisting me in research with intelligence, sensitivity and constant supportive interest. And last, thanks to Trish Roccuzzo, who painstakingly prepared this manuscript for publication with ever-pleasant precision and energy.

Introduction ────────────────────────

This is a book about people. About *relationships*. About self-medicating—with drugs, alcohol, food, sex, gambling or any excessive behavior—the emotional pain that is the result of trauma. It is also about the subsequent trauma created by addictions to these substances. This is a book about *relationship trauma*, about the internal earthquake or loss of solid psychological and emotional ground that happens when people you love and need in order to feel secure in the world are lost in their own addictions, psychological illnesses or addictive behaviors, when the relationships you depend upon for survival are ruptured.

The Chinese say that "The deepest pain has no words." I observe that, often, trauma has no words and does not evidence itself as we might imagine. The face of trauma might be a small boy staring intently at the floor without movement, trying to be still enough to ward off danger. Or the middle-aged man exploding into road rage at being cut off. It is the college girl who, in a low drone, finds fault with her roommates at every turn—deadening spontaneity, creating subtle distance in relationships. It is unmetabolized pain that sits within the self, leaking out in all the wrong places. It is not necessarily the woman biting her nails and seeming like an anxious mess. In fact, "The 'agitation' in anxiety serves an expressive function"; it is when we feel that the situation is hopeless that "a placid, tense, immobile, catatonic, inhibited reaction develops" (Krystal 1998). Two basic types of trauma are *situational*, resulting from circumstances such as war, death, natural disasters or family breakups; and *cumulative*, which can result from an accumulation of experiences such as abuse (emotional, physical or sexual), or persistent school or family problems. All too often, when we are traumatized (by either type of trauma), we become the proverbial "deer in the headlights," frozen and immobilized.

Giving words to trauma begins to heal it. Hiding it or pretending it isn't there creates a cauldron of pain that eventually boils over. That's where addiction comes in: In the absence of sharing and receiving support, pain feels overwhelming. The person in pain reaches not toward people, whom he or she has learned to distrust, but toward a substance that he or she has learned can be counted on to kill the pain, to numb the hurt. Such actions are attempts to self-medicate, to manage emotional pain, but the relief is temporary and had at a huge price. Addicts may initially feel they have found a solution, but the solution becomes a primary problem: addiction. The longer traumatized people rely on external substances to regulate their internal worlds, the weaker those inner worlds become and, consequently, the fewer their available personal resources. Addicts become out of practice for living. Emotional muscles atrophy from lack of healthy exercise. Personality development is truncated or goes off track. Thinking becomes increasingly distorted and secretive as addicts strive daily to justify to themselves and others a clandestine life. Authentic, honest connection slowly erodes as relationships turn from sources of support to targets of deception and means of enabling. Thus, more trauma accumulates on top of the original pain. The supposed solution becomes the source of new problems, followed by a now ever-expanding reservoir of pain that begs for more medication to assuage it.

Trauma and addiction go hand-in-hand. The traumatized person who experiences deep and intolerable emotional and psychological pain or suffers from such states of physiological arousal as rapid breathing, racing heart or anxiety, may discover the dangerous lesson that a little bit of alcohol, some heroin, cocaine, a joint, sugar or sex brings quick and reliable relief. Initially, pain goes away and a sense of equilibrium is restored. "Ahh, that's better, I feel okay again." Eventually, however, the brain and body become addicted, and larger and larger amounts of the addictive substance are needed to produce the same effect. Then feeling great is no longer possible, because the body and mind have been damaged by years of addiction, and the addict has to use just to feel normal. What starts out as an attempt to manage pain evolves into a new source of it.

The person in an intimate relationship with an addict also becomes traumatized. Life is a constant struggle. Will the addict be drunk or sober, cruel or effusively affectionate? For children, life with an addict is an endless game of trying to adjust to ever-changing circumstances and rules. Such family members live in two different worlds—the sober one and the using one—and the worlds pull in different directions. Children's development wraps itself around both like a vine climbing up a tree that has been split by lightning. There is significant undermining of "emotional literacy," or the ability to *put feelings into meaningful words*, that occurs as a result of trauma. When we are traumatized, we lose contact with our real and authentic emotions. They become covered by psychological defenses and emotional armoring. When we cannot access our true emotions, we cannot put them into words and create meaningful scenarios out of the events in our lives. We become, instead, emotionally illiterate, unable to describe our inner world to ourselves or another person.

SURVIVAL BONDS

Nature has designed it so that in order to survive, we need to have close, bonded relationships with our primary caregivers. I call these survival bonds. Nature rewards these close bonds, which contain the secret of the survival of the species. When mother and infant are in close, intimate contact, the brain of each releases spurts of beta endorphins, similar to morphine, which is known as a "reward chemical." This forms an invisible "chemical glue" that is part of the survival bond. When these bonds are threatened, the results can be terror or rage. In the animal kingdom, mothers may engage in selfless acts of heroism if their young are threatened, attracting danger to themselves in order to preserve the lives that nature assigned them to protect.

Emotions are a vital part of the survival bond and travel through us in the form of pleasure chemicals which, when released, produce feelings of closeness and equilibrium inside of us. Nature has encoded this physiological and emotional survival bond into all higher species. Parents are designed to protect these bonds, to sustain life and to train, through their own behavior, future generations of parents. When these bonds are ruptured, it feels as if our inner and outer worlds are falling apart. We feel as if our very survival is threatened because that is the way nature meant it to feel. *This is why a rupture in a relationship bond is traumatic.* Ruptures in early parent/child bonds are some of the most traumatic because our dependency and risk for survival are at their highest in infancy and childhood. Bonds with partners are also traumatic when ruptured because we are encoded to respond powerfully to them; the mating game is a survival game. If someone has experienced a rupture in a "survival bond," subsequent bonds may be harder to form and subsequent ruptures may be more devastating because they return us to the pain of the original one.

Our need for closeness rivals even our need for food. Witness the famous monkey studies of the 1960s. In an attempt to further understand the need of an infant for its mother, researchers at the University of Wisconsin set up two "wire monkey mothers." These were pieces of wire shaped into the form of a monkey to act as a substitute for a real primate mother. One wire mother had food strapped to her in the form of a bottle, the other had soft padding covered with cloth. The infant monkey chose to spend more than seventeen hours per day with the cloth mother and less than one hour with the wire mother who had the food. A sense of closeness and comfort was more consuming than physical nourishment to the infant primate. *We need intimacy in our primary relationships more regularly than we need food.* Researchers who observe primate groups find that over 90 percent of their time is spent in social interaction. This interaction may take the form of grooming, reassurance, discipline, play or comfort. Again, we see that nature has a purpose behind seemingly random activity. Intimate and playful interaction releases opiates that act as "brain fertilizers." Without these molecules, brain cells cannot connect effectively. These "chemicals of emotion" contribute to pleasurable bonds that, when ruptured, can leave us desolate.

When survival bonds are ruptured either by single traumatic events such as abandonment or death or chronic experiences such as prolonged abuse or neglect, people are at risk for developing post-traumatic stress disorder (PTSD), which can interfere with a person's ability to form healthy relationships and live a comfortable life.

People who have experienced the rupture of survival bonds and the resulting lack of naturally stimulated reward chemicals often use other ways of activating pleasure centers in the brain. Exercise produces endorphins—this can be a good thing. High-risk behaviors do, too—this is not such a good thing. And heroin literally floods the brain with dopamine, creating a state of ecstasy that "cannot be described—better than the best sex." It also creates a life-threatening addiction and destroys a person's health, life and relationships. In addition, when addicts finally sober up, they may have used up significant supplies of dopamine for a few great highs, and they are forced to face life without sufficient natural tranquilizers. This is a bad thing. The cycle of trauma and addiction is endless. Emotional and psychological pain lead to self-medicating substances and behavior, which lead to more emotional and psychological pain, which lead to more self-medicating, and so on.

Research on infant/mother relationships reveals that each tiny interaction between the child and primary caretaker becomes a part of the hardwiring of the child's brain (Schore 1994). Lessons on love are communicated through the tactile and auditory world of mother and infant. Is a plaintive cry met with soothing touch or rejection? Is the gnawing feeling of hunger fed with a tender breast and enveloping embrace, a propped bottle, or denied altogether? Is the child fed on demand when hunger calls or on schedule when the clock strikes the hour? Is the child being taught to self-regulate or to be regulated by another?

Self-regulation is one of the earliest tasks of childhood. Self-soothing is one of the primary tasks of development that needs to be mastered (Greenspan 1999). Addicts are characterized in part by poor impulse control, or a lack of ability to self-regulate. Surely one of the things an overeater or a drinker or a drug addict is attempting to do is to self-soothe, to bring calm to an anxious inner world. Those with unresolved childhood trauma are considerably more likely to develop PTSD symptoms in adulthood, which can and often do lead to addiction.

We might imagine, then, that the ability of the child to self-regulate and self-soothe—as learned from the mother or primary care-giver—is part of what allows for a sensory integration that acts as a buffer to the harsh realities of the world. It may follow that an inability to self-regulate and self-soothe opens the door to the need for soothing substitutes.

For the past decade-and-a-half, I have been researching the relationship between trauma and addiction, and how psychodrama, sociometry and group psychotherapy can be used in their treatment. Since trauma responses are stored in the body, a method of therapy that engages the body through role-play proves to be extremely effective in accessing the full complement of trauma-related memories. For this reason, it has become the therapy of choice for survivors of trauma and addiction.

Psychodrama works not only with emotions and cognition, "the feeler" and "the thinker," but with the body as well. Somatic roles such as "the mover," "the eater" and "the sensual being" enter the therapeutic space as well, so that they can be healed and integrated on a sensory level. Through psychodrama, clients who do not know what comfort feels like or how to take it into their self-system can have that experience simulated for them in a therapeutic environment. This experience enters their *soma*, where it can be imprinted as a building block for other similar experiences.

In this book, I use a combination of case studies from my own clients and psychodrama trainees, as well as excerpts, with their permission, from my New York University psychodrama students' journals and papers. Into explanations of my own use of psychodrama and experiential techniques, such as journaling and working with photographs to treat PTSD and addiction, I have woven the trauma theories of Bessel Van der Kolk, Judith Herman, Jonathan Bowlby, Henry Krystal and others. PTSD is the cluster of symptoms first identified in soldiers returning from war. It is now recognized that those same symptoms appear in those who have grown up in addicted homes or in homes where emotional, psychological or physical abuse are prevalent. A dual diagnosis of PTSD and addiction is common for adult children from such homes. Recent trauma research is providing for more effective treatment of these clients, as well as uniting the addiction field and the broader mental health field by opening up a common ground between them.

In my own practice, I witness this approach working most effectively in resolving issues of PTSD, reducing relapse and allowing addicts, adult children of alcoholics (ACOAs) and spouses an arena in which to confront their issues and work through them toward successful healing. The combination of trauma theory and psychodramatic method is ideal. In this day of managed care, it offers cost-effective, group-oriented therapeutic alternatives that are effective.

This is the approach we use at the Caron Foundation/ Chit Chat Farms, where I work as Director of Program Development and Staff Training. Staff at Caron have accumulated decades of clinical research regarding the efficacy of this and other approaches in treating addiction, relapse and the debilitating life complications of children and spouses of addicts, and are devoted to restoring persons and families negatively affected by addiction to satisfying lives. We have found addiction and trauma-related symptoms to be highly treatable. Since positive treatment outcomes with addicts, ACOAs and dependents of addicts are more frequent than negative ones, all of us feel optimistic about the long-range implications of our successes.

This book is designed to be accessible to all readers and

useful to therapists. The end-of-book glossary provides definitions of terms readers may wish to check, and the appendix specifically outlines uses of psychodrama in the treatment of trauma and addiction. I present psychological stories that will draw you toward them and allow you to identify with them, and then I decode their meaning with theoretical narrative. It is my hope that by this book's end you will have taken a journey of your own. Like all journeys, it will be exciting and scary, mysterious and illuminating, joyous and painful. At the close you may feel what I do—great hope and optimism.

It is so often through pain that we crack through our own reserve and defense system into what is real and authentic about us. Nothing is better, no reward greater than our true connection with ourselves, and through that we can reach out and really touch another. Working through trauma pulls us from the surface of life into the wellspring from which we learn who we really are. It is this holy and good work that purifies our spirits and deepens our souls. It is in this way that we spin straw into gold and turn our wounds into wisdom.

ONE

The Connection Between Trauma and Addiction

*Bacchus hath drowned more men
than Neptune.*

Thomas Fuller, M.D.
Gromologia, 1932

*O God! that men should put an enemy
in their mouths to steal away their brains;
that we should, with joy,
pleasance, revel, and applause,
transform ourselves into beasts.*

William Shakespeare
Othello, II, iii, 293

THE ORIGINS OF TRAUMA

*He that conceals his grief
finds no remedy for it.*

Turkish Proverb

Trauma, by its very nature, renders us emotionally illiterate. Life events that we experience as traumatic can feel senseless, out of the norm, hard to pin down, elusive and strange, so we don't integrate them into our normal context of living. The brain, like any good computer, categorizes information by type. Traumas such as the school shootings in Littleton, Colorado, or a devastating hurricane or being raped are not part of our daily routines; consequently, we don't have well-developed mental categories for organizing our impressions of them. They seem unreal, out of the ordinary. They need to be talked through in order for us to make sense of them. Talking about trauma, going over what happened, helps us to understand and integrate events and our reactions

3

to them. If we do not process trauma, ongoing life complications such as depression, anxiety, sleep disturbances, anger, feelings of betrayal, and trouble trusting and connecting in relationships can persist for years after the traumatic experience occurred. Such are the symptoms that, when unresolved, lead people to seek pleasure or self-medicate with alcohol, drugs, food, sex, spending and other addictions.

Because of the unpredictable, uncontrollable and inherently traumatic nature of substance abuse and addiction, people who are chemically dependent, or those in an addict's family system such as spouses, children and siblings, usually experience some form of psychological damage. Family members as well as many addicts present disorders that extend across a range of clinical syndromes, such as anxiety disorders, reactive and endogenous depression, psychosomatic symptoms, psychotic episodes, eating disorders and substance abuse, as well as developmental deficits, distortions in self-image, confused inner worlds with disorganized internal dynamics, and codependence.

Chronic tension, confusion and unpredictable behavior, as well as physical and sexual abuse, are typical of addictive environments and create trauma symptoms. Individuals in addictive systems behave in ways consistent with the behaviors of victims of other psychological traumas. For example, trauma victims often develop "learned helplessness"—a condition in which they lose the capacity to appreciate the connection between their actions and their ability to influence their lives (Seligman 1975) as do individuals in addictive systems.

"Persons are traumatized when they face uncontrollable life events and are helpless to affect the outcome of those events" (Lindemann 1944). Living with a person suffering from addiction or other forms of mental illness can be traumatic. After repeated failures and disappointments while trying to gain some semblance of control, feelings of fear, frustration, shame, inadequacy, guilt, resentment, self-pity and anger mount, as do rigid defense systems. A person who is abused or traumatized may develop dysfunctional defensive strategies or behaviors designed to ward off emotional and psychological pain. These might include self-medicating with chemicals (drugs or alcohol), as well as behavioral addictions that affect their brain chemistry (bingeing, purging or withholding food), or engaging in high-risk or high-intensity activities such as excessive work behaviors, risky sex or gambling). These behaviors affect the pleasure centers of the brain, enhancing "feel-good" chemicals, thus minimizing pain. This means of handling trauma can lead to the disease of addiction.

Scientific research, mainly in neurobiology, has produced significant studies of PTSD. The findings through brain imaging demonstrate that trauma can affect the body and brain much more than had previously been understood (Van der Kolk et al. 1996). Traumatic memories are stored not only in the mind but throughout the body as what scientists call cellular memory. Psychodrama, because it is a role-playing method that includes the use of normal movement, provides a natural and immediate access to those memories. Long before the scientific research had yielded these conclusions, J. L. Moreno was developing his psychodramatic method, one of the earliest methods of body psychotherapy. Moreno taught that "the body remembers what the mind forgets" (Moreno 1964).

Based on observations of role-play, Moreno saw the importance of involving the body in remembering. He hypothesized two types of memory: content (mind) and action (body). Content memory is stored as thoughts, recollections, feelings and facts. Action memory is stored in the brain but also in the musculature as tension, holding, tingling, warmth, incipient movement and the like. The best route to recapturing action memory, according to Zerka Moreno, his wife and cocreator of the field of psychodrama, is through expressive methods that use the whole person (mind and body) in action and in space; that is, our lives occur in a context, *in situ*. When we act out rather than talk out situations from our lives, the recollection of memories occurs more completely. The action itself stimulates memory, much in the same way an old song or a familiar smell is followed by a flood of associations.

"People have been aware of a close association between trauma and somatization since the dawn of contemporary psychiatry" (Van der Kolk et al. 1996). The link between mind and body (psyche and soma) is again supported by the current research of neuroscientist Candace Pert (Pert et al. 1998): "Intelligence is located not only in the brain, but in cells that are distributed throughout the body. . . . The memory of the trauma is stored by changes at the level of the neuropeptide receptor. . . . This is taking place bodywide."

THE HIGH PRICE
OF SUBSTANCE ABUSE

At any given time, 10 percent of the drinkers in the United States will become alcoholics, those addicted to the drug of alcohol (Johnson Institute 1986). It is estimated that seven out of ten people in the United States are in some way affected by addiction. Children of alcoholic parents are conservatively estimated at twenty-two million people (Deutsch 1982). The significant characteristics of the diseases of alcoholism or chemical addiction are that it is primary (one of the most serious types of disorders a person can have), progressive (it gets worse over time), chronic (it doesn't go away by itself) and fatal (it leads to death). The Johnson Institute describes four stages from alcohol and drug use to alcohol and drug dependence:

1. The *Initial* drug experience (presymptomatic phase) may be experimental, socially motivated and provide relief from tension. A person learns that using the substance can change a mood and through experience develops a relationship with the substance.
2. The *Onset* phase comes when the drug use switches from recreational to medicinal with a beginning preoccupation with a drug of choice. The individual seeks a mood shift. This stage may be accompanied by "blackouts," or periods of time where the addict has no memory of what he or she said or did.
3. The next phase, *Harmful Dependence*, is characterized by excessive use and loss of control when engaged in the use of drugs or alcohol. It is accompanied by a progressive deterioration of self-image, acute phases of

self-destructive behavior, and distorted emotional and psychological attitudes.

4. In the *Chronic* phase that follows, a person needs to use just to feel normal. Because the illness is progressive, this phase often results in death.

Addictions have been subject to multiple understandings over the last hundred years, moving from being seen as a moral failure to being diagnosed as a disease to pharmacologically mediated brain dysfunctions (Gray 1999). The National Institute on Drug Abuse recently cited between fifty and seventy risk factors for drug abuse that are found in the addict's community, that is, within the individual's peer cluster, within the individual's family and within the individual. The largest risk factor for drug abuse is an untreated childhood mental disorder (Gray 1999) (including PTSD). Two other major reasons people take drugs are to awaken a "feel good" sensation (sensation-seeking) or to feel better (self-medication) (Leshner 1998).

Years of brain studies on addiction by the National Institute on Drug Abuse suggest a common and worrisome biological thread to all addictions: Drug use changes the brain. "Most recently the action of all drugs of abuse has been traced to the action of dopaminergic neurons in the mid-brain" (Gray 1999). Recent knowledge that many areas of the brain other than the base are affected by drug use has caused researchers to explore those other areas and has also inspired new behavioral studies to determine why those areas of the brain might be triggered (Schultz et al. 1997).

In addition to the interpersonal and intrapersonal costs of addiction, addicts also place a high financial burden on society. As of 1995, the cost of substance abuse to society was about $276 billion, and the cost of drug abuse and addiction itself was about $110 billion (Leshner 1998). These costs include lost productivity, crime leading to incarceration, and mental illness. Actually, it is cheaper to treat addiction than to let it go.

The cost to public support systems, productivity in the workplace, and family cohesion from addiction is such that it tears at the infrastructure of society itself. It is one of the most serious health problems in America today.

THE ROVING "ISMs"

All too often, one addiction leads to another; that is, when an addict sobers up from alcohol and/or drugs he or she picks up another medicator such as food, nicotine, sex or gambling. When the anesthetizing effect of drugs or alcohol is removed, we are left in raw pain. Food, sex, spending, cigarettes or combinations of these become addiction number two. In my office recently, I saw a young woman who very successfully sobered up several years ago. Today, she weighs over two hundred pounds. Her weight fluctuates according to her emotional state. She is the one at the office who everyone relies on. The one who takes on extra work, gets it done without complaining and feeds her frustration with her favorite comfort foods. Though she is well paid, she is generally unable to pay her bills on time and she juggles a complicated schedule of late payments. I suspected after a few visits that she was hiding a painful secret. Sure enough, over time, she revealed that a close uncle had sexually abused her for a period of several years. She was lovely as a teenager, it attracted his attention and ever since she has been medicating, with one thing or another, her profound loss of personal safety and the terror that created. Her boundaries were violated, she couldn't say "no" then and now she cannot say "no" to herself: She cannot tolerate her own neediness, intrusive thoughts and body sensations without somehow getting rid of them. First alcohol, then drugs, then when those were removed, food and spending. The roving "isms." The pain remains the same but the medicator changes.

THE COST OF SILENCE

We have a human need to confess and to share our feelings. There are examples throughout cultures of the various types of confession—ranging from dream sharing in African tribes to confession rituals in North and South American tribal cultures, as well as confession in the church and a sharing of stories in support groups in our culture.

According to James Pennebaker, author of *Opening Up* and researcher on the physical effects of withholding versus expression of emotion, inhibition has three serious effects on us physically. Inhibition is physical work: When people actively inhibit their thoughts, feelings and behavior, they have to exert significant effort to restrain and hold back feeling. In the case of emotional inhibition, the work is constant. Inhibition affects short-term biological changes and long-term health. In the short term, inhibiting feelings results in immediate physical changes such as increased perspiration, which can be measured through methods such as lie detector tests. "Over time, the work of inhibition serves as a cumulative stressor on the body, increasing the probability of illness and other stress-related physical and psychological problems. Active inhibition can be viewed as one of many general stressors that affect the mind and body. Obviously, the harder one must work at inhibiting, the greater the stress on the body" (Pennebaker 1990).

Inhibition Influences Thinking Abilities

When we inhibit parts of our thinking and feeling, we are not able to think through significant events in our lives. Hence, we are prevented from understanding and then integrating that understanding into the larger context of our life pattern. "By not talking about an inhibited event, for example, we usually do not translate the event into language. This prevents us from understanding and assimilating the event. Consequently, significant experiences that are inhibited are likely to surface in the forms of ruminations, dreams and associated thought disturbances" (Pennebaker 1990).

Pennebaker has also found that, "Confrontation reduces the effects of inhibition," reversing the detrimental physiological problems that result from inhibition. When we make a lifestyle of openly confronting painful feelings and we "resolve the trauma, there will be a lowering of the overall stress on the body." Confrontation "forces a rethinking of events. Confronting a trauma helps people understand and, ultimately, assimilate the event. By talking or writing about previously inhibited experiences, people translate the event into language. Once it is language-based, they can better understand the experience and ultimately put it behind them" (Pennebaker 1990). This is a crucial part of developing the emotional literacy necessary for recovery.

The Long-Term Effect of Childhood Trauma

Pennebaker's research was done with a research team that examined the progress of people who lost spouses by suicide or suddenly through accidental death—that is, recent traumas—as well as childhood trauma such as sexual abuse that occurred early in life. He found that childhood traumas affect overall health more than traumas that occurred within the last three years, because of the cumulative stress on the body through long-term inhibition of feelings. When traumas are not resolved, they are not converted into language, thought about and integrated into our overall pattern of thinking, feeling and behaving.

The obvious result of this, as I have observed over years of clinical experience, is that clients arrive at therapy, say in their mid-thirties, feeling as if their lives are puzzles with significant pieces missing. They may have trouble settling on a life's direction. They may be experiencing problems in intimate relationships, or the thought of a long-term committed relationship overwhelms them.

Intimate relationships trigger unresolved pain from the past. Early childhood traumas such as sexual abuse, physical abuse, divorce—or seemingly lesser traumas such as being ignored or misunderstood by those whom we most wish to understand us and are dependent upon for our sense of healthy connectedness—lie dormant within us if our coping style has been inhibition rather than confrontation and disclosure. Then the pain gets triggered without the understanding and self-awareness that we would have, had we gradually and over time resolved our feelings related to the trauma. The result of this is often a projection of early pain into the current relationship. That is, we see the trigger event or our current intimacy as the problem in and of itself. All too often it follows that our idea of the solution or way out of the pain is to dump or exit the relationship.

The deep excavating work of therapy is to make conscious these early wounds and convert them into words so that they can be felt and understood—to use the skills of emotional literacy. Only then can we place them in their proper perspective, give them a context (where, when and how), and integrate them back into ourselves with understanding as to what happened and what meaning we made out of it that we currently live by.

Construction of Personal Meaning

In addition to inhibition of emotional expression, we need to understand a broader range of the effects of trauma. The meaning that we make out of traumatic childhood events is affected by several factors. What was our developmental stage at the time of the trauma? Was it a one-time event or a cumulative trauma that occurred over time? What were our sources of support at the time that the trauma occurred? What meaning did we make out of the trauma that got incorporated into our core belief system and affected the way we learned to see ourselves, relationships and the world in which we live?

Kathryn's situation is a compelling illustration of this. One of a set of identical twins, Kathryn and her sister

Karen were sexually abused by a caretaker over a period of five years between the ages of four and nine. Though the abuse was basically the same, their reaction to it was completely different. Kathryn felt actively loathed by her mother and had no recollection of ever being hugged or even talked to by her father. In her mind this meant that she was bad, not a good child. Her profound confusion over being abused by the caretaker, who with his wife gave her more attention than her own parents, caused her to fall completely silent. She fused the experience of care and attention with pain and abuse. She never complained, never acted out, and always saw herself as responsible for the pain she was in. She was, in her mind, not worth paying attention to, and she had no place to go to break her silence and reach out for support. As she saw it, she had no alternative but to bear up to the inner chaos of betrayal, terror and abandonment that arose out of the horror of the repeated incest and the loss of comfortable connection from parents and caretakers. Now, as an adult, she experiences herself as "an outline, a cardboard cutout, the vision of a person with no one inside." Because she had foreclosed on her inner world and inhibited any expression of what was most primary in her life, she "went away."

Karen, by contrast, complained, yelled, kicked and rebelled. Although the abuse did not change for either of them, Kathryn split off into fragments inside of herself and became a multiple personality who self-medicated with drugs and alcohol while her twin went on to an integrated life. In fact, Karen has a much clearer recollection of the episodes of abuse than Kathryn does. The simple act of confronting, however primitive and childlike the expression of feeling, allowed one twin to stay within the context of her own life and continue to develop while the other disappeared into the silence of her tormented inner world. Karen's escape from living, forever locked in unresolved childhood pain, was the *expression* rather than the *inhibition* of feeling.

Kathryn's work today is to learn to feel, and the hardest place she has to feel is that place where she shut feeling down in her childhood. Generally, she has no sympathy for herself as a child. Rather, she calls that part of herself "dumb one" or "dead one" and sees herself as stupid and ineffectual. "Both post-traumatic stress disorders and multiple personalities appear to be problems related to the separation of traumatic emotional experience from language" (Pennebaker 1990), which results in emotional illiteracy. One of Kathryn's breakthroughs was when she began to cry; a second was when she became able to complain in the present. Once, when she felt I was paying too much attention to another group member and ignoring her, she told me how mad she was for several days after that. "I was so jealous, I wasn't sure I'd come back to the group. I just hated seeing Amanda get what I wanted but couldn't ask for." The connection with her inhibited ability to reach out in childhood was only too clear, and this anger and jealousy, along with converting those feelings into words and sharing them, represented a great deal of healing.

Pennebaker has fascinating charts that he generates by connecting clients to a device which measures physical changes as they talk about significant events in their lives. These charts tell with crystal clarity the story of how inhibition affects the body. This is the chart of Warren, who was a very bright student and valedictorian of his high school class. "After performing quite well his first year and a half of college, he suddenly developed test anxiety. Midway in his fourth semester of college, he began to fail every test he took. He was soon placed on academic probation and later forced to withdraw from school. Over the next year, Warren saw a therapist who specialized in behavioral treatments. Several weeks of relaxation training and behavioral modification failed to produce significant improvements." A year later, Warren visited Pennebaker and agreed to talk about his life while his heart was measured. Though Warren's words told one story, his body told quite another.

Topic	Heart Rate	Warren's Comments
Girlfriend	77	Some disagreements about sexuality
College courses	71	Most have been interesting . . . tests have been another matter.
Failing exams	76	It's been hard on my ego. I can't explain it.
Parents	84	We were a close family until the divorce.
Parents' divorce	103	It was no big deal.
The future	79	It scares me. I can't bear the thought of failing again.

From *Opening Up* by James W. Pennebaker

Warren was amazed to see the results of this measurement. The source of the trauma was evident but repressed. The body held what the mind disowned. The trauma led to a psychological fear of the future but the source of the fear was related to the trauma of the divorce. Warren began to talk about his feelings about his parents' divorce and to acknowledge both to himself and his parents how deeply upsetting it was to him. Though he still has some of these feelings, his test anxiety completely disappeared.

A VICIOUS CIRCLE

We are biologically set up to meet our needs for dependency and nurturing through our early kinship relationships. When our basic life needs are met inadequately early in life, we can develop an emotional hunger that is never met and is characterized by our seeking to redo the past—to meet our early unmet need with the wrong people at the wrong time and place. When we ask present-day relationships to make up for the failures of past relationships without awareness of how those needs are affecting the relationship, we burden them in a way that impairs healthy functioning.

The basic psychological response to uncontrollable trauma is a two-phase reaction of protest and numbing. "The protest phase may be marked by anger, verbal hostility or acting out. In time the initial reaction is followed by numbing: a state of emotional and interpersonal withdrawal from active participation in one's environment. The major signs of numbing include difficulties solving problems, withdrawal from social activities and isolation" (Flannery 1986).

Important research by Bessel Van der Kolk establishes the connection between trauma and addiction. The research shows that trauma victims attempt to control their internal state of hyperarousal, social withdrawal, emotional pain and anger through the use of substances that quiet their inner struggle and restore a sense of control over their tumultuous inner world. The substance of choice becomes a reliable source of mood management that temporarily masquerades as a restoration of the trauma victim's equilibrium. However, this method of mood management actually has the effect of denying trauma victims access to their own internal worlds. The emotional states and signals that would allow them to comprehend and come to terms with their internal struggle are numbed by this method of self-medication. While trauma victims gain the temporary relief they are seeking, they do so at the expense of self-knowledge and the potential for self-mastery.

To complicate matters further, the addictive process comes to have a life of its own. The withdrawal from authentic emotion and alienation from the self that the drug induces leave trauma victims helpless before their own internal worlds, and the "learned helplessness" (Seligman 1975) of the trauma victim is thereby reinforced. When the self-medicating substance wears off, the person is again overwhelmed by the pain, which now has further isolation, shame and unresolved pain added to it. Hence, the need for a substance to assuage a stormy inner world becomes even more pressing. Thus, the trauma victim enters a vicious circle: *emotional and psychological pain—self-medication with drugs, alcohol, food, sex, etc.—sobering up—reemerging of unresolved pain—more medication,* and so on. If the trauma issues that lie beneath the desire to self-medicate are not resolved, an addict may lay down one addiction only to pick up another. The addictive process takes over and births a life of its own, rendering the trauma victim more and more helpless with each sinister turn of the wheel of addiction.

THE WHEEL OF TRAUMA AND ADDICTION
(DAYTON 1999)

Life complications get deeper, more overwhelming, and harder to solve as drugs and other addictions take over, invading all aspects of one's life.

Emotional and psychological pain, shame, and turbulent inner world related to trauma.

Greater need for larger amounts of drugs, alcohol, food, sex, nicotine or combinations of several of these due to increased physical tolerance of medications and persistent and pervasive emotional and psychological problems.

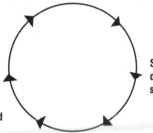

Self-medication through drugs, alcohol, food, sex, etc.

More emotional and psychological pain, shame, and turbulent inner world, and weakened personal resources to deal with them due to drug dependence.

Life complications—trouble with relationships, work, loss of true play and enjoyment as a result of unresolved trauma and drug use pervading and controlling inner world.

Children who have been traumatized will be left with significant deficits in psychological development as well as in the ability to engage in nurturing relationships. They will go through life attempting to fill in these developmental gaps. If there were such a thing as an imaging test that could evaluate the emotional and psychological state of a person, it might evidence gray shadows that portend disease. But there is no such test, and we can only see the extent of damage through symptoms of rupture, abuse or neglect, such as emotional withdrawal, shutdown, hypervigilance, hyperarousal, and loss of trust and faith. People who carry these invisible wounds seek relief. Their locus of identity has not been built slowly within themselves, they have not learned to be self-sustaining, they have not been shown what nurturing feels like and how to bring it into their own self-system. Rather, they seek to meet their unmet needs in what we might call emotionally unintelligent ways. Substances such as food and alcohol and behaviors such as sex provide temporary relief, but the underlying emotional pain from trauma remains unchanged or, even worse, becomes more complicated and intensified because, rather than being processed consciously, it is being self-medicated, which leads to addiction.

According to Bessel Van der Kolk (1996), "A traumatized person does not have access to the left hemisphere of the brain which translates experience into language, therefore, they can't make meaning out of what is happening to them or put it into any context. The right hemisphere evaluates the emotional significance of incoming information and regulates hormonal responses. Traumatized people have been known to have trouble tolerating intense emotions without feeling overwhelmed and thus continue to rely on disassociation [as is the case with Kathryn]. This interferes with their ability to utilize emotions as guides for action. Such individuals go from stimulus to response without being able to figure out what upsets them. They overreact, shut down, or freeze."

This renders people emotionally illiterate. They are not able to fully process experiences and put them into context because they have lost access to the part of themselves that tells them how they feel about what goes on around them. They feel confused and overwhelmed, and when that state gets too uncomfortable, they shut down like an overheated computer, and their emotional circuit breakers flip in order to keep them from blowing up.

THE HIDDEN KEY:
WHY PAIN IS NOT NECESSARILY
AN INDICATOR OF WOUNDEDNESS

One of the confusing things about resolving trauma-related issues is our defensive structure surrounding them. The things that hurt us deeply are those we can be the most out of touch with on an emotional level. Because one of the most common defenses when we are hurt or traumatized is to go numb—or to freeze—we have little or no feeling in those areas of disowned pain. We are anesthetized like when we have Novocain. Therefore, we lose access to the feelings that would serve as indicators of where our wounds are. This, in my opinion, is one of the reasons we reenact them. They are out of consciousness. We remember the dentist's drill, his or her office, the smells and sounds, and maybe the general unpleasantness and anxiety of being there, but not the pain exactly. Somewhere inside of us we hurt but we don't know just where and, more often than not, we bump into that place accidentally. A particular behavior from another person presses on an old wound, triggering a response in us that is clearly an overreaction. This is perhaps the site of the original wound. But this is also where we are numb and out of touch. So, instead of seeing our overreaction for what it is, we project our unfelt pain onto the situation or person triggering it and create so many more problems on top of the original ones that we get lost or highly distracted by them. But they are red herrings keeping us away from the spot that, although we cannot feel it, holds the truth.

DIAGNOSTIC CRITERIA FOR POST-TRAUMATIC STRESS DISORDER

According to the Diagnostic Criteria from the DSM-IV put out by the American Psychiatric Association (Washington, D.C., 1994), a person can develop PTSD if,

The person has been exposed to a traumatic event in which both of the following were present:

(1) the person experienced, witnessed or was confronted with an event or events that involved actual or threatened death or serious injury, or a threat to the physical integrity of self or others;

(2) the person's response involves intense fear, helplessness or horror.

Scenes of rage with yelling and throwing objects, physical violence, sexual abuse, or the breakup of families can make children feel overwhelmed and as if their safety is at risk. These circumstances are traumatic for those involved. The effects can remain with the traumatized person and may be re-experienced in one or more of the following ways:

1. Recurrent and intrusive recollections of the event(s) in a variety of images, thoughts and perceptions;
2. Recurrent, distressing dreams;
3. Acting or feeling as if the traumatic event were recurring (includes a sense of reliving the experience, illusions, hallucinations and dissociative flashback episodes, including those that occur on awakening or when intoxicated);
4. An experience of intense psychological distress when exposed to situations that symbolize or remind the person of the traumatic event (including the intimacy of subsequent relationships);
5. Physiological reactions such as rapid heartbeat, sweating, a generalized sense of anxiety, stomach queasiness, head pounding, etc., when exposed to situations that symbolize or remind the person of the traumatic event.

People who have been traumatized tend to change the way that they live their lives after their trauma. They may adopt three or more of the following:

1. Efforts to avoid thoughts, feelings or conversations associated with the trauma
2. Efforts to avoid activities, places or people that arouse recollections of the trauma
3. Inability to recall an important aspect of the trauma
4. Markedly diminished interest or participation in significant activities
5. A feeling of detachment or estrangement from others
6. Restricted range of affect (i.e., unable to have strong or varied feelings including loving feelings)
7. Sense of a foreshortened future (i.e., does not expect to have a career, marriage, children or a normal life span)

If someone has been traumatized he or she may experience two or more of the following symptoms:

1. Difficulty falling or staying asleep
2. Irritability or outbursts of anger
3. Difficulty concentrating
4. Hypervigilance
5. Exaggerated startle response (DSM-IV)

People who grow up in homes where addiction, chronic physical, sexual or emotional abuse, or neglect are present are frequently traumatized by the experience. They exhibit some of the symptoms we have listed. In their attempt to manage their states of psychological, physiological and emotional arousal, they may use drugs and alcohol to make those symptoms less severe. This type of self-medication can and often does lead to addiction.

Two

Emotions and Emotional Literacy

Every vital development of language
is a development of feeling as well.

T. S. Eliot

EMOTIONS

All emotions are pure which gather you
and lift you up;
that emotion is impure which seizes only one
side of your being and so distorts you.

Rainer Maria Rilke

The Origin and Evolution of Emotions

Emotions, like all things in nature, have a purpose and order of their own. They are part of what has ensured survival of the species; slowly selected over time according to their importance in our human evolution. The brain as a whole has no function; rather, it is a collection of systems called modules, each with different functions. Evolution has acted on these modules over time in order to adapt to pressing human (or animal) needs. Joseph Ledoux, author of *The Emotional Brain*, has come to the conclusion that emotions are mediated by different brain networks. In other words, there is no all-purpose emotional system in the brain; instead, different emotions act within different brain systems. For this reason he has focused his research on the emotion of fear, with the intent of exploring further emotions one at a time as they move through their particular paths.

In *The Expression of the Emotions in Man and Animals*, Darwin stated that, "The chief expressive actions exhibited by man and by the lower animals are not innate or inherited—that is, have been learned by the individuals." Nature has selected for the traits that ensure its own survival. Is love, then, part of what ensures that we will care for our young and each other—the bond of familial love that runs so deep and that carries with it our deepest hopes and our final breath? Is fear what allows us to avoid danger and stay alive? The special adaptive behaviors that are crucial to survival might define which emotions occur over and over again throughout the evolutionary process until they become part of the hardwiring of the brain of humans, animals, fish and so on. Each emotion, says Ledoux, has a different brain system and should be studied separately.

Darwin felt that an important function of emotional development and expression was communication between individuals. Hostile or vicious sounds, snorts or, in animals, hair that stands on end, all signal other individuals to stay away. Cooing sounds, soft strokes and soft movements invite others to come near. Part of the evolution of emotion was to create communication; our survival is interdependent, and emotions grow and adapt in accordance with those evolutionary needs. The mother who smiles at her child's positive behavior encourages more of it, while her frown of disapproval curbs another action from persisting. Emotions that are expressed through changes in facial expression or body posture are easily read and a very important aspect of emotional communication, probably stronger in evolutionary terms than more subtle feelings. Darwin felt that fear and rage were part of the palate of expression of our very early ancestors while grief, suffering and anxiety came closer to human evolution.

Ledoux says that emotional traits traveling through bloodlines can be selected. "For example, identical twins (even those reared in separate homes) are far more similar in fearfulness than fraternal twins. This conclusion applies across many kinds of measurements including tests of shyness, worry, fear of strangers, social introversion/ extroversion, and others. Similarly, anxiety, phobia and obsessive compulsive disorder and addiction tend to run in families and to be more likely to occur in both identical twins than in both fraternal twins."

Ledoux discusses the various thinkers who put forward theories of emotions. These researchers gain their information by studying a wide variety of cultures from around the world, including isolated indigenous tribes less exposed to other cultures' social norms. They propose that these emotions are hardwired into the brain, slowly selected for through centuries of evolution. Experiments by Joseph Ledoux show how the fear response in particular gets set up. Fear-conditioning experiments are basically used to induce a fear response in an animal. A rat might be placed in a small cage where a loud sound and a small shock are simultaneously applied to its feet. After a very few such conditionings, the rat will act afraid when it hears a loud sound because of the "shock" that accompanied it. Even when the shock is no longer used, at the sound alone the rat will freeze, its fur will stand on end, its blood pressure will go up and it will be flooded with stress hormones. It may only take one or two pairings of shock and sound to set up the fear response. Nature has built this response into our biology over centuries of evolution to ensure survival. Nature doesn't necessarily allow for second chances, so learning has to be quick.

"Not only is fear conditioning quick, it is also very long lasting. In fact, there is little forgetting when it comes to conditional fear. The passing of time is not enough to get rid of it" (Ledoux 1996). However, repeated exposure to the *sound without the shock accompanying it* can lead to extinction of the fear response. The fear response will be deconditioned, that is, the rat will no longer fear the loud sound by itself.

People who begin therapy often come to individual sessions or group expecting the kinds of responses they are used to encountering—perhaps criticism, disgust, belittling, lack of interest or being treated as if they don't matter. Slowly, over time, they decondition those responses by being exposed to different behaviors like support and acceptance. This is why therapy takes time. Insight alone does not necessarily produce change. It is the new relationship dynamics, over time, that recondition a person's conditioned responses.

In Ledoux's book, Robert Plutchick proposes eight basic emotions: joy, acceptance, anticipation, anger, disgust, sadness, surprise and fear. Like primary colors, these emotions, when mixed, can produce other emotions, e.g., joy plus acceptance equals friendliness. Ledoux goes on to describe how Paul Ekman introduced the idea of "emblems" and "illustrators." Emblems are a specific movement that could have a verbal meaning attached, such as nodding a head yes or no or shrugging shoulders to signify not knowing. Illustrators fill in gaps of communication where words do not necessarily exist, somewhat like talking with your hands if you're Mediterranean—describing, with gesture, nuance or meaning. These movements help individuals explain something beyond or in addition to words, or fill in where words cannot be found or fall short.

Do I Feel What I Think or Think What I Feel?

One of the greatest myths my clients bring into therapy is that emotional wellness, once attained, is a state that lasts forever. They enter sick and will become well. But think of it this way—we would never expect to go to a hospital with one particular illness, get well and never be sick again. We go to the hospital for a particular ailment—liver disease, gallstones, breast cancer, etc.—in other words, a part of our body gets ill. Entering therapy can be very similar; a part of us is ill—our relationship, unresolved grief or trauma over a past loss, and so on. Though in body as well as mind, if we are ill enough, the whole body or mind may be at risk, most often part of us is ill and part of us remains well.

For centuries, it seems, we have seen emotions as sort of a quagmire of generalized, nonspecific feeling. We talk of emotions, but we do not differentiate in type of emotion, intensity and depth, passing or persistent. We have not subjected emotions to the same rigorous study that we have applied to cognitive functioning. Countless studies are related to cognition, while only a few deal with emotion.

Dr. Kenneth Isaacs, author of *Uses of Emotion*, suggests a new way of looking at emotions. It isn't necessarily our emotions, but our emotions about emotions, that give us problems, says Isaacs. ". . . [C]ognition and affect each appears to include its own underlying system of cataloguing and indexing of experience (memory) with separate lines of associative connections. That makes a dual system of indexing of memory of experience available to pursue content and meaning of early experience analytically. Thus associative process may be pursued through either a cognitive path or an affective (feeling) path."

A feeling can lead us to thoughts or thoughts can lead us to feelings. We remember events in intricate webs of association—our grandmother's kitchen, the smell of biscuits, a red linoleum floor and crisp linen are all woven together to form what feels like one single memory. Feelings operate in much the same way. A feeling of well-being might be laced with a sense of contentment, belonging and love—all separate feelings, but associated to each other in what we experience as one memory. Then the feelings are associated with the cognitive memory. Often the feeling acts as a stimulus for a particular memory. In other words, if we feel sad because we have just had a quarrel with our spouse, the feeling of sadness triggers other seemingly unrelated memories that also have sadness associated with them, and we enter into a sort of despairing state of mind that calls other despair-type memories towards it. Or an upbeat sense of accomplishment tends to stimulate other memories in which we feel upbeat, accomplished and happy, because the feeling of well-being acts as a stimulus for other times when we have experienced the same feeling. This state, too, is self-perpetuating. This is why a therapeutic method such as psychodrama that allows easy access to both a cognitive and feeling path and connects it to the body can be so effective in allowing a full range of expression.

The Canadian neurosurgeon Wilder Pennifield conducted research on patients with epilepsy in the 1950s. When Pennifield stimulated the cerebral cortex, he saw snatches of the mind in action. In response to the electrical stimulation, patients sometimes recalled passages of music, interactions with friends and family, and even entire scenes from their childhood with lavish detail. These were sometimes experienced with "movie-like" clarity. Pennifield wrote:

> M. heard "a mother calling her little boy," when point eleven on the first temporal convolution was stimulated. When it was repeated at once, without warning, she heard the same thing. When it was repeated twice again at the same point, she heard it each time and she recognized that she was near her childhood home. At point twelve nearby . . . stimulation caused her to hear a man's voice and a woman's voice "down along the river somewhere." She saw the river. It was a place, "I was visiting," she said, "when I was a child." Three minutes later when the electrode was held in place at thirteen, she exclaimed that she heard voices late at night and

that she saw the big wagons as they used to haul the animals (of a circus) in (S. Vaughan 1997).

Though we may not be conscious of certain memories, Pennifield's research suggests that they are, nonetheless, stored in our memory system and can be "triggered" or recalled through a reminder or association.

Psychologist Susan Vaughan postulates that the seat of the mind has within it a sort of story synthesizer. This synthesizer carries with it certain themes that get enacted throughout our lives. This would seem to contribute to self-image and self-fulfilling prophesies, depending upon the meaning of the story to us and how we see it relating to ourselves. That is, we make our own particular meaning out of events in our lives and live according to that meaning. In therapy, Vaughan feels we actually alter the story neuronically. That is, through extended deep examination we alter the memory as it sits within the brain. Freud and others have postulated that we form a sort of memory template from which we operate throughout our lives. Through it memories are triggered or coalesced into a particular form. Imagine a stained glass window when light shines through it. The floor onto which the light shines reflects the constellation of colors determined by the design of the stained glass window. The memory template might operate similarly. Our way of seeing a particular situation may manifest in a variety of ways, depending upon the brain templates from which we operate.

This is the conclusion I have come to in my own clinical work. As clients tell pieces of their story and their inner world begins to unravel itself, we witness the narrative of their life through new eyes. New insight replaces old meaning. The memory is now altered. First it became conscious, that is, we recovered the original memory as we saw it at the time it occurred. Now added to that original interpretation of events is our current one. The wisdom of today alters in some measure the impact particular events may have had at a given developmental stage, when they were seen altogether differently. One could not help but alter the inner world as it is brought forward slowly and painstakingly over a long period of time and witnessed all along in the light of today. We are both thinking and feeling beings. That is, we think about what we feel, and we have feelings about what we think. These functions are meant to operate together along with behavior in order to create a whole person who can be guided by both mind and heart into action.

"Being endowed with a marvelous dual mental system gives us great advantage and comprehension of our world—if we use both parts of the system. Attempting to function with only affect [feeling] or only cognition [thinking] is to function as a cripple. With the former, we comprehend feeling without ideational content. With the latter, we comprehend thought content without knowing significance. . . . There is a vast literature of studies of cognitive processing. In comparison, studies of affective processing are fewer, and those that exist include many that appear to be fumbling, cloudy and quite imprecise in what they work with. Many are self-contradictory. This may be a result of our being more accustomed to feeling about what we think than thinking about what we feel" (Isaacs 1998).

According to Isaacs, emotional "storms" are often the result of "impairments placed in the path of access to one's own emotions. Most people make the mistake of trying to 'deal' with their emotions. They mistakenly work at trying to manage them, control them, tolerate, suppress or get them out. Instead, we are better off noticing our emotions and using the information they bring because acting on them is optional" (Ibid.).

I recall when I was studying yoga and meditation in India twenty-five years ago a swami describing emotions as being like a fish swimming through the waters of the mind. He advised that we not overreact to the fish, but rather observe its path through the waters of our mind. Without emotion, we would not know what we feel personally about a given situation. Life would have no color or depth. It is emotion that connects us to the meaning of the material of our own lives. In therapy, as in meditation, we learn to sit with our feeling states, not run from them but observe and witness them. Then we put words to feelings so that we can describe our inner world to ourselves and others. In this way we can use our thinking to decode our feeling and our feeling to inform or color our thinking.

But emotion itself may not be viewed as the whole story. We have a saying in Twelve-Step programs: "Feelings aren't facts." Trauma freezes feeling states so that we experience them as facts, as if they have only one interpretation. For those of us who have grown up in alcoholic homes, our feelings can become so rigid that they seem like facts. We let them run us; we let them define who we are and how we relate to our lives. They have grown like an actor who has exaggerated his role on stage and lost its proper proportion within the context of the story, until all we are watching is the actor and we have lost sight of the play. We are taught by the yogis to seek a balance between mind and emotion. A thought without feeling is passionless, colorless and heartless; and feeling without thought can be rash, ruthless or foolish. The balanced person is one who can bring thought and feeling together in such a way as to give life meaning, purpose and beauty.

There are really very few true emotions, Isaacs argues. He feels we confuse emotions with what he calls *para emotions*, or *affective attitudes* which include expectations, beliefs, aims, etc., but do not function as pure emotion. Healthy states:

> such as love and hate are examples of our emotions that include emotions but, being affective attitudes, also include expectations, beliefs, aims, etc. . . . the word depression is often taken to mean 'a lot of sadness'—that is why people commonly say they feel depressed about . . . when they are 'sad, grieving or mourning about . . .' Getting to the root of feelings of our inner states allows us to work through them. Depression can be a combination of feelings that are more or less in a traffic jam. The individual cars need to move so traffic can flow freely. Perhaps the depression is part anger, part sadness and part fear. Working with each feeling gives us a place to start. 'What are you sad about? What are you angry about? Who are you angry at, yourself or someone else? What are you afraid might happen if . . .' Temper is an example of a para emotion that can be understood as a personality attribute related to (one's) degree of control over actions. . . . Obsequiousness is an example of a characteristic attitudinal stance that is not an emotion but a derivative of emotional

experience. . . . Hostility is a para emotion that
belongs in the category of affective attitude. It
often includes components of anger or other emotions such as disgust and contempt. It has often
been confused with emotion (Isaacs 1998).

The idea is that emotion is as precise an experience as
seeing color. In other words, if we are not color-blind, we
are sure that we are seeing red, yellow, blue or gray, and
if we are not "feeling blind," we can also be sure that we
are feeling sad, fearful, angry, joyful and so on. For many
years cognitive and behavioral sciences have left emotion
out of the picture, as if people who were fully in touch
with all of their emotions would be in some way over the
top or even pathological. But those who are in tune with
their emotions are simply able to read on a feeling level
those emotions that are moving through them as they
operate in the world. Reading emotions is what allows us
to function freely. We are *emotionally literate*, able to
accurately tune in to our internal world and to act
informed by the information we're receiving. It is in
repressing, denying, rerouting and minimizing emotions
that we get into trouble in our daily lives. The urge to
repress and deny comes more from our fear of our emotions than the emotions themselves. Once we lift this
stigma that we feel about feeling, we are able to allow the
emotions to move through us without taking them either
too seriously or not seriously enough.

Talking About Trauma

Part of what makes a situation traumatic is not talking
about it. Talking reduces trauma symptoms. When we don't

talk about trauma, we remain emotionally illiterate. Our most powerful feelings go unnamed and unspoken. We're emotionally confused while wandering around in the darkness of our own internal world. What we care about the most we don't talk about, while underneath we are constantly preoccupied with feelings related to the trauma—feelings that go unnamed and unarticulated. Because of this, they often also go unfelt, but they are there, whirling around our inner world, pulling on us from within.

Emotional literacy is the ability to put feelings into words so that those feelings can be understood within some sort of psychological context. The ability to identify and name an emotional state allows us to find it again when we wish to, much like an address gives us a way to locate a person. It gives us a way to communicate our inner world to someone else and to understand what another person might be saying to us. Trauma shuts down access to our own feeling states in ways described in this book. It therefore undermines emotional literacy, because feeling feelings is essential to eventually naming them. Therapy or psychodrama might be seen as schools in which we learn to become emotionally literate, which is how we build emotional intelligence.

Since memories of trauma can bypass the cortex, or the part of the brain associated with conscious thought, they are stored in other parts of the brain, such as the basal forebrain, which influences arousal, reward and emotional function, or the amygdala, which is associated with long-term emotional memory, reward and the fight-flight-freeze response. This means traumatic experiences don't get thought about. In other words, trauma memories can be stored where we do not have access to them.

Recent research on addiction has begun to focus on these "emotional memories" and the way in which we store our mental records of events, either wonderful or horrible, which aroused intense emotions. Many researchers believe that memories of being drunk or high on drugs are stored as emotional memories, which then contribute to an addict's craving, compulsion and relapse. The way we begin to heal such traumatic emotional memories is by talking about them.

Talking about trauma allows us to name the related feelings, which has the effect of lifting the memories out of a shadowy, semiconscious state into light and air. Because we have a name, we can now categorize: "I am mad" (anger, rage and the like). Then we can identify the extent: "I am very mad/sort of mad/in a white rage/slowly simmering," etc. This way we can begin to modulate our emotions, which is part of mastery. Once we understand our own emotions, we can share or communicate them to someone else. This is the beginning of feeling okay and expressive in the world—we know how to say what's on our minds in appropriate ways. Next, we can listen. Because we felt, named, categorized and understood our own emotions, we have a basis for doing the same for someone else. That is to say, we have reference points within ourselves that we can use to understand others. We can actually hear what they are saying and empathize with them. This is the beginning of intimacy.

In alcoholic families, emotional truths that pervade the family system frequently go unspoken. The effect of this is to suppress feelings, which creates disease in the emotional system in much the same way bacteria causes infection in the body.

People in alcoholic family systems come to doubt their reality and learn to deny the truths in front of them and their responses to those truths. They cannot sort through, categorize, modulate or communicate their inner worlds, because their environment does not allow for the development and practice of those behaviors. People who have been traumatized tend to alternate in their emotional responses between intense fear or rage and numbness, dissociation or shutdown. Consequently, they do not develop the ability to modulate the intensity of their emotions because their internal world moves from numb to red hot without conscious knowledge of why. They cannot talk about what matters most, what presses hardest from within.

The longer talking is avoided, the more threatening the prospect of opening up becomes. The addiction looks for a while like the relief: heroin and the world feels alive; liquor and it looks rosy; cocaine and it comes into focus; food and we numb it out; pot and we transcend it; sex and we release and feel powerful; buy, spend or gamble and we feel relieved, alive or temporarily empowered. But not talking is riskier than the risks inherent in the temporary pain of opening up.

Despite having said this, "there is no intrinsic value in dredging up past trauma if one's current life provides gratification and the present is not invaded by emotional, perceptual or behavioral intrusions from the past" (Van der Kolk et al. 1996). Denial, however, is such a pervasive defense around addiction and its effects that symptoms such as reenactment dynamics (constantly creating life situations that recreate painful emotional dynamics related to the trauma), hypervigilance (scanning the

environment looking for signs of danger), and relationship problems such as poor communication and discom-
fort with intimacy, can get written off as being of less
consequence than they are.

EMOTIONAL LITERACY: CREATING AN EMOTIONAL AND PSYCHOLOGICAL MAP

Most of us have trouble at some point or another finding just the right words to say what we mean. We say too
much or too little. We say part of what we mean and leave
out the other part. We get lost in overexplanations or we
reduce our communication to too few words to get our
point across.

The more emotionally laden the material, the harder it
is to communicate. How do we ask for a raise, say we're
hurt, express anger or describe a subtle inner state?

Emotional literacy is the ability to convert feelings into
words, to decode our inner world through the use of
words. At its core it gives us the ability to "talk out" rather
than "act out" our feelings. For example, "I feel like hitting her" allows the child to express the feelings of helplessness and anger which might lead to a conflict that can
only escalate if he acts out by actually hitting.

Each of us has an emotional experience that is unique
to us. In order for inner harmony to prevail, we need to
understand ourselves. In particular, we need to know
what it is that makes us happy, frustrated, sad or content,
and what motivates us in a way that will have staying

power and allow us to actualize our own unique talents. Trauma and addiction interfere with emotional literacy by blocking access to our internal worlds. Fight, flight, freeze—i.e., raging, dissociating, shutting down and self-medicating—are all designed to numb the effects of our emotional reactions, to block us from feeling our feelings.

In my clinical work I see the process of emotional literacy as spanning significant territory. I have broken it down into four stages that I observe clients move through in translating feeling into words and communication. Sometimes, when there has been trauma, it can take years to identify internal states and bring them into literacy. Other times it happens in a few seconds. Following is an outline of these stages.

The Four Stages of Emotional Literacy: Developing an Internal Map

Stage One: Feel the Fullness of the Emotion

Sitting with and feeling what we're feeling is obviously necessary for any sort of understanding of our inner world to take place. Without it, we live as strangers to our own insides. It is like being color-blind—we see brown as black, we are blind to subtle nuances of color or we misread them altogether. Though sitting with all of our feelings is clearly the obvious and necessary first step of helping ourselves to grow, it is amazing how many of us can't do it. This is where we suddenly find we have a million other things to do in an unconscious attempt to distract ourselves from our inner world. This is where we mindlessly down a bag of Oreos, a pint of Häagen-Dazs or a fifth of Scotch. Trauma undermines this first step when the feelings we are asked to sit with feel overwhelming or frightening. However, if we are willing and able to take this first step, then this is where we derive our "Aha's," our sense of connectedness, our sense of aliveness, excitement and trust in life.

Stage Two: Label It

Next, we need to give our emotional experience a name so that we can order it into the contents of our inner world. Labeling also makes us feel better. Labeling feelings, according to Dr. James Pennebaker, actually elevates the immune system. However, the elevation is only temporary, and something needs to happen to sustain it. In a research study, participants were divided into two groups. The first group watched Nazi war movies, and the second saw films about Mother Teresa. Group One had lowered immune readings after watching, while Group Two had elevated ones. Immune system readings for both groups returned to normal shortly after viewing the films. However, when each group viewed the movies and then was asked to think of them throughout the day, Group One remained low and Group Two remained elevated or high. Thoughts are powerful.

Labeling emotions and sustaining awareness has physical, psychological and emotional benefits. Emotional literacy is a way to sustain an understanding of the connections between feeling states and provide a word map by which to further explore their foundations. The best offense is a good defense. Emotional awareness creates resilience, so that when confusing emotional states arise, they can be decoded and the brain will know where to store them. Calm and equilibrium can be restored through accurate labeling. The brain is, after all, a computer. It creates categories, subcategorizes and cross-checks. Information is filed according to its label, so when we label emotions, we also create categories and deepen our capacity for holding. In addition, we recondition our fear response, because each time we feel a feeling it is less unknown, less threatening. This increases our capacity to feel more deeply, to take on greater feeling risks or challenges, which can lead to an increased sense of aliveness and attunement.

Stage Three: Explore the Meaning and Function Within the Self

Am I saying no when I want to say yes but I am too afraid of rejection to risk saying yes? Am I making nice-nice to someone because I truly want to throttle them and I'm afraid of the power of my own feeling and its possible consequences? Am I saying something doesn't matter a bit to cover up, even to myself, how hurt I feel? Am I using psychological defenses such as denial or projection to keep myself from knowing what is truly going on inside of me?

Meaning is deeply personal. We create it out of our own minds, and it is based on what we have experienced at this point in our lives, our personal value system and developmental stage. In-depth research on the efficacy of eyewitness accounts got those accounts thrown out of courts unless they were corroborated. This is because each of us sees the same situation differently—each of us perceives truth through our own lens. How we see a situation depends on what is already stored in the brain.

A child who has been struck may flinch away from an

arm that goes up suddenly. A child who lived through World War II bombings may freeze at the sound of a siren. A child who is held, loved and valued is likely to assume that the world is a friendly place and people mean him no harm.

The meaning we make out of something depends on many things. How old are we? How do we already see ourselves? Do we have someone to talk things over with and check out our perceptions, or are we isolated, locked in our own point of view? What is our state of mind and life circumstances at the time of a particular incident? Is there a power imbalance in the situation—child/parent, boss/worker, tall or short, big or small? Are we a man or a woman, gay or straight, young or old?

Understanding meaning is complicated, and no cookie-cutter approach can do any individual justice. Understanding the function that a particular behavior or way of thinking has within the self system requires individual reflection. That's not to say there won't be central themes that unite many, but each of us needs to explore and decode our own meaning and function in order to be true to ourselves and in order to attain an emotional literacy that we can wear with comfort.

Stage Four: Choose Whether or Not to Communicate Our Inner State to Another Person

At this point, we have a choice. We have the information. We know enough about what's going on inside of us so that we can choose what to do with it.

Relationship is critical to health and well-being, so part of emotional literacy is what happens on the inside and part is what happens on the outside. It isn't only clarity within ourselves about what we are feeling and the meaning and function it has for us. Full emotional literacy involves the ability to share that information with others if we choose to, to decide when and with whom such sharing is necessary or appropriate, and to engage in back-and-forth communication. It can take courage to communicate honestly with another person. But, if you pass through the stages of emotional literacy, communication can be done in a compassionate manner rather than dumping in order to get rid of the feeling at another person's expense. One helpful hint is to mentally "reverse roles" with the person you wish to talk to and imagine how it might be for them to hear it. This can help you communicate in a way that is "hearable" for someone else, so that you can expand rather than contract the relationship.

This informed ability to choose gives us a great deal of power and self-confidence. Choice means:

- That we can *talk out* rather than *act out*.
- That we can decide whether communicating our feelings will help our cause or hurt it.
- That we can decide how much to communicate, according to our own needs and according to a realistic assessment of who we are talking to and what we are talking about.
- That we can figure out our most effective mode of communication.
- That we can do what is truly in our own best interest instead of what we may feel like doing in a heated state of emotional arousal.
- That we can deepen understanding, communication and intimacy with another person.

As a society, we really don't understand that emotional literacy is a learned skill. We are not born emotionally literate, any more than we are born knowing how to read. We need to be taught about our inner world in just the same way that we need to be taught about our outer world. "The big fireball in the sky is called the sun, and it sets in the west and rises in the east." "The feeling that I am experiencing right now is called frustration, and it can lead to anger and rash action." By understanding the problem, the solution may present itself naturally. The sun will set; my frustration can subside if I am patient.

Normally, each age has its own developmental tasks in acquiring emotional literacy. For the small child, it may be simple descriptions of basic emotional states: "I am sad, I feel scared, I want to see my mommy." By adolescence, it gets more complicated: "I feel anxious when I haven't done my homework" might lead in teenage years to "I am forgetting to bring in my homework, which perhaps is a defense against my feeling that I can't succeed even if I try."

Ideally, as children grow, they will be encouraged to feel and label their feelings and practice the stages of emotional literacy. However, children who grow up with trauma and addiction are not given the opportunity for such practice—quite the opposite. So an important part of recovery needs to be guidance, encouragement and practice in developing the skills of emotional literacy.

Emotional Literacy and Intimacy

Emotional literacy is the cornerstone of good relationships. It is generally accepted that meaningful communication is central to successful intimacy. Emotional literacy provides the content for that communication. Without it, communication is vague and doesn't go anywhere. Classic grunts, monosyllabic answers—"I dunno," "just because," "because I do"—and a plethora of other dead-end communiqués are the result of emotional illiteracy. People who are emotionally illiterate cannot tell you how or why they feel the way they do.

Trauma and addiction exacerbate this condition. Those who have been traumatized cannot decode their inner world or understand, label and communicate what is going on inside of them. And because they don't have their own codified emotional world as a blueprint, because they are in the dark about themselves, they are unable to understand another person. What really complicates this, however, is that they generally don't know that they don't know. Consequently, they may perceive probing questions as intrusive, pestering or mean-spirited. When asked a direct question about their emotional world, they can feel defensive, criticized or brought up short.

Whether we understand them or not, we take our inner worlds with us wherever we go. When we see the solution to relationship problems as changing, fixing or replacing the other person, we are missing one of the critical points of emotional literacy. That is the fact that we can only hope to have mastery over our own inner world (if we're lucky), and that in order to have an emotionally literate partnership, we first need to become an emotionally literate partner. Then we have a chance at an emotionally literate communication. Until we can clearly feel and decode our own inner world, communicating it well rarely happens. When we are lost in and overwhelmed by our own internal goings-on, we are equally lost in and over-whelmed by communicating in a partnership.

Take a typical scene from Lucy and Harry's relationship. Little hurts have built up in Lucy's mind, but nothing has seemed important enough to mention. Harry is absorbed in work and doesn't seem to want to connect and chat at the end of the day. Lucy, who is working part-time, tries to be understanding and feels that it would be selfish to put pressure on him when he is already feeling pressured. He seems remote, and she feels lonely. He is more short-tempered than usual and she is getting hurt. Because she doesn't feel comfortable saying anything, she withdraws and hopes that he will notice. He does notice, but assumes that she is remote because she is losing interest in him. He feels hurt but too vulnerable to ask her if this is true. He withdraws and hopes that she will notice and ask him why he is withdrawn. She does notice, but assumes that he is mad at her (after all, she's mad at him underneath it all). She is afraid to ask if this is true, because if it is, then they might have a fight and she'll feel that she caused it.

They have made plans to go out for dinner and to a play on Saturday night. Lucy is hoping that having some fun on a date will bring them closer. Harry is hoping that Lucy will come closer to him if they go out together. They are each sure the other one took responsibility for the tickets. They have not checked in about this because they have been distant and withdrawn. They have no tickets. This triggers an explosion in which they each blurt out all of their small, piled-up hurts at once—talking or yelling on top of each other, neither one hearing the other. The more they don't listen to each other, the more unheard each of them feels, and the more defensive they become. Soon they are exaggerating their hurts in order to get their points across because they are each stonewalling. Now they are both yelling, Lucy is crying, and Harry is storming around, huffing and puffing. Emotional illiteracy! Nothing gets solved, their weekend is marred and the things that were bothering them never get talked about.

Let's correct this scenario by giving Harry and Lucy some emotional literacy.

There are a few ways this could go that would improve the result. The first is that when Lucy feels ignored by Harry, she sits down with herself and tunes into her own feeling. *(One, feel the fullness of the emotion.)* To do this, she'll need to accept the feeling as her own and at the same time keep an open mind—so that when she checks it out with Harry, her mind won't already be made up as to what he is feeling. Then she can name her internal state: I am feeling ignored. *(Two, connect the label to the internal state.)* Maybe my feeling ignored isn't only about Harry. I do feel he is ignoring me, but why am I reacting to it so strongly, why am I feeling so defensive and isolated; what's getting triggered, what's being ignored, covered up? Then she will need to decide why she is feeling this way. *(Three, understand the meaning or function within her.)* Maybe Lucy feels ignored because she herself feels less productive and creative than Harry and she is a little jealous. Maybe she is worried that Harry will judge her the way she is judging herself. Or perhaps she witnessed her father losing interest in her mother over years of married life and has an unconscious fear that this could happen to her. As she goes through this process, she becomes more enlightened as to the workings of her own inner world and less likely to project unexplored, painful feelings onto Harry.

Once you understand the meaning and function of feelings within the self system, you are free to *(Four, choose whether or not to communicate them to another person)*. Lucy can decide to take the feelings to therapy, talk to a friend, use a support group or talk to Harry. The fight, flight, freeze response that is discussed in chapter 1 is altered, and her responses move from rigid and reactive to resolution.

Another path this might take is that Harry tunes into his urge to withdraw and passes through the same four stages: First, he can feel his urge to withdraw. Second, he can name it. Third, he can explore its personal meaning. Perhaps he feels a lack of self-esteem at work and his feelings about himself are down; and he is projecting that onto Lucy, assuming she does not truly respect him. Or maybe his father modeled withdrawal and disinterest and he is acting that out. Finally, he can choose how and where to communicate this to Lucy or to another trusted person for further exploration.

Still another possibility is for the couple, after going through this internal process, to risk feeling vulnerable and communicate their feelings to each other. This is not easy. It brings up fear of rejection or looking weak. But ultimately, when couples do this they generally can come closer together and feel safer and more trusting, rather than driving each other away. It is best, in this scenario, to focus on communicating your own feeling and your "feelings about the feeling" or its personal meaning to you without assuming that you know what your partner is feeling. Listen as your partner communicates his or her feelings and personal meaning, then work toward mutual acceptance and understanding. Notice I did not say agreement. We can understand our partners without agreeing with everything they say. Fusing in order to avoid dissension is not closeness. Fusing leads to a loss of a sense of self in both partners. Fusing is the opposite of distant withdrawal. Neither tactic brings a couple closer.

Still another and probably more common direction this might take is as follows. The scenario is the same up until the explosion, but rather than turn the explosion into a marathon of hurt feelings, Harry and Lucy explode, then back off and calm down. They realize that they got into a spot of trouble and that they need to talk things out. Together they use the steps of emotional literacy to work their way through their hurt and angry feelings into a better place. Mutually, they reflect on the emotions behind the blowup and name them. Together they sort out the meaning they were making out of their feelings (their feelings about their feelings). They share their more vulnerable sides with each other. Lucy talks about her feeling that she is not very creative or constructive these days. Harry shares his feelings of low self-esteem at work. In this way, they are able to feel better through sharing and opening up and by receiving understanding and support. In this way, a couple can deepen their empathy for each other while retaining a sense of autonomy and selfhood which, of course, deepens intimacy. This does require that each person in the couple is willing to accept the other as human and imperfect. We all have fantasies of the perfect partner who has no insecurity or frustration. But, alas, there is no such person to come along and save us. Listening to a partner's insecurity can be hard but, in the long run, it is better to accept each other as flawed and love and be loved, warts and all.

Emotional Literacy as an Evolving Life Skill

Emotional literacy is not a cure. It is not an end point. It is not something that, once gained, lives inside of us in a finished state. Emotional literacy is a learned process, a set of skills or techniques that, once internalized, can be applied over and over and over again to each new situation. We are in a constant state of change. Each new phase of life presents its own challenges. While we may have seen the world one way as young people, suddenly we become parents and see it from an entirely new perspective. Raising children is different from having a career. Going to college is one type of experience; working is another. While we may have been cool and calm as a single person or part of a married couple, give us a couple of kids and we're anxious wrecks—new memories of our own childhood are being stimulated and we constantly feel inept. Or we get a job and our boss makes us feel like a teenager—and we start to act like one until we figure out what's going on. Each new stage of life triggers different responses inside of us. Each new stage requires daily reapplication of the skills of emotional literacy.

We make our most critical life choices based on how well we know ourselves, love and work, partner and career. The better we understand what makes us tick, the more able we are to make good rather than bad life choices. Once we are in a partnership or a life's work, it is emotional literacy that allows us to understand at any given time where we are, how we are "living in" our lives, thriving or not thriving, coping or disintegrating. It provides us with the tools to manage our own experience. We cannot assess our internal experience without the language through which we map out the terrain of our own inner world. Happy, sad, mad, glad does not begin to cover the intricacies, complexities and variety of complicated functions that are part of our emotional makeup. Without this knowledge of our inner world, it is virtually impossible to explain ourselves to someone else. We don't know where to begin. Consequently, we go along with the hand we are dealt and try to adjust our inner world to fit, rather than consciously reaching compromises with partners and career situations that accommodate our own needs, desires, dreams and drives, as well as those of others. Also, emotional literacy provides the skills necessary for the victim of trauma to learn to negotiate issues with another person. Our "trauma reads" on a situation are often rigid and defensive. We need to slowly negotiate our way toward a middle ground when we get triggered by another person so we can hang on to a sense of self and let someone else do the same.

When we begin to blend cultures, races and classes into a more unified whole, emotional literacy takes on still a more vital role. What is the emotional experience of the African American? The white American? The Asian or Latin American? How do we know each other and come to understand our similarities and differences, to appreciate each other's strengths and deal with each other's weaknesses? And as the world shrinks through technology, what about the Japanese, Chinese, Italian or Russian person? Without the tools of emotional literacy, we are left to think in stereotypes, keeping a polite or hostile distance from what we do not understand.

Emotional literacy offers a way to understand our responses to all of the various situations that life inevitably confronts us with. It gives us the skills to get the most out of ourselves, our relationships and our careers. And, just when we think we've got it all figured out, it changes again. We retire, our children leave the nest, we become grandparents, we meet the final years of our lives. But emotional literacy is there to help us figure it out all over again—keeping us young, fresh and ready for life.

THREE

How Trauma and Addiction Undermine Healthy Styles of Relating in Families and Intimate Relationships

Happy families are all alike;
every unhappy family
is unhappy in its own way.

Leo Tolstoy
Anna Karenina, 1876

Confusion is a word we have invented for
an order which is not understood.

Henry Miller
Tropic of Capricorn, 1938

THE EFFECTS OF TRAUMA ON FAMILIES AND CHILDREN

Families that experience addiction experience trauma. Trauma as a rupture in a relationship bond is fundamentally isolating. In order to stay "in relationship" with people who are hurting us, we develop strategies that *seem* to allow us to stay safe—like hiding our true feelings while putting on a false face. These disconnects are our attempts to stay safe while being engaged in pain-filled relationships. This chronic pattern of disconnection becomes a relationship strategy. That is, when as adults we attempt to get close to someone, these patterns of disconnection come along, so that part of our connection includes a built-in disconnection. They were our strategies for staying safe as kids, so we continue to use them as adults. According to Steven Krugman, the impact of trauma on family organization has three main components:

1. Constriction, leading to enmeshment.
2. Avoidance, leading to disengagement.
3. Impulsive behavior, leading to chaos.

Children from trauma families develop "an intense need for closeness and support combined with a fear of being hurt and abandoned," says Krugman. This makes it very hard to build mutually satisfying and authentic relationships. With each nonmutual, pain-filled relationship, subsequent connection is harder to form because we have formed a pattern of disconnected relationships alongside an "intense need for closeness and support."

For women, nonmutual relationships can be especially traumatic. According to research done by Carol Gilligan, Jean Baker-Miller and others of the Stone Center in Boston, Massachusetts, women tend to develop differently from men. They call this type of development Self-in-Relation. In other words, women gain part of their sense of self-esteem through connection—mutual relationships. The ability to form relationships of mutuality is a central organizing principle of feminine personality development. Nonmutual relationships promote a sense of disconnection and isolation, thus undermining the sense of mutuality so important to a woman's sense of well-being. This is certainly true for men as well, to varying extents.

Jean Baker-Miller, author of *The Healing Connection*, has identified three factors that both emerge from and perpetuate nonmutual family relationships. They are present in virtually all addicted families to some extent:

1. Secrecy in the family in which family members deny "unacceptable reality."
2. Inaccessibility of parents; children are denied opportunity for consistent and reliable connection with their parents.
3. "Parentification" of children.

Secrecy, says Baker-Miller, tends to bind the abused to the victimizer—it isolates the child or family member from honest connection. Secrecy affects feelings of self-worth and self-esteem, because children and family members tend to blame themselves for the crazy-making or bad feelings they experience when holding secrets. Family members learn to "shut their eyes to what's in front of them"—to deny significant parts of their world and reality—which undermines the fabric of the family. Members do not turn to each other for an authentic read on reality, because reality is being denied. Also, "secrets create power inequities—those who know versus those who don't." In this case, family subgroups develop, some members with information and some without; some are in the know and others feel outcast or confused. Family members avoid subjects that would lead near the disowned, emotionally charged territory, which means they cannot talk about what is happening around them. When family members have to "walk on eggshells," issues cannot be faced and resolved. Family members are forced to go outside the system for authentic connections and feel false within the family itself. Secrets isolate children and family members from the world—"they fear that people might find out." Consequently, they lose access to outside support, which perpetuates the effects of trauma on the family system. Trauma and addiction build on each other. Initially, this creates isolation; then, because of the secretive nature of addiction, that isolation becomes a perpetual cycle which builds in intensity.

Baker-Miller goes on to describe the effect of inaccessibility of parents on children. Children experience profound confusion of feelings when a parent appears to be there but is not truly present. Their thinking gets fuzzy;

they rationalize, repress or idealize in an attempt to keep their sense of a good parent alive. This occurs at the expense of authentic connections. To further complicate matters, parents "may not recall what transpired when they were drinking" and drugging. Pockets of reality are forgotten or denied. Problems cannot be resolved because information is missing. "Parents may make promises that will later be denied." Children from alcoholic families learn not to count on adults to follow through on what they say. This produces a loss of trust and faith in relationships. Children feel that they are on their own, that people are unreliable and will eventually let them down, lose interest or turn away. Another reason for loss of access to parents is that a parent drinks not to feel, so the alcoholic becomes barely present at all, explosive and rageful, or guilty and overindulgent. The child internalizes a relationship model that is inconsistent and "based on the needs or state of the parent rather than those of the child" (ibid.).

Many children grow up with depressed parents, particularly mothers, since depression is more prevalent in women than in men. Typically, children feel their parent's depression is their fault. They feel terrible about not being able to "help the parent with the obvious sadness." When the parent withdraws, the children have no one to depend on and feel guilty at not being able to reach their parent. Children with addicted or depressed parents suffer a deep sense of helplessness and profound disconnection. When parents are emotionally numb or restrict their emotional experience, they cannot be empathetic and responsive to their children. Parents who shut down or medicate their own internal world are unable to show their children how to relate well through their own behavior. They are poor models of emotional literacy or how to conduct intimate relationships.

Parentification, according to Baker-Miller, reflects lack of mutuality—because the parents cannot respond to children's needs but cast them instead in the role that suits them. "The parent doesn't recognize the contributions and efforts of the parentified child." Parentified children may put their own needs for being taken care of aside and learn to make connections through taking care of others. Parentified children may come to view relationships as burdens. The sad truth is that, "The parentified child doesn't take care of their parent or siblings out of love and mutual connection but out of fear of the parent's anger or a desperate attempt to maintain some sense of normalcy. Also, these situations force children to develop skills before they are truly developmentally ready to perform them with ease and a sense of mastery, which can leave them with a sense of failure and inadequacy. They end up with a feeling of dissonance between how they are perceived by others and how they experience themselves" (Baker-Miller et al. 1997).

These three patterns, *secrecy, inaccessibility of parents* and *parentification*, can lead to psychological problems because developmental needs are not adequately met in the family. Often, permission is not freely granted in such families to seek connection and help from those outside the family.

Families like these do not particularly support individuation and often take attempts of children to separate as assaults on the system. They do not necessarily encourage gradual, healthy separation while maintaining connection. Children separate at the peril of losing their place.

Some children try to resolve these issues by leaving home early through marriage, geographic distance and so on. However, they carry the preoccupations and worries with them, and their issues get triggered when they again attempt to enter into and create their own circle of relationships.

Adult children from alcoholic families and addicts learn to form disconnected types of relationships; for example, marrying workaholics or people who are not responsive to mutual connections is common. We use strategies that keep us disconnected in order to feel safe and prevent further violation of attachment bonds. In order to resolve these problems so we can learn to connect in healthy ways, we need to grieve what we never had. This removes the block in the way of new learning and leads to a willingness to take the risks that will be involved in creating new kinds of relationships. It opens the path, the Step One, of emotional literacy.

A Torn Heart

This is a direct quote from one of my clients: "My wife and I fight constantly, but we've really managed to keep our own problems separate and we're great parents." Though on the face of it the idea of keeping their problems separate is a good one, there is a significant piece of denial operating in thinking that it is not affecting the children.

Children grow up in the arms of their parents, in the atmosphere of their parents' relationship. The feelings, thoughts and actions that exist in the container of the parents' relationship are naturally felt by the child. Part of being a good parent is being a good partner. Modeling is, perhaps, the most significant part of parenting. Who we are speaks louder to our children than what we say. We teach children emotional literacy and healthy communication by practicing them ourselves. Children constantly scan the environment of their parents' relationship, picking up on all of the subtle signals sent out from one parent to another. The emotional atmosphere between the parents is not invisible to children—quite the contrary, it prints itself indelibly on the child's mind. When we ask our children to get along with each other, their friends and the adults in their lives, but we don't set an example or show them how to do this by having a decent relationship with their other parent, we confuse them at a very deep level. They cannot make sense of having parents who don't get along but tell them that they should. When words and actions don't match, there is a cognitive dissonance within the child, a confusion; they feel crazy

Recently, I was doing a sociometry exercise with my class at NYU. (Sociometry is the concrete representation of our relationship choices. It involves the attraction, rejection or neutral response between people. We will illustrate this in chapter 9 through the social atom.) I asked a series of questions. "If you chose someone to play your cousin, who would it be? Who could play a childhood friend? Who could play your brother, your sister? Who would you choose to play your mother, your father?" Most of the group members found it easy to make these choices. Andrea, however, stood on the sidelines unable to move forward. When I asked her what was going on she answered, "I'm so confused. I can't move. I can't choose. I feel paralyzed."

I inquired into her parental situation. She said, "I never

heard my parents say a kind word to each other. They hated each other. They each loved me, but they wouldn't speak to each other."

I asked her to show us what she meant with role-players. She chose someone to play her mother, father, stepmother and stepfather. She set them up, each couple facing the other and herself. You could have cut the tension with a knife. She looked from one to the other and cried—a deep, muffled sobbing that spoke to years of held hurt. "If you love me, why won't you be civil to each other? It hurts me so much. I can't stand it. I didn't ask for any present for my graduation. I only wanted a picture with me in the middle of the two of you on either side and you wouldn't do it. You wouldn't even give me this picture. I wanted it so much. It meant so much to me. Couldn't you put aside your hatred just long enough for this?"

Andrea had grown up in the hostile gaze of her parents' mutual hatred. Their unresolved issues with each other were lived out in every tiny interaction over their daughter. She became the container of their rage and hurt, the carrier of their pain. She endured years of small slights and innuendo, of tones and facial expressions that hinted at the anger constantly vibrating just beneath the surface of their cold and distant interactions. Andrea was left wondering if these two people had ever loved each other at all or if she was the product of mutual hate and nothing else. It terrified her. It made her feel as if she had somehow ruined their lives, and she carried this sense of failure into her own life. It wrapped itself around her dreams of ever having her own marriage and stood in the way of her faith in a happy future.

Andrea had never articulated the pain of being caught

between two warring parents, and though it was extremely painful to open up this wound, it began her process of healing.

So often the subjects that are nearest and dearest to our hearts go unspoken—the painful ones especially, as if to put them into words will make the situation worse. Just the opposite is true. It is when we don't talk about traumas that they become huge inside of us, co-opting our internal world, silencing the voice within us that wants to speak. Talking about trauma pulls the emotional pain past our defensive system and into the part of our brain where we can think about what we're feeling—where cognition meets emotion. This process—pulling emotions out of hiding, sorting and labeling them, then reflecting on their personal meaning and the myriad ways that the meaning we make out of them influences our thinking, feeling and behavior—is what allows us to make sense of our lives. Then we can use emotional wounds to expand rather than contract our experience of self, others and life. Until then we are prisoners of what we cannot feel.

In Andrea's case, she had been using drugs and alcohol, so available on college campuses, to soften the pain of a splintered inner world. She was well on her way to dropping out of college due, at least in part, to her excessive drug use. So many hurting young people do just this. Especially when the traumatic rupture is with their parents, the very people they grow up wishing to come to with little and big hurts. But Andrea's big hurt was with these two and she could not bring it to them, so it sat inside her like a stone weighing her down, making life feel exhausting and burdensome. Andrea's process of exhuming this pain that was eating away at her was rocky, and it shook an already shaky foundation. But she stuck with it, slowly integrating the new awareness of how living in the gap of her parents' unresolved history had affected her personality and the way she conducted her life. This allowed her to build inner strength where once there was decay and to develop the courage to make choices that were good for her. Drugs and alcohol began to fade from the scene as she no longer needed them to take the edge off of emotional pain.

Andrea's painful situation, unfortunately, all too often leads to continued complications such as addiction, divorce or both. Separated and divorced men and women were three times as likely as married men and women to say they had been married to an alcoholic or problem drinker. Almost two-thirds of separated and divorced women and almost half of separated or divorced men, under the age of forty-six, have been exposed to alcohol in the family at some time (World Health Organization). We repeat what we knew growing up. Without the intervention of recovery, adult children of alcoholics tend to marry back into the disease in one way or another.

The Effects of Trauma on Intimate Relationships: When Adult Children of Trauma Fall in Love

Unresolved childhood trauma resurfaces in adult intimate relationships. Feeling dependent and vulnerable in partnership, as we all do when we open our hearts to love, can make old wounds feel new. First, there is the damage to self that living with trauma and addiction engenders, which undermines our ability to be ready for healthy intimacy and internal stability. Then there is the emotional and psychological pain from ruptured relationships that gets projected onto the current partnership which, in fact, belongs at least partly to the past. In this section, we will explore the areas of relationships that are negatively affected by early experiences of living with trauma and addiction.

Intimacy: Because survivors of trauma have been deeply hurt by significant relationships in childhood, it can feel perilous and frightening to try to become intimate with others later in life. Simultaneously, they have a deep longing for love and connection and a deep fear of staying connected. Those who are willing to take the risk of being in an intimate relationship may find that it provides an opportunity for healing and growth.

Commitment: Trauma survivors carry contradictory fears—of being abandoned and of being engulfed. Both of these fears can create anxiety around the subject of commitment. The result may be running rashly into commitments without allowing time to know the other person or trying to stay clear of any relationship that feels permanent.

Communication: Genuine communication is subtle and complex. It requires understanding our own internal state and being able to put it into words, listening without overreacting or under-reacting, and picking up on verbal and nonverbal signals from others. Trauma undermines these communication skills, distorting interpretations, shutting down access to one's inner world, and leaving repressed wounds that are vulnerable to being triggered. It is no wonder that the ability to communicate in intimate relationships is seriously impaired for trauma survivors.

Boundaries: In healthy relationships, those involved are able to share a co-state while each maintains a sense of self. They tend to have flexible boundaries that allow each of them to get what they need as individuals and as a couple, not necessarily every moment, but in the overall relationship. Survivors of trauma may have trouble maintaining healthy boundaries. They tend to try to create safety by either withdrawing into themselves or attempting to fuse with the other person out of fear of abandonment. This over-closeness can become smothering and makes them wish to withdraw again.

Modulating Emotion: Trauma survivors tend to leap from zero to ten in their emotional responses, alternating between high-intensity feeling states and emotional shutdown. They have trouble modulating emotions between these extremes towards a state that is appropriate for a given situation. Learning and practicing modulation is part of the process of recovery from trauma and an important part of living in healthy intimacy.

Trust and Faith: Because early relationships have been undermined by trauma, survivors may be left with a sense of betrayal and an undermined ability to trust. As a result, they may hesitate to form deep attachments. Because no relationship is without problems, trust and faith are the glue that's necessary for any intimate relationship to succeed over time.

Accepting Love and Support: Traumatized people lose some of their ability to take in caring and support from those around them. In intimate relationships receiving is as important as giving, accepting support and being supportive are core to happiness in partnership.

Having Fun: Having fun requires that we let go of control and enter a world in which fantasy can play a role, and to allow others in through a spontaneous give-and-take. Trauma undermines all of these abilities. Activities and therapies such as games, creative arts therapies and psychodrama can help retrain spontaneity and restore the ability to play.

[The foregoing material was adapted from my book *Heartwounds* (Health Communications, Inc. 1997). Please see that book for a more detailed discussion of the topic.]

Trauma survivors struggle in intimate relationships because they act and react according to unconscious but deeply held patterns they have learned. Those dynamics include *chronic disconnects, reenactments, transference, triggering, fusion, splitting, hypervigilance* and *perfectionism*. We'll turn to a discussion of these now.

Chronic Disconnects in Relationships

All relationships, even healthy ones, cycle through periods of connection, disconnection and reconnection. It's the natural ebb and flow of family, friendship or partnership. In healthy patterns the reconnection is usually "a small step up" (Baker-Miller et al. 1997), that is, we learn a little something about getting along from our temporary feeling of disconnection and bring it into the reconnection. For those who have grown up with trauma, however, the types of disconnection that occur are much more serious.

Therapy is about working on disconnections. According to Jean Baker-Miller, this is why it is difficult. The movement toward reconnection is tough because it "threatens a person's strategies for disconnection, which are in some broad sense adaptive." That is, we develop them for a reason, to stay safe or to survive. These strategies allow us to stay in the primary relationships that we need so much. When we change these strategies in therapy, it feels as if we are giving up a piece of ourselves.

"These experiences of disconnection lead people to form relational images of others as people who cannot understand them, cannot feel with them, will leave them in isolation, will not be there for them, will scorn, humiliate or abuse them. Then they develop a variety of responses such as compliance, silence, serving and responding to others' needs, not asking anything or outwitting, controlling or triumphing over others" (ibid.). For example, a son of an alcoholic mother may develop a strategy of taking care of her by being a sort of magical lover, a good listener, caretaker, etc. Or a daughter of a sexually abusive father may develop a pattern of compliance, idealization or collusion.

Hiding authentic feelings, such as sadness at rejection or hurt at abuse, is also a strategy, as children feel they appear "weak, ugly or like a loser" (ibid.) if they reveal their true emotions. These patterns get played out in adult relationships. When we attempt to connect we bring along with us the full pattern—that is, all that encompasses connection within our experience, including disconnection.

In one sense, the surfacing of these patterns is a good sign. It means that we are breaking our isolation and trying to get close to someone. When our traumas have occurred through ruptures in relationships, they need to be reconstructed and reworked in relationships. Reaching out for a relationship is nature's attempt to heal early wounds—to take a leap of faith and try again. Remember, trauma is a rupture in a relationship bond. The rupture may arise out of neglect, physical abuse, constant humiliation, sexual abuse, divorce or having a parent who is addicted to alcohol, drugs, sex, gambling, food or work. When these ruptures occur in childhood, our emotional pain associated with them may go underground for years. Then as adults, when we try to reenter committed, intimate relationships, that repressed pain gets triggered.

That pain affects our relationships in significant ways, including how we handle conflict. According to a recent ten-year study conducted in the state of Washington, psychologists Cybil Carrere et al. could predict with 95 percent accuracy which couples would divorce before the six-year mark by watching the first three minutes of a fight. Couples who had a style of attack, defensiveness or counterattack often ended up divorced.

1. **Problematic fighting**
   Wife: "You never pay any attention to me, all you care about is your damned computer!" *Attacking immediately with blame.*
   Husband: "Well, if you were more fun to be with I might want to spend time with you." *Counterattacking and continuing blame cycle.*
2. **Healthy fighting**
   Wife: "I'm bothered by the fact that we aren't spending more time together." *Opening the subject nonaggressively.*
   Husband: "I thought we were having a good time, what do you mean by that?" *Gathering more information for clarification and communication.*

Those who have histories of trauma and addiction have generally seen couple number-one in action more than couple number-two, and that is the training they take into their own marriages. However, new styles can be successfully learned. On the following pages, we will examine some of the underlying dynamics that get in the way of healthy fighting.

Reenactments, Transferences and Triggering

Three of the most common dynamics I see in couples with histories of trauma and addiction are *reenactments, transferences* and *triggering* of old wounds leading to explosion or withdrawal.

Reenactments, or those relationship dynamics that get created over and over again, reveal to us where our deepest wounds lie. Sandy, who fears abandonment as a result of her parents' divorce, her mother's addiction, and the deaths of her parents and her loving grandmother, drives Michael away constantly. It is as if she would rather alienate him through behaving in an irrational and hostile manner than give herself and risk being abandoned. As if she's saying, in her relationship, "You can't fire me, I quit."

Michael, on the other hand, is terrified of being a fool—of trusting someone as he did his first wife who, out of the blue, announced that she was leaving him for another man, at which point both his personal and professional worlds fell apart. He protects himself by remaining in a constant state of ambivalence—withdrawing into a protective shell, fearful of making a long-term commitment lest it go sour on him once again. The more noncommittal he is, the more enraged Sandy becomes as her fear of abandonment gets constantly triggered. She acts out through yelling and insulting, he becomes terrified of trusting someone who appears to be so volatile and gets withdrawn, sullen and ambivalent, she feels even more abandoned—and, boom, both of their worst fears are lived out over and over again. They constantly recreate the very situation that has traumatized them and they want never to experience again. This pattern is, of course, largely unconscious. Were it conscious, they could talk it through and come to understand the source of their reenactment.

Transference is that piece of unresolved history from past relationships that gets projected onto people in the present. Sandy *transfers* the deep pain of being abandoned physically by her father and emotionally by her mother's alcoholism onto Michael. At some deep level, she assumes that it will only be a matter of time until Michael leaves her, that she matters to him only to a point. This devaluation of his love leaves him feeling confused and ambivalent. On the one hand, he feels sure she will not leave him as did his previous wife. On the other hand, she constantly accuses him of walking out or wanting to "walk" or end the relationship.

Michael's life fell apart when his first wife left him. He trusted her and she betrayed him. He lost his ability to be effective on the job, which resulted in his being fired. With this double trauma, love and work, his life fell into shambles. He cannot put words on his pain so he can grieve and understand the power of these losses over him. Consequently, the fear of re-creating the same situation has him paralyzed. He cannot commit himself to a relationship where he feels vulnerable, even in therapy. He cannot move forward and risk building a relationship and a career that could fall apart again. His *transference* of unresolved pain is largely unconscious, since he is not fully aware of how traumatized he was, it hurts him too much to "go back there," he feels he should be "over it by now." His unconscious transference is that a marriage attachment to Sandy will somehow, somewhere along the line, blow up in his face, that deep down she is not trustworthy, and, ultimately, she will come to hate him.

It is the unconscious piece of these transferences that makes them tricky. You could say that Sandy and Michael are adults, aware of their behavior and therefore able to change it. But the extent to which they were traumatized by earlier ruptures is not fully understood by either of them. Who wants to go back into these wounds and feel the vulnerability, pain and desperation that were originally too much to bear? And yet it is just this grief work that is necessary in order to move on. Without it we go for a premature resolution of the pain. We tell ourselves that it is or should be over and we need to move on, but the hidden camera in our unconscious loads scenes from the past onto its reel and projects our disowned past onto the screen of our present-day relationships.

When unfinished business does not get resolved, it sits inside of us in what we refer to in psychodrama as a state of "open tension," or in a more common vernacular, "a time bomb waiting to go off." The pain from the old wounds forms what T. S. Eliot calls "undisciplined squads of emotion." These emotions are neither named, categorized nor put into some sort of context that the mind can understand and make peace with. In relationships, these old wounds are triggered through the feelings of dependency and vulnerability that are part of intimacy. When we feel neglected or hurt we become, in an instant, the wounded child or adolescent or young adult that still lives within us. Then the unhealed contents of the wound explode. Yelling, shouting, crying, raging, accusing, withdrawing, shutting down—bits and pieces of the emotional and psychological pain that have been stored in the memory as fragments of the truth fly around the room like down in a pillow fight. Feeling flashes, flashbacks and memory fragments are ignited and zoom to the surface at split-second speed. Like actors who arrive suddenly on stage with an old script, they look for another character with whom to play out this scene. And so it goes, a buried grenade from a previous war gets stepped on and explodes its contents into another time and place.

Fusion, Withdrawal and Splitting

Three other relationship dynamics that commonly play out are fusion or "enmeshment," altering with *withdrawal* and *splitting*, or "black-and-white thinking."

If we look again at Sandy and Michael, we see that one of the ways they try to assuage their fear of abandonment is through fusing with each other. If they are one in all they think and feel, then how can anything ever come between them? This oneness we refer to here is not a spiritual sort of union, which can be a beautiful part of a relationship, but a fusing of identities driven by a fear of feelings of loneliness, alienation or abandonment. The trouble with this is that it is unnatural, and because it's unnatural, a couple needs to become rigid in their fused identity in order to maintain it. The unconscious motto is "there is only room for one here"—one point of view, one perspective on the world, one way of thinking and feeling about a given subject. Dissension will not be tolerated and disagreement is discouraged.

When all of this togetherness becomes stifling and intolerable, as it inevitably will, couples may unconsciously seek ways of breaking loose and withdrawing from each other. Fights, in order to create some distance, are common. When Sandy and Michael's fantasy of closeness caused them to have to submerge their own personalities for too long, somehow they ended up in a fight. It was the only way to get some space, since their individual needs for space were viewed as threatening to the relationship. Or, if the couple stays fused, children can feel on the outside.

Those who grew up with addiction and/or trauma have often had problematic individuations from their families of origin. Feelings of being alienated or cut off from their families are common. They are often torn between longing for the family they lost and relief at finally having escaped. Normal children can feel significant guilt at wishing to be separate individuals, but the guilt of children who feel they escaped or fled can be profound. That guilt, the unfulfilled longing, the conflicting wishes both to escape and crawl back into the womb all get carried into adult intimate relationships. The traumatized or addicted family often does not allow its children to separate and stay connected. All too often they are in or out of the "family unit." If they are in, they may feel they need to hide their authentic selves; if they are out, they carry deep feelings of rejection and loss. Hence, their distorted reasoning, their "trauma reasoning," tells them that, if their partnership is going to work, they need to either hide their authentic selves or leave the relationship in order to be who they are.

Trauma victims tend to see the world in *black-and-white* terms. This dynamic grows out of and mirrors their inner world, which alternates between high intensity and shutdown (Van der Kolk 1987). In relationships, this can translate as seeing a partner as all good or all bad when upsets occur. When Sandy's abandonment issues get triggered by Michael's inability to decide whether or not to make a marriage commitment, he becomes all bad, a person incapable of loving, a lover out to hurt her and abandon her (as her father did). She completely loses touch with the side of him that she loves. She *splits* him into two extremes. She feels much like a disappointed small child who wants to pack a suitcase and run away from the parent she hates, unable to hold and integrate the feeling that this is also the parent (or partner) she loves. Her inner world has only two sides, and the doorway that leads from one to the other is locked shut. In Sandy's case, this split expresses itself in calling Michael horrible names, blaming him for being the person who is blocking the relationship from moving forward without examining her piece in it. She drives him away before he has a chance to leave her, since being left is her greatest fear.

Michael, on the other hand, comes to a full stop emotionally and psychologically. He cannot move forward, backward, sideways or in any direction at all. At the prospect of marrying and risking being left again, he freezes like a deer in the headlights. His defense is to shut down and withdraw, he goes numb—which enrages Sandy so she screams at him, then he feels terrible and he goes even more numb.

Hypervigilance and Perfectionism

People from traumatized and/or addicted homes have been so hurt by their primary relationships that they often become hypervigilant in marriage and partnerships—constantly scanning these relationships for signs of a problem, waiting for the other shoe to drop.

As a defense against feeling this constant angst or experiencing the natural anxiety that is part of any relationship, adult children of trauma can become rigid and perfectionistic in their expectations about what a relationship should be and what it should do for them. They may have unrealistic expectations of their partners or impossibly high standards. Underneath is the wish to be rescued and taken care of that grows out of unmet child-hood needs. Because they worry so much about signs of problems, they wind up creating them. Small problems that a less anxious couple would see as "not that big a deal" get read through the lens of trauma and blown out of proportion. The couple's deep fear of the relationship falling apart or engulfing and subsuming them can tax it so much that it becomes a self-fulfilling prophecy.

Adult children of trauma are deeply hurt people who often unconsciously want their relationships to fix their pain and make their wounds go away. It comes as a shock when, instead of going away, they actually surface with extraordinary intensity. Not only does the couple not know what to do with these wounds or where they are coming from, they think it means that their relationship is bad. "I keep choosing the wrong people." "I married my mother." The tragedy of this is that relationships which could work out don't have the opportunity to. Adult children of trauma can lack that inbred sense of what "nor-mal" feels like. Consequently they aren't sure what to dismiss and what to take seriously as it arises in marriage and family life.

The Distancer and the Pursuer

Still one more common couple dynamic is the *distancer* and *pursuer*. When Sandy pursued Michael, he became distant. Sandy felt that she needed full commit-ment immediately, and Michael's reluctance to grant it felt like a torture. The more in pursuit Sandy was, the more distant Michael became. Generally, this was the way things played. However, when the dynamic reversed and

Michael was in pursuit of Sandy, she suddenly withdrew and became ambivalent. The truth of it was that they both feared intimacy and used these alternating roles to keep a safe and constant distance from each other. One minute Sandy was the one who wanted to be "close," next it was Michael. When one came closer, the other grew distant. The roles changed, but the distance between the two remained the same.

Unresolved trauma and addiction issues are a breeding ground for anger and hostility. Anger that masks old hurt spills out into the container of the relationship that triggers it. This means that adult children of trauma are more likely to have relationships characterized by conflict than others. In research done by Timothy Smith at the University of Utah (Williams and Williams 1993), it was found that couples that scored high in tests that measured levels of anger and hostility (high HO scores) had more "dominating, acrimonious interchanges than those with low HO scores." The test instrument used was the popular Minnesota Multiphasic Personality Inventory (MMPI).

Next in our progression come the children born to the couple. Unless the couple resolves their trauma-related issues, those issues get passed down in a myriad of ways. In the following pages we will examine some of the mechanisms through which attitude and behavior get handed down through the generations.

PARENTS GIVE WHAT THEY GOT WITHOUT KNOWING WHY: WHEN ADULT CHILDREN OF TRAUMA HAVE CHILDREN

Our daughter was born in September. Her first winter was spent in our arms in a snuggy. By her second winter she was walking, and I knew that she needed a winter coat and a muff. Somehow, I got it into my head that a winter coat meant a blue or pink coat with a white fur collar and a muff—until I had these items, I felt that she was not prepared for the cold. I searched every store and catalog I could find, but I couldn't locate them. As a last resort, I bought powder blue and pink wool, fur and a pattern, then gave them to a seamstress to sew what I was convinced were compulsory parts of her winter wardrobe. As time-consuming as this project was, I never questioned the fact (in my mind) that these coats were absolutely necessary for my daughter's first winter on her own feet. Once I had them, I felt at rest. She was prepared, winter was possible, it could come.

Fifteen or so years later, I was looking through some old photographs with my mother that I hadn't seen for thirty years at least. We came upon one in which I was wearing a little blue wool coat with a white collar and my hands were tucked into a winter fur muff. I said, "Oh, I had a little blue coat," to which my mother replied, "You had a pink one, too. You loved them." It was at that moment, I think, that I fully accepted the power of an unconscious childhood memory.

All during my intense search for my daughter's coat, I never once recollected that, at that same age in my own life, I had worn the very same coat that I was so convinced she absolutely needed. Never once did I understand that my drive toward finding (or re-finding) this coat for her was the direct result of my own experience at this same age in my own life. Though the memory of my coat was unconscious, it reappeared at this moment in my daughter's life as a projected need for her. The coat I wore and had forgotten, I needed to put on her so that she would feel as I had felt—cozy, adored and looked after. The muff that had kept my hands warm became the muff I felt she needed to keep her hands warm. These coats and muffs were what little girls wore in the fifties, but time collapsed and was meaningless with the reappearance of my own little girl. What I could not find in the stores of the seventies, I had made, because my coat and muff had made such an impression on my child mind. It held a meaning for me that I needed to pass on to my little girl.

The Age Correspondence Reaction

This is known as an *age correspondence reaction*. So much of parenting is a passing on of just this sort of memory, just this sort of meaning. We clothe our children in the memories of our own childhood past. With precise accuracy, these memories are triggered when our children enter the stages of development that are captured in our unconscious minds, recorded and forgotten—waiting to reemerge when our own children enter that same stage in their own lives. Our children's reaching a particular age stimulates memories from when we were that age ourselves. Good memories beget good actions; painful memories beget painful actions. The child who was beaten as a four-year-old later becomes the father who beats his four-year-old. The age correspondence reaction is, in my opinion, the key to unlocking how trauma thinking, feeling and behavior is passed down through the generations. If we wish to "break the chain" of an inner world that is prone to addiction or trauma, we need to transform the memory from unconscious "acting out" on reenactment to conscious "talking out." We need to use these moments of truth, such as the one we will see in our next story, as guides of where we need to do our personal work, where we need to seek out help and healing.

The Role as the Dynamic Aspect of Self

Trauma survivors also pass on what they have learned because of the roles that have been modeled for them. One way that people develop and express themselves is through *roles*. The role, according to J. L. Moreno, is the tangible form the self takes (1964). Thinking, feeling and behavior are role-specific. That is, we think, feel and behave according to the particular role we are playing. A daughter thinks, feels and acts like a daughter while a father thinks, feels and acts like a father. The self emerges from the role being played.

Moreno describes three stages of role learning. The first is *role taking*. This stage is something like modeling or imitation, where we take in the role exactly as we see it or experience it from some outside source. For example, we learn to be a mother from how we are mothered.

The second stage he outlines is *role-playing*. This is playing the role we have learned, while aspects of our own personality intrude on the original learning and find their way to the surface, so we play the role as we learned it but with our own personality giving it light, flavor and color.

In the third stage, we enter *role creation*. At this point we have learned the role, have recognized that we are able to play it, and have made the dynamics of playing it conscious enough so that we are more or less in charge of it and can play it consciously. Ideally we would parent from this stage in our role development.

History seems to repeat itself most frequently when we play the role either just as we learned it or by doing the opposite to the way we learned it, referred to as *reaction formation*. While aspects of the role remain unconscious, we tend to pass on what we got in more or less the form in which we got it, with bits and pieces of our own personality interlaced, or else we play out the opposite if we reacted against what we got. An example of this might be a woman who as a child felt ignored by her mother to such an extent that she felt she was disappearing. As a parent, she may have a tendency either to ignore her own children and play the role exactly as she learned it (passing on the pain) or to overprotect and smother them (reaction formation).

One other dynamic that passes down dysfunctional patterns is *triangulation*. For example: The mother and father use the daughter for a scapegoat. Then, when the daughter grows up and finds a husband, they use her as a scapegoat for their painful issues, repeating the previous dynamic.

Here is another illustration, from one of my psychodrama students at New York University, of the way parents unconsciously pass down what they have learned.

John brought up an incident from the past that we worked out psychodramatically. He set up a scene in which he was about sixteen. He was standing in the kitchen when his father walked in. He said, "Hi, Pop," thinking he was making a friendly overture to his father. His father gave him a slap and said, "Don't ever call me Pop!" Shocked and confused, John replied with something like, "What's the big deal? What did I do? Why did you slap me?" His father grumbled something and left the room. John stood in anxious silence as he went over in his mind all of the possible negative interpretations that his father might have inferred from "Hi, Pop." He strained his intellect as far as it would go; it made no sense, which was scary, because who could tell when some other comment he made in innocence might set his dad off? About two hours later, his father finally figured out what had happened. Troubled by the power of his own reaction, he reflected on its origins until he recalled that he was forbidden to call his father (John's grandfather) "Pop." It was "too disrespectful." Suspecting that this might have cultural origins, I asked John to choose someone to play his grandfather. John reversed roles with his grandfather, and I interviewed him.

Tian: "What's your name?"

John (in the role of grandfather): "John."

Tian: "Where are you from?"

John (as grandfather): "Sicily."

Immediately, I understood that two cultures had clashed. The Sicilian father in America had seen the behavior as disrespectful. No good Sicilian son would address his father in so offhand a manner, and he had not allowed his son (also named John) to use it. That made sense; it went along with his cultural norms. But when young John, as a second-generation American kid, affectionately called his American-born dad "Pop" and got hit, that made no sense. The role behavior was passed down, but the context was no longer appropriate. It was a transference reaction where John Number Two transferred something he got from John Number One onto John Number Three. An old role relationship was transferred onto a present-day role relationship.

This story also illustrates *identification flipping,* as John Two identifies with John One, then acts the contacts out with John Three.

In the case of the three Johns, John Number Two was an emotionally literate person who had the psychological health to reflect on his own behavior. He sat with the feelings surrounding his overreaction and named them: shame, embarrassment and regret. He put together the meaning "Pop" had had for him and traced it back to a painful situation from his own past. He had been hit for calling his father by a name at this same age (equivalent to "Pop") that his father found disrespectful (an age correspondence reaction on the part of John Number Two). Once he understood all the ramifications of the interaction, he chose to go to his son, John Number Three, and apologize. He broke the chain of the cycle of reenactment. This greatly relieved John Three, transformed his fear of John Two into understanding, and became a very bonding experience in which the two of them talked about John Two's childhood for a couple of hours. It gave John Three a deeper understanding of both his father and himself and allowed John Two to let go of an old piece of baggage.

Children aren't the only people in a family who grow and change. The family is a container for all concerned. The atmosphere of respect, support and nurturance is a source from which each member of a family draws strength throughout life. Families are dynamic units, and each role shapes, affects and defines the others. Communication is key to allowing family members to self-actualize while still staying in touch emotionally. Intimate relationships with partners and children are one of our truest vehicles for stimulating unresolved pain because they so closely mirror our early sense of connection. They trigger our conditioned fear responses. They show us where our wounds are and motivate us to work through them. This is a gift we give to ourselves and those we love. This need to connect and correct can help us to surrender and become willing to change if we make the dynamics conscious. It is this surrendering and willingness that open the door to change. Then—because of our need for connectedness—we are willing to let others share that pain to help us as we help them.

Nature Plus Nurture—How Relationships Develop Emotional Intelligence

Today's research shows that the interaction between parents and children actually forms the hardwiring of a child's brain.

Psychological and emotional development in a young child is a process of continual "organizing, disorganizing, and reorganizing within its internal world" (Schore 1994). Everything that occurs in a child's social world affects neurochemical and neurobiological structure. Nature and nurture do not compete, but work hand in hand, two systems constantly influencing and shaping each other.

Development is not a solitary activity that takes place

only within a child. Rather, both neurochemical development and neurobiological development occur in response to the give-and-take between child and caregiver. Such social interactions actually alter the neurochemistry and neurobiology or the hardwiring of a child's brain. Next, children encounter and express themselves as the persons they have become, and their personalities elicit particular responses from their caregivers and social worlds, which continue to shape their development (Schore 1994).

The mother is the primary mediator of an infant's social world. She serves as a sort of transistor or translator between the environment and the child, showing the developing child through each subtle, emotionally laden interaction what the world is made of. Is it safe or scary, supportive or denying? Actually, the naturally attuned mother will not construct an either/or world but one that is well-modulated, creating safety, love and nurturing alongside slowly teaching how to tolerate frustration and postpone gratification. A subtle process of feeding and weaning constantly occurs in the mother-child relationship so that the infant, through the caregiver's attuned response, learns about regulating from the mother until such regulation evolves gradually into self-regulation.

The development of the infant/mother relationship is part of the deepest process of using language as symbol. The infant needs the presence of the mother and in her absence may use such transitional objects as "security blankets" to keep the feeling of her presence near. A blanket that carries her scent might later be converted to teddy bears that the child can cuddle in her absence. Eventually, the child will use the word "mommy" to evoke the image and feeling of nearness that is required for comfort. The conversion of this primary need into language is central to a child's psychic organization and sense of personal security. This concept of *mommy* held by the word is the beginning of what will allow a child to introject or take into the self the image of the mother upon which gets built a sense of comfort and security. The child may not always have the physical presence of the mother but will be able, at will, to call her into itself.

This is touchingly illustrated by a psychoanalyst friend of mine. His two-year-old son has a blue toy phone and when the father stays away for the night for work, he presses the large square buttons, incanting, "Daddy, Daddy, Daddy" over and over again. Without the experience of "daddy" converted into the word symbol, he would surely not understand that the voice at the other end of his real telephone is indeed his father. It is this naming of the initial experience that allows him both to call forth the image of his father for a sense of connection and to use his phone game as his method of accessing that connection.

This is how a child begins to learn to *self-soothe*. Self-soothing is one of the primary developmental tasks. For those who have lived with trauma, learning healthy ways of self-soothing is critical and will help them not to seek comfort in addictive, self-destructive ways.

The psychoanalyst Mme. Spielrein has surmised in her studies of early language that the word "mama" uttered in so many languages is actually an extension or a prolongation of the act of sucking, that primitive instinct inborn in every child designed to sustain life in its earliest stages. The sounds produced by an infant are then attached to a sort of command to the mother to satisfy the need for food and by extension, nurturing and soothing. Much early language, according to Jean Piaget, seminal researcher on child development, is not being related to concepts but to the satisfaction of basic needs. The child utters its primitive command and its need is fulfilled as if by magic "or at least," says Piaget, "connected with peculiar modes of behavior which should be studied for themselves and quite apart from adult mentality."

The following story is an example of such meaning from my own life. It illustrates how the interactions that occur within a child's universe are imbedded with a magical sort of meaning.

Our little corner of the balcony was like Mount Olympus. The sun streamed in on our little chats, bathing us in its radiance: All of the world was morning. My father owned the mountain, his hair was made out of the sun and when he moved his powerful limbs to caress my forehead or lift me miles through the air up to his lap, the earth moved. I flew like a small animal being plucked out of the grass. I sailed through the air and felt the wind brush up against my cheek. Then suddenly, I was put down onto the arms of a redwood chair and I was of equal stature to my father—I was as tall as the heavens and the top of my head brushed against them. For a moment, I was smarter, braver than anything in the world below me. My little words fell with pleasure and amusement upon my father's waiting ears. Now and again he rolled his head back in laughter and amusement and the air around him shook. He was my hero beyond all other heroes, my knight in shining armor—the person I adored most of anyone in the world. *Tell me your stories, Daddy. I will listen. I will listen with my heart, my soul and my body. I will listen better than any little girl has ever listened before. Tell me what you want and I will magically grant it. There is nothing that this love of mine can deny you—nothing I would not do to bring a smile to your face or to bring calm and peace to your brow. You cast your glow into my soul and I am special. There is nothing beyond our corner of the earth, our mountain perch—all the world issues from this point outward. This is the center of the universe—where it all began. This is my place in the sun.*

I share my own experience to illustrate the almost magical, archetypal meaning that children make out of events in childhood. It is impossible to separate emotional literacy from these early interpretations because they are the meaning that we attach to words and events. The brain remembers best material that has a high emotional charge, be it positive or negative. The common thread is that they are both experiences with intense emotional content that burn themselves into the neurochemistry of the brain and act as a template upon which we print future pages of life.

The magical thinking is an outgrowth of the meaning children make out of these subtle interactions that occur repeatedly in their young, egocentric world. The child experiences a sense of oneness with the mother or father through such interactions that actually influence the hardwiring of their emotional brain, so to speak, and the meaning that they attach to early language. Their emotional intelligence and literacy grows out of this partnered experience of themselves and life. "The earliest substantives of child language are very far from denoting concepts, but rather express commands or desires." This early language retains "for many years in the child's mind a significance that is not only affective but also well-nigh magical . . ." (Piaget 1981). Traumatic memories can also take on meaning that can be terrifying for the small child. If goblins lurk under the bed and monsters might be hiding in the closet waiting to pop out, then imagine what a drunk and out-of-control parent becomes in the mind of a child.

All of these early experiences are the seeds of emotional literacy. Until children know an experience internally, they cannot name it. The more attuned the caregiver is in interactions, the less confused and overwhelmed children will be. A well-ordered, modulated world allows children to better understand what is going on internally, and that makes it easier for them to name and communicate their inner world to another person. A disorganized, murky and pain-filled world produces the opposite effect.

It is important to understand that the root of emotional literacy is nonverbal. It is the experience of comfort that precedes the naming of that feeling, the feeling of love that tugs for a word to encapsulate it, the burst of anger that seeks a label to reflect the intensity of the feeling. Without the emotion, there is nothing to name.

Electrophysiological studies using animals as models of cerebral development show that, compared to those of adults, the higher centers of young brains are able to deal with only a small amount of information per unit of time, and their brain circuits function more slowly than those of adults. In the book *Forsyte Saga*, the protagonist of the story refers to that magical period in his childhood where everyone spoke in "special voices" just for him. Adults intuitively understand that children need to be spoken to differently than adults do: slowly, with greater emphasis on particular words, along with emotion integrated into the tone, tempo, touch and facial expression.

Brain structure develops daily during the accelerated period of brain growth in infancy. In the first year of life, the weight of a child's brain goes from four hundred grams to one thousand grams, more than doubling its size in twelve months. This critical period is influenced by social forces. The rapid growth continues until around eighteen to twenty-four months and is particularly sensitive to outside stimuli. There are late-maturing areas of the cortex, the area of the brain that oversees conscious thought, which mature after subcortical brain-stem areas.

Stanley Greenspan, in his extensive research on child development (1999), speaks of growth-producing or growth-inhibiting environments. A growth-producing environment is one in which the parent is attuned to the child and the child can become attuned to the parent. It is one in which there is no great gap between what is said and what is done or between words and actions. Such environments, in which consistency and authenticity are the norm, allow children to internalize behavioral norms and routines that they can count on. This means that children's energy is freed up to meet the challenges and opportunities of their own lives. In the growth-inhibiting environment such as is found in an alcoholic family, the child's energy has to be devoted to developing strategies to ward off painful, confusing and inconsistent behavior. In such cases, children become internally preoccupied with bringing sense and order to external and internal chaos so that they can feel safe.

FOUR

Trauma in the Body and in the Brain: The Body-Mind Connection

The mind is hurt and the body cries out.
Italian Proverb

The body remembers what the mind forgets.
J. L. Moreno

I ache all over.
She's a pain in the neck.
You make me sick to my stomach.
He's a pain in the butt.
My gut's telling me. . . .
I feel it right in the small of my back.
He's got a heartache.
My head is bursting.

My father's hand used to shake violently whenever we crossed a border. I remember him repeating in his thick Greek accent, "I am an American citizen." I noted that other people's hands didn't shake that way, but whether we were driving to Canada and I was watching from deep in the back seat of the Cadillac or trailing my family like a little duck as we passed through European customs, my father shook and his eyes darted around like a fox looking for a hole to hide in before he got ravaged by the hounds. Now I know that is what trauma looks like. It's physical—stored in the body. It makes you shake and become hypervigilant, scanning the environment for danger when anxiety gets triggered.

When I asked my mother why Daddy shook so, she explained, "Your father came here when he was sixteen years old and he had only his guts and his faith in God with him. He got a job on an ocean liner, and when they were in port in New York he summoned up all his courage and ran down the gangplank onto the pier. He still remembers all the voices saying, *'Pyastone, pyastone!'*" ("Catch him!" in Greek.) Mom said that he sometimes woke in the middle of the night and sat bolt upright in bed with his eyes wide open and his ears hearing those words even thirty and forty years later. I never liked to wake my father out of sleep because his eyes startled open with a haunted, terrified look. This exaggerated startle response was another sign of trauma.

Poor Dad, now I understand that liquor was like medicine to you, a way of calming you down, quieting intrusive memories and taking you out of this terrible place like insulin for a diabetic. If only we had known.

How Traumatic Memory Gets Stored

Traumatic memory is stored in what is referred to as the "old brain." This part of the brain is older in evolutionary terms than more recently developed parts of the brain, such as the cortex. This older part of the brain was developed at a time when our species was less evolved. Therefore, the memory that is stored here tends to be encoded with responses that were helpful to early humans and their survival. Fight, flight and freeze responses, common to both animals and humans, are sur-vival skills that were especially needed by early humans. They are also the response to trauma in both humans and animals.

Van der Kolk describes what happens when memories are stored without much conscious thought attached to them; they become what we refer to as "body emotions." According to Bessel Van der Kolk (1987), "In PTSD fail-ure of declarative memory may lead to organization of the trauma on a soma sensory level (as visual images or physi-cal sensations) that are relatively impervious to change. The inability of people with PTSD to integrate traumatic experiences in their tendency to continuously relive the PTSD are mirrored physiologically and hormonally in the misinterpretation of innocuous stimuli as potential threats." The person will revert to earlier defenses of fight, flight or freeze, which might include fighting, withdrawing, becoming emotionally numb and non-communicative, leaving, or dissociating, thus creating or re-creating the very situations that they wish to put behind them forever.

Consequently, when we are triggered in everyday life into trauma memories that are stored in the old brain, our responses tend to be inhibited in accordance with the inhibitions of the stored memory.

In other words, if we shut down as a kid being yelled at, we may well shut down as a spouse being criticized—or do its direct opposite when shutting down doesn't hold any more and we burst like a hot water pipe. Trauma memo-ries reveal themselves also through flashbacks and somatic sensation. They are not organized into the memory system in the same contextualized manner in which more benign memories are stored in the brain, because our defenses are in high gear to protect us against feeling the pain at the time the trauma occurs. Memory storage is affected at such times, so only bits and pieces get past our protective guard. Consequently, people who have been traumatized misread current life events. Events that a nontraumatized person might pass over or have only a temporary reaction to can send a previously traumatized person into an emotional tailspin that might include withdrawal, anger, belligerence, fear, hurt or rage. The traumatized person is reacting to a currently upsetting situation—be it bad traffic or a fight with a spouse or crossing a border for a simple family vacation—with the intensity of feelings appropriate not to this situation but to the original trauma. They are getting triggered, stuck in yesterday, constantly reliving the cycle of intense feeling associated with the original traumatic episode or the cumulative trauma of an earlier pain-filled relationship. The misinterpretation that occurs is important to note in understanding trigger reactions. The person being triggered may insist that what is bothering them is exactly what is going on. They hang onto their misinterpretation as the absolute and only possible interpretation of what is taking place. Obviously, their spontaneity is greatly limited because they are reduced to very few responses when they are feeling traumatized. When memories are synthesized, "metabolized" and processed or thought about in the cortex, choice is possible, and we are able to operate well enough to come up with "adequate responses" rather than those limited by trauma responses.

When, through therapy, we can dredge up from our memory bank enough pieces of the puzzle of our own

lives, we can make sense out of our experiences by syn-
thesizing them into stories with beginnings, middles and
ends, and themes that make sense in the context of our
own lives. It is very important, according to Judith
Herman, author of *Trauma and Recovery*, that survivors
telling the full trauma narrative or story go back to the
time in their lives *before* the trauma took hold. There is so
much confusion and memory loss that follows a traumatic
episode that we simply cannot remember life before the
trauma. We lose touch with the happy child we were
before the family fell apart or the self-confident teenager
we were before the accident and so on. We need to put
the story back into the overall context of our lives so that
our whole life (and self) becomes ours again.

The Emotional Body

Measurement is the foundation of modern science.
According to scientists, if we can't measure it, it doesn't
exist. Hence, heart, emotions and spirit get relegated to
the fringe—incarcerated in prescribed substrates, such as
church, temple, talk therapy or New Age ideology. That is,
until Candace Pert discovered (measured) something
called the *opiate receptor* (1997). Market-driven interest
and acceptance came from pharmacologists who develop
drugs, as it provided them with a way to understand the
action of drugs in the human organism.

According to Pert, each cell of our body is covered with
vast numbers of tiny receptors, something like satellite
dishes. "Basically, receptors function as sensing molecules," says Pert, ". . . scanners. Just as our eyes, ears,
nose, tongue, fingers and skin act as sense organs, so, too,

do the receptors on a cellular level. They hover in the membranes of your cells, dancing and vibrating, waiting to pick up messages carried by other vibrating little creatures, also made out of amino acids, which come cruising along—*diffusing* is the technical word—through the fluids surrounding each cell. . . . All receptors are proteins . . . and they cluster in the cellular membrane waiting for the right chemicals to swim up to them through the extra cellular fluid and mount them by fitting into their keyholes—it is a process known as binding."

This is the path through which information enters a cell and is distributed throughout the body. The binder itself is called a ligand, and the process of the ligand bumping into the cell, skipping off and bumping back on again is called cell binding. After the binding has occurred "the receptor, having received the message, transmits it from the surface of the cell deep into the cell's interior where the message can change the state of the cell dramatically" (ibid.). Then a chain reaction occurs as "tiny machines roar into action directed by the message of the ligand" (ibid.). According to the information and the resulting chain reaction, changes in behavior, physical activity and mood occur. This process has its own order in that receptors ignore all ligands but those that are made to fit it or those that vibrate to the same tune, so to speak. "The smallest, simplest of molecules, generally made in the brain to carry information across the gap, or synapse" (ibid.) are called neurotransmitters. These are the names we have heard bandied around in journals and magazines—like dopamine, histamine, serotonin, norepinephrine, GABA, acetylcholine and glycine.

The second category of ligands is comprised of

steroids. These include the sex hormones testosterone, progesterone and estrogen. The third category, which comprises 95 percent of all the ligands, is called peptides, which play a large role in regulating most all life processes and play a pivotal role in what Pert calls molecules of emotion. What we are talking about is information—how it travels around the body, is altered by what it encounters and gets into cells, where it orchestrates and drives the functions of our body and mind, which are so intimately interwoven that they are more truthfully referred to as *bodymind*. Francis Schmitt of MIT referred to this dynamic process as *information substances,* which describes the "messenger molecules and their receptors as they go about their job of linking brain, body and behavior" (Pert 1997). Schmitt included in his new generic category both long-familiar substances such as the classical neurotransmitters and the steroid hormones, and newly discovered ones such as peptide hormones, neuropeptides and growth factors—all ligands that trigger receptors and initiate a cascade of cellular process and changes.

What Candace Pert is telling us is that emotions, in the form of biochemicals, are constantly circulating throughout our bodies, received into cells distributed and located all over our bodies and encoded into the cells with which they bind. Having a "gut reaction," experiencing someone as a "pain in the neck," feeling "queasy" when we see that our kids are cut or bruised—all speak to the constant passage and storage of emotion in the body.

There is a clear link between emotions and memory that has a physiological base. After all, feelings have to be stored somewhere or we wouldn't be able to recall them. One case study refers to how liquor acts as the stimulus for recall. People in a study were taught tasks while under the influence of alcohol. Those same tasks were difficult to recall while these people were sober, but when they were again given alcohol, the tasks were easily remembered. "The emotion is the equivalent of the drug, both being ligands that bind to receptors in the body," says Pert. "What this translates into in everyday experience is that positive emotional experiences are much more likely to be recalled when we're in an upbeat mood, while negative emotional experiences are recalled more easily when we're already in a bad mood. Not only is memory affected by the mood we're in but so is actual performance. We're likely to be helpful to others and perform in altruistic ways when we're experiencing a good mood. Conversely, hurt the ones you love enough times and they will learn to feel threatened in your presence and remember to act accordingly."

Emotion has played a pivotal role in what gets remembered and what gets forgotten throughout evolution. "The cave woman who could remember which cave had the gentle guy who gave her food is more likely to be our foremother than the cave woman who confused it with the killer bear," quips Pert. "The emotion of love (or something resembling it) and the emotion of fear would help her secure her memories."

Moods and emotional states are generated, then, by neuropeptide ligands. These neuropeptide ligands exist both in the brain and in the body, which runs contrary to earlier research that saw all emotion as solely within the brain. But we are now discovering that "what we experience as an emotion or a feeling is also a mechanism for activating a particular neuronal circuit—simultaneously through the brain and body" (ibid.). Much like the stimulus of alcohol we discussed previously, the emotion acts as a trigger of behavior in the entire person on all levels, physical, emotional, mental, spiritual and so on. What is not known to date is whether or not there is a peptide for each feeling, but for our purposes we are breaking down the wall between the body and the mind, recognizing that they are the parts of a whole, a network of systems that interact to produce the sum total of who we are.

Darwin referred to the emotional facial expressions common to both animals and humans that have been preserved and used throughout the evolution of the species in *Expression of Emotions in Man and Animals*. In a Learning Channel series on primates, it was shown that monkeys exhibit a sort of widening of the lips showing teeth that looks like a smile. In fact, monkeys use this facial gesture to communicate to each other that they are not intending to act aggressively. I was reminded of one of my son's teachers who used a smile similarly. The kids used to imitate it. Intuitively, they knew that it wasn't a real smile. Instead, he seemed to use it to show that he did not intend to act aggressively even though he was feeling aggressive inside. In my own dealing with the teacher, I interpreted it in this way also. The smile always came over this teacher's face when he was about to say something aggressive but wished to signal that he still intended to maintain a friendly communication. Emotional signals are constantly traveling through our bodies both consciously and unconsciously, and they affect the way we look, stand, sit and move.

The Body Remembers—Cellular Memory

Candace Pert's research, along with that of many other biophysiologists, has come to prove that memory is stored, not in the brain alone as we previously thought, but throughout our bodies. Information moves through the body at split-second speeds, carried by a vast network of neurotransmitters, and attaches itself to receptors surrounding each cell in the body. This "cellular memory" opens the door to understanding why, for example, we experience a particular memory when we are pressed in a certain area of the body.

"The living tissue retains records of memory of the influences that have been exerted upon it" (Oschman and Oschman 1995). When vibrations pass through tissues, they are altered by the signatures of the stored information. In this way, our consciousness and our choices are influenced by memories stored in soft tissues.

"Memories are stored not only in the collagen network but in the elastic fibers and even in the various cells found throughout the connective tissue: histocyte, fibroblasts, osteoblasts, plasma cells, fat cells, etc. One has the impression that every movement of the body is recorded in the living matrix. The repeated movements in, say, learning how to play tennis, alter our connective tissue architecture. If we add a sport such as speed walking to our repertoire, we will forever alter that architecture" (Oshmann and Oshmann 1998). This is why we are able to respond automatically. Throw us a ball and our hand flies up to receive it; we get caught in a gust of snow and our eyes narrow; expose a man who was beaten as a child to verbal abuse and his palms sweat and his heart rate increases.

"Researchers have noted that the psychological effects of trauma are stored in somatic memory and expressed as changes in the body's stress response." This is why when we get triggered our throat goes dry, our heart rate speeds up, our gut churns and our head starts pounding. In other words, buried memories that were somatized, repressed or dissociated from in the past because they were too scary to feel are getting triggered.

Intense emotions cause memories of particular events to be dissociated from consciousness and stored instead as visceral sensations (anxiety and panic) or visual images (nightmares and flash-backs). Traumatized patients seem to react to reminders of the trauma with emergency responses that had been relevant to the original threat but that are inappropriate for the current situation. . . . Unable to put the trauma behind them, victims have trouble learning from experience: their energy is funneled toward keeping their emotions under control at the expense of paying attention to cur-rent exigencies. They become fixated on the PTSD, in some cases by being obsessed with the trauma, but more often by behaving and feeling as if they were traumatized over and over again without being able to locate the origins of these feelings (Van der Kolk et al. 1996).

The Somatizing Personality

There emerged out of the research of psychoanalysts two notable concepts of mental functioning in people who suffered from forms of psychosomatic illness. The first,

La pensée opératoire (Paris School: Marty, de M'Uzan and David 1963), is translated as "operatory thinking." This is a type of mental functioning that is totally affectless, where a person is completely out of touch with their emotions relating to a particular event or circumstance. Joyce McDougall, in *Theaters of the Body* (1998), describes two clients with this affectless manner of living.

A patient who had fallen gravely ill with ulcerative colitis was asked what events had occurred in her life just before the outbreak of her violent loss of bowel control. After some searching she recounted in a flat unemotional tone of voice that her parents and her fiancée had been killed in an automobile crash from which she had escaped unhurt. When asked what her reactions to this tragic event had been, she replied, *"I just knew I'd have to pull myself together."* A sensitive listener might read behind the spoken lines and understand that the young lady felt her whole life had been suddenly shattered and that much pulling together of the broken pieces would be required. She, however, had no conscious knowledge of such feelings and made no connection between the traumatizing event and her subsequent psychosomatic illness, in which her body exploded in an uncontrollable, life-threatening way.

Another patient who suffered a sudden outbreak of psoriasis that covered almost his entire body revealed that shortly before this he had run his automobile into a woman pushing her baby in a pram and had severely injured both. When asked what he felt at the time the accident occurred, he replied, *"It was okay. I'm totally insured."* Like the preceding patient, this man saw no connection between his own repressed emotion and turmoil that may have contributed to his psychosomatic outburst and the accident.

The findings of the Paris School led to further research in Boston (Nemiah and Sifneos 1970, Nemiah 1978) and the development of the concept of *Alexithymia*. Alexithymia refers to a condition in which people have no words to describe their emotional states, either because they have no awareness of their inner states or because they cannot distinguish one emotion from another. Earlier we discussed Kathryn, the victim—along with her twin— of sexual abuse, who feels she has no insides. At times in therapy she says, "I know you all think I'm here and I'm relating to everything that's going on, but inside I'm completely disconnected." She refers to herself as having "thought-feelings"; that is, she can figure out through thinking what she should or might be feeling, but within her she cannot distinguish one feeling from another.

Somatic patients need not fall into these categories of alexithymia. Somatization may occur, according to McDougall, when "the emotion aroused is not recognized in a symbolic way (that is, within the code of language which would have allowed the affect [feeling]-laden representations to be named, thought about and dealt with by the mind) but instead is immediately transmitted by the mind to the body, in a primitive non-verbal way such as fight-flight impulses, thus producing the physical disorganization that we call psychosomatic symptom."

The Emotional Brain

It is our limbic brain, or as some refer to it, the emotional brain, that directly governs mood. What goes on in the limbic brain directly affects the relaxation or the constriction of the organs of our body. It is our mood, not our thinking, that affects our heart. Emotions, then, are directly coded into how our body performs. When we talk about stress, we tend to divorce it from our emotional life and imagine that we can create activities that will manage it completely. However, without working with emotions that originate in the emotional brain, stress persists because the emotional brain exerts power that comes from behind.

According to Candace Pert, when asked about the relationship between emotions and health during an interview with Bill Moyers on PBS: "It leads us to think that the chemicals that are running our body and our brain are the same chemicals that are involved in emotion. And that says to me that we better seriously entertain theories about the role of emotions, emotional suppression and disease, and that we better pay more attention to emotions with respect to health."

Elaine de Beauport, in her research on the brain, adds: "I believe that the continuous lack of permission for feeling and, especially the lack of satisfactory experience with negativity, is a direct cause of the high rates of strokes, heart attacks and other organic weaknesses so prevalent in Western society. To restrict feelings is to restrict the organs of our body, and it leads to eventual weakness." Pert, Dreher and Ruff refer to the extensive research done by Pennebaker which "has shown that disinhibition of emotional expression and processing has solitary influence on immune functions and resistance to illness. In experimental studies, subjects who wrote their deepest thoughts and feelings about past traumas experienced enhanced

T-cell responsivity and improved overall health compared with control subjects who wrote about trivial events." Pennebaker has shown that, for this inhibition to foster health or healing, previously blocked emotions must not only be expressed but also cognitively processed, understood and resolved. He structures this through journaling over three or four twenty-minute writing sessions on successive days. The degree to which the subjects disclosed previously inhibited painful memories and emotions was linked to better health outcomes. (Later in our chapter on using journaling, photographs and letter writing you will see examples of how this can work.)

Memory Editing—Can We Create an Edited Life Script?

Giving voice to these emotions, using the skills of emotional literacy (i.e., naming, articulating, expressing, describing) allows us to come to see the emotional experiences we have stored in long-term memory and bring them for ward for other viewing. I call this "memory editing."

Learning is a process of tearing down and building up brain cells. Memory is stored in clusters. When, *through our desire to remember*, we bring one of these clusters forward—as we watch the memory unfold within the screen of our mind—we are actually paring down and building up brain cells. When we re-view the memory, we see it differently. We may discard old meaning that we had attached to particular events and introduce new meaning, new understanding, from now being able to see it in a new light. Then, when we re-store this memory—that is, when it returns to a less conscious state—it is stored differently in a new cell assembly. It is, in fact, *reframed* with new insight and new understanding.

We may feel that focusing on the positive is equivalent to working through negative feelings. In truth, ignoring or repressing those feelings is what can cause us problems in both psychological and physical health. What we need to do is to draw them out of our memory, feel them and think about them. Focusing on the positive and having optimistic attitudes about life is indeed one of life's great secrets. But we need to do both, to face trauma that drags on our inner world, then transform it into learning and growth. Trauma is part of life; it doesn't need to be seen as something that can devastate us forever. We can get over it, just as we can get over a physical ailment. Then our focusing on the positives has real power, and comes from an inner domain large enough to hold all of life.

Emotional literacy is the skill that integrates all of these processes. To give language to our inner world, to draw it from its hiding place onto the stage of our mind where we can dwell, look, wonder, feel and otherwise process, and to translate that experience into appropriate language— this is a skill that promotes physical and mental health.

Many of us set up coping strategies in childhood that we felt kept us safe from experiencing overwhelming emotions that we perhaps didn't understand or felt helpless in the face of. The power balance between ourselves and authority figures kept us from being able to process difficult emotions. Instead, we adopted strategies for not getting hurt: shutting down, running away, idealizing the abuser, repressing or hiding emotions, denying or minimizing. Although these coping mechanisms may have served to get us through in the short run, in the long run the feelings we hid and our strategies for dealing with painful feelings come to have a life of their own that gets played out in the "theater of our body" and relationships and situations in our present-day.

If we learned to hide our feelings as a coping strategy, we continue that pattern in adulthood. If we learned to repress them, we become grownups who white-knuckle it when the going gets tough emotionally. But emotions do not disappear. Rather, they are stored out of sight, perhaps even out of conscious mind, but certainly not out of the picture altogether. They remain stored in the brain and body where they exert a powerful influence over our healthy functioning.

It is my clinical experience that with enough reexamination through therapy these memories can be worked through and edited. Some seem to be permanently changed, while others, much like a tape in a recorder, get taped over rather than eradicated altogether; in other words, traces are still there but new memories have been formed on top of them that change our automatic responses to life. People can and do change if they put in the hard work to do so, but, luckily, inherent in each difficult stage of healing is relief, internal expansion and the joy of self-discovery.

TRAUMA IN THE BRAIN

The mind is a trickster when it comes to taking in information from the outside. Interestingly, what we take in and store as knowledge and how we categorize that knowledge largely depends on what we've already stored internally. In this sense, early experience shapes later experience, which is why making the unconscious conscious is so important. If we don't know what's in our minds, our choices are made largely unconsciously.

Let me give you an example from my own life—one that is not pleasant or easy to talk about but is an extremely clear example of what I'm describing. When I was a little girl, on several occasions I witnessed a man exposing himself while masturbating. Because as a child I felt frightened and overwhelmed by this sight, I relegated it to a part of my memory system that I held out of consciousness. In fact, I would not have known that it happened at all, had my mother not told me as an adult that I had told her about it when it occurred. (Even as I write this, I feel nauseated and my throat is going dry. The physiological responses to this traumatic sight are still with me. My body and my unconscious know something that I strongly resist knowing.)

The event that is so revealing occurred about twelve years ago, during a lunch break with two colleagues when I was attending a conference in New York. As we were walking back from lunch, we passed a homeless person on the street. I felt both drawn to and repelled by the state of the person. I reached into my wallet to pull out a dollar. A five-dollar bill was on top, and for some reason I made a split-second decision that I could not take the time to leaf through for a dollar. I quickly put the five in his hat and walked on. Both of my therapist friends noted all of this and ribbed me for my donation and quick exit. They assumed that I had seen what they had seen and understood why they didn't go near this man. The full impact of what I had done didn't become clear to me until they explained, with some incredulity at my seeming blindness, that this man was openly masturbating. I had blocked out what I was seeing, just as I had done as a child, while some other part of me registered it, panicked and made a fast exit. At that moment I truly understood the power of the human mind to relegate traumatic information to a portion of the mind that remains inaccessible. Had my colleagues not explained to me what I saw, I would not have seen it. I would have looked without seeing and acted without knowing why.

Traumatic memories are not stored the way other memories are stored, nor are they accessed the way normal memories are accessed. They return as body sensations and flashbacks, if at all, and they are stored in fragments of the truth, pieces of reality that are disconnected from one another. They remain unmetabolized, decontextualized and unsynthesized until such time as they are either triggered by life circumstances, causing confusion and disruption, or excavated in therapy (temporary, monitored confusion) and restrung to make sense, to create a context and a story line. While this memory remained unconscious, I had no choice regarding how to act. There was no decision made between a five-dollar and a one-dollar gift. All I could do was act and get away. Now that I have made this memory conscious and worked with it, I doubt that I would react that way again. It is in life itself that we test our healing and our new set of responses.

Our minds make split-second decisions as to what information they will take in and what information gets relegated to other areas of psychic storage. Information taken in by the brain, according to Jonathan Bowlby, renowned British psychoanalyst, can undergo one of several selection processes:

1. It can be completely excluded without leaving a trace—that is, the brain will not take it in at all.
2. It can be retained long enough outside of consciousness in a sort of buffer storage to influence judgment, autonomic responses and mood.
3. It can reach a stage of advanced processing associated with conscious thought and intelligent cognitive functioning, and in doing so influence all levels of thinking, thereby becoming eligible for long-term storage.

This description of the subtle selection process the brain goes through helps us understand how a person can avoid or dismiss information that the brain "forbids knowing." That is to say, the brain is influenced in what it accepts or rejects by what it already knows or is willing to accept. With split-second timing, it scans the flow of information, analyzing and evaluating it in terms of knowledge already stored or filed on the subject, and then sends commands to an encoder as to what should be kept and what should be rejected or discarded. This is how information that feels painful or traumatic can get stored in the brain without awareness or memory. Thus, someone who has a pattern of repression or denial can maintain this pattern with little conscious awareness, as perception happens so quickly and is largely subliminal (Dayton 1994). This helps us to see how we can be so blind to our own dark sides, even though we may be intelligent and perceptive in other areas.

The upshot is that, provided these representational models and programs are well adapted, the fact that they are drawn on automatically and without awareness is a great advantage. When, however, they are not well adapted, for whatever reason, the disadvantages of the arrangement become serious. As anyone who has developed a bad style in some physical skill knows well, to review the cognitive and action components of a system that has long been automated and to change it is arduous and often frustrating, moreover, it is not always very successful. Hence, some of the difficulties encountered during psychotherapy. You can't teach an old dog new tricks. This, however, is not the only problem nor the greatest. For the task of changing an over-learned program of action and/or of appraisal is enormously exacerbated when roles long implemented by the valuative system forbid its being reviewed (Bowlby 1973).

Trauma survivors who have adopted and repeated maladaptive or dysfunctional relationship styles that they learned as children find it difficult to retrain those styles in adulthood. To add to the problem, retraining those styles requires that they first be reviewed—which, in the case of survivors of trauma, requires that the survivor re-experience the emotional helplessness and vulnerability associated with the original hurt before "retraining" the subsequent behaviors.

Perceptual defenses, along with what the brain has learned, are core features determining whether or not a person is emotionally set up and capable of healthy mourning later in life, which is critical to reexamining trauma memories, rescripting and resolving them.

Accepting the full reality of a situation is a requisite of healthy mourning and eventual healing. However, people who are prone to splitting off painful or unwanted thoughts and feelings, relegating them to a part of the brain that is excluded from conscious awareness, are not able to sit with the full reality of a painful circumstance and process their thoughts and feelings associated with it. All of these are a part of mourning, which we will address more fully in chapter 7. Those for whom defensive exclusion is pervasive in their personalities are handicapped in their relationships. They are more likely to suffer breakdowns in functioning for periods lasting weeks, months or years, because they are impaired in dealing effectively with problems that arise in their lives (Dayton 1994).

Response to trauma, then, is bimodal. There is *hyper-reactivity* to stimuli on the one hand, which produces *anxiety* and a *feeling of reliving the original emotions.* Or, on the other hand, there is *psychic numbing,* which leads to *avoidance* and *amnesia.* These responses to extreme experiences are so consistent across the different forms of traumatic stimuli that this bimodal reaction appears to be the normative response to any overwhelming and uncontrolled experience. As an apparent attempt to compensate for chronic hyper-arousal, traumatized people seem to shut down: on a behavioral level by avoiding stimuli reminiscent of the trauma and on a psychobiological level by emotional numbing which extends to both trauma-related and everyday experience (Van der Kolk 1996).

The freeze or numbing response when humans are confronted with traumatic events is designed to protect the person from fully experiencing traumatic situations. Therefore, the memory is not stored the way other memories are stored, which also prevents learning from that experience. It complicates life later because the trauma survivors are thrown back on their earlier defenses and are not able to experience, work through and integrate current situations when confronted with a situation that feels frightening. One might say that trauma survivors have not learned that fire burns, so they keep putting their hands on a hot stove.

"In addition to the reactions to discrete, one-time traumatic incidents documented in these studies, interfamilial abuse is increasingly recognized to produce complex post traumatic syndromes that involve chronic affect disregulation, destructive behavior against self and others, learning disabilities, dissociative problems, somatization and distortions in concepts about self and others" (Van der Kolk et al. 1996).

The problem is that PTSD victims tend to lose the ability to use their emotions as signals. They are not able to use the emotions of their inner worlds as indicators of what is going on inside of them. Their reactions to emotionally painful situations can become fixed in nature as they lose their ability to react spontaneously. It is, then, no surprise that they tend to misread subtle signals from other people, either overreacting or underreacting to what communication they perceive another person is sending out to them, even on a subliminal level. This greatly complicates learning the skills of emotional literacy because core emotions are unavailable or confused with other internal dynamics.

FIVE

Personality Characteristics of Adult Children of Trauma and Addiction: What Happened to Me?

The child is the father to the man.

William Wordsworth
"My Heart Leaps Up When I Behold," 1802

If you bring forth what is within you, it will heal you. And if you do not bring forth what is within you, it will destroy you.

from the Gospel of St. Thomas

POST-TRAUMATIC STRESS DISORDER

I n 1980, after the war in Vietnam, the illness underlying the psychological symptoms often created during war was given a name: post-traumatic stress disorder—PTSD for short. What was called "shell shock" in World War I, "battle fatigue" in World War II and "operational exhaustion" in the Korean War was studied anew. Ten years after the war, soldiers who "lost their innocence with an M-16 in their hands and a license to use it" (Eric Gerdman, psychologist, Silver Springs, Maryland, commenting on shell shock), exhibited the symptoms we now understand to be a part of PTSD. These included sudden appalling flashbacks to events in Vietnam, recurring nightmares, emotional numbness, periods of panic, depression and rage, sometimes exploding acts of violence, and often guilt about having survived. For soldiers even years after the war, symptoms surfaced that may have been vibrating beneath the surface all of that time.

There were other factors that made the PTSD of Vietnam veterans different from that of other wars. First, this was an adolescent's war, a surreal experience in which young men of an average age of nineteen, who were still in the process of developing a sense of self and a coherent self-image, were put into circumstances that they did not have the maturity to handle. It shattered their not-yet-developed sense of self. And this was a hated war that alienated these young soldiers from their peer group. They returned home with no parades or fanfare, no reentry rituals to reintegrate them back into life and society. As soon as their twelve-month tour of duty was finished, they were put on a plane alone to return to a society that didn't want them. The camaraderie and support received by soldiers in other wars who returned in groups to a country with open arms was denied to them. And this was a pointless war, it made no sense; hence, they were deprived of the sense of moral rightness that might have helped them cope and feel justified in the atrocities they were forced to commit.

Secrecy was another factor that exacerbated symptoms of PTSD. Sarah Haley, a psychiatric social worker at Boston's VA outpatient clinic, talks of David, who was drawn into "Operation Phoenix" at a vulnerable point after a personal injury. Against his deeper wishes, he "participated in nighttime raids, interrogations and assassinations in villages that were suspected to serve as havens for Vietcong" (Langone 1985). The "severity and persistence of his symptoms" led Haley to "believe he was harboring some secret from his Vietnam days. Five months into his psychotherapy during the anniversary month of his three narrow escapes from death, David told me of his participation in Operation Phoenix. It included night raids, interrogations and other horrors. He was tremulous and ashen, yet also greatly relieved. 'I've waited for years to tell someone about it'" (ibid.). The guilt that David felt about his actions locked him in a secrecy that made his PTSD symptoms more severe than they might have been had he felt a sense of moral rightness about his cause or a forum of support for his actions. Such survivor's guilt is common among Vietnam veterans; also among addicts who get and stay sober, and children or spouses of addicts who discard sick relationships and lifestyles for healthy ones.

As research on Vietnam veterans infiltrated the field of psychology, professionals in the mental health fields identified similar symptoms in those who had been victims of natural disasters such as earthquakes and floods or who had been exposed to prolonged periods of physical, emotional or sexual abuse—or who had lived with addiction.

The responses of those who have survived trauma will, of course, vary in intensity. Van der Kolk has identified several factors affecting the duration and severity of the trauma response:

1. *The severity of the stressor.* Research among 226 survivors of Nazi concentration camps showed 99 percent had some psychiatric disturbances, 87 percent had cognitive disturbances, 85 percent showed persistent nervousness and irritability, 60 percent suffered from sleep disturbances, and 52 percent (similar to Vietnam veterans) had nightmares.

2. *Genetic predisposition.* The central nervous system reacts differently in different people.

3. *Developmental phase.* An adult with a firm sense of identity and a good support system is infinitely better protected from the effects of trauma than a

child with less advanced cognitive skills.

4. *A person's social support system.* Disruption or loss of social support is intimately associated with inability to overcome the effects of psychological trauma. Children are particularly vulnerable to this when they are physically, emotionally or sexually abused by the very people on whom they depend for safety and nurturance.

5. *Prior traumatization.* People with a prior history of traumatization are more likely to develop long-term symptomatology in response to later trauma. This was true also for Vietnam vets.

6. *Preexisting personality.* People with pre-existing, untreated phobias and maladaptions to stressful life circumstances are more likely to have psychiatric reactions to trauma (Van der Kolk 1987).

Research has shown that living with chronic abuse can produce PTSD symptoms. The factors we have discussed above that contributed to the PTSD of veterans are also present in moderated forms in living in homes in which trauma and addiction are present. Children of addicts do not have the maturity to cope with parents who are more involved with their addiction than with them. Living with addiction can "shatter their not yet developed self." Addiction is a "hated war" (Langone 1985). It isolates families and children from feeling they are normal and a part of the mainstream. Children feel different, bad and shameful, and may lose their ability to take in love and support from others. And, like the war in Vietnam, this disease makes no sense. One day we're winning, the next losing. The enemy is not easily identifiable. Addicted families live under constant threat, in a siege state with intermittent reprieves that contribute to the feeling of senselessness, like the Vietnam soldier who returns from a day of killing in time for the evening movie—which tells the story of a culture from which he feels alienated and for which he is yearning at the same time.

Also, like the soldier David, addicts have lived secret, debasing and humiliating lives, over which they carry great shame. And along with the addict, family members are dragged into emotional and psychological places of pain and horror. One such memory stands out for me. After my parents' divorce, my father, having disappeared off my radar screen for a few months, resurfaced in Florida with a new house and a new partner. I would visit him there. Sometimes he was sober and we would have a great visit, and sometimes he was drunk and it was a trip of tears.

My father had a swimming pool that, in his drunkenness, he had let go after fighting with the pool man, and now it looked like a swamp. When my father was drunk he took on a diabolical cast; it's hard to describe, but there was a sort of crazy evilness pouring out of his eyes and a cat-like agility that belonged almost to another world. Each day he said, "Tianna, dive into the swimming pool." I was horrified. How could my father, who loved me more than "anything in this world," want me to swim through slime? I couldn't make sense of it. I liked to do what my father asked me to do because it made me feel secure in some strange way—as if I still had a father who cared about me. I was confused. Who was asking me to do this? I had no support. I was a teenager alone visiting him in a strange home. I said no, stop it, you're not serious (he couldn't be), but he kept at it again and again. "Go on, Tianna, dive in." At a weak, vulnerable and confused moment, I couldn't handle it anymore. I wanted him to stop, and I reasoned in my lonely and frightened state that two minutes of suffering would get him away from me, would make this scary daddy stop. I dived in. Suddenly, his humiliation and degradation became mine. I felt myself, young and fresh and clean, swimming through this drunkard's swamp that my father (whom I loved) had pushed me into. I pulled myself out of that pool, and I felt my head hanging down in shame and sorrow. It had come to this—this metaphor made flesh. I walked dripping to the shower and stood under it, wondering if I would ever be clean again. I think that was the moment when I knew in my soul that I had better save myself, because this person whom I loved so much and who loved me so much was going to drag me into his underworld if I let him. These are the kinds of stories those of us who grew up in addicted homes, as well as addicts themselves, keep secret.

When I came home after that visit, I must have seemed very different. My sister looked at me and said, "What happened?" I don't remember saying anything to anyone, I just put it away somewhere inside of me among the many other things that I had, as T. S. Eliot put it, "Forgotten and remembered." But I was shattered inside. This kind of deep confusion, these alternating, crazy-making realities are a seminal part of the addict's, ACOA's or codependent's world. Simultaneously, as the world we depend upon disintegrates we lose our accustomed sources of support. So the more we need help, the less we get it.

Over and over again people that I work with all across the United States share stories such as these; not openly and easily but through clenched faces, tightly held or trembling bodies and tears fighting their way up through the emotional constriction that has held them in check for so long. They feel alone, ashamed, as if no one will understand. They feel they are bad and carry a sense of guilt that, if they had done something else to ward off danger, the outcome might have been different. Those whose lives and relationships are working out suffer a profound sense of survival guilt that can lead to relapse or some form of self-sabotage.

The research on PTSD has opened the door to understanding how early childhood experiences with repeated abuse or chronic addiction can lead to the cluster of symptoms we now call PTSD, one of which is a *desire to self-medicate*. It is not surprising, given the complexity of these symptoms and their power to undermine a person's ability to live a comfortable and productive life, that those from addicted families seek solace in what seems like an alleviation of pain and anxiety, namely self-medication. It is a misguided attempt to manage a misunderstood illness. In addition, for those who have become damaged by living with addiction, the feeling often is: "Why should I be stuck going through the painful excavation process of therapy to get better from an illness that wasn't mine in the first place—one that I have done nothing but suffer through for years? I want things to get better the easy way." This and the learned helplessness of survivors of trauma make it hard for them to undertake therapy in an active way. They resent having to work that hard, and they want it to be done for them—and fast. That's why part of the healing is to engage the client in a full range of services that address not only the disease of the mind and heart but that of the spirit as well. An underpinning of Twelve-Step work provides both a new design for living and a spiritual path in which each recovering person realizes that the disease is not their fault, but it is their responsibility to see that it is healed and the chain of pain is broken in their generation.

THE LEGACY OF TRAUMA AND ADDICTION

As we will see throughout the stories in this book, trauma changes a person's personality. Krystal calls this profound change the "disaster syndrome," and describes it as characterized by:

- Loss of capacity to use community support.
- Chronic recurrent depression with feelings of despair.
- Psychosomatic symptoms.
- Emotional "anesthesia" or blocked ability to react affectively.
- "Alexithymia" or inability to recognize and make use of emotional reactions.

He lists secondary reactions to psychological trauma as being emotional constriction, sensation-seeking, re-enactment, and drug and alcohol abuse. These reactions make it difficult to identify PTSD (Krystal 1978).

Such personality changes contribute to the generational

nature of trauma and addiction—the endless cycle of parenting in ways that engender emotional and psychological pain, due either to addiction or the post-traumatic stress syndrome that occurs from living with addiction. Simultaneously, substances are being used to self-medicate that pain, which keeps a family and the individuals in it stuck in destructive modes of behavior.

On the following pages we will look in more detail at personality changes that are common to individuals and families that have experienced both trauma and addiction. Furthermore, at the end of this chapter [pages 157–158], I have included a brief self-test to help you evaluate per-sonal levels of involvement with the symptoms listed below. You may wish to take this self-test either before or after you read the following material.

1. Learned Helplessness
2. Anxiety
3. Depression
4. Emotional Constriction
5. Disorganized Inner World (Disorganized Object Relations)
6. Traumatic Bonding
7. Cycles of Reenactment
8. Loss of Ability to Modulate Emotions (Black and White Thinking
9. Emotional Triggering
10. Distorted Reasoning
11. Loss of Trust and Faith
12. Hypervigilance
13. Loss of Ability to Take in Support
14. Fused Feelings
15. Emotional Numbness (Alexithymia)

16. Loss of Spontaneity
17. High-Risk Behaviors
18. Survival Guilt
19. Development of Rigid Psychological Defenses
20. Desire to Self-Medicate

1. Learned Helplessness
"Nothing I Can Do Will Change Anything"

Imagine Jay as a six-year-old being screamed at by his father, insulted and verbally battered. He freezes. He learns to be physically present but emotionally frozen, shut down, unavailable.

Or the four-year-old girl whose father comes to her after bedtime and runs his hand across her body and along her private parts, arousing physical sensations that both alarm her and feel strangely exciting. She is confused; where is Mommy, isn't this a bad thing for Daddy to do, does this mean I'm like Mommy, Daddy's little wife, when can I get away and play or fall asleep with my stuffed animals? She is overwhelmed. She numbs her body in order to get rid of sensations she doesn't know what to do with. She dissociates by almost leaving her body and going to another place.

Picture the little boy who is being hit repeatedly with a ladle all over his head and body by his drunk mother. He hides and she makes him return, he defends himself and she twists his childlike reasoning into a scenario where he is at fault. This child has few alternatives to use in order to keep himself safe. He is faced, as are the others, with a need to defend himself against the person upon whom he needs to depend for his very survival. His caretaker is his perpetrator.

When we feel that we are powerless to change a painful situation, that nothing we can do will stop the abuse or rectify the problem, we give up. This giving up can become *learned helplessness*.

2. Anxiety

"I Feel Like Jumping Out of My Skin"

Maryanne is standing in line at the supermarket. She is not in a particular rush, but the idea of wasting time, of being kept waiting, of wanting to be somewhere else begins to grate on her. She is starting to find the cashier incompetent and the person in front of her irritating. She finds herself counting the items in other people's carts—eleven in one, thirteen in another—in a ten-item-or-less aisle. She wants to scream.

Larry is sitting in traffic. Someone cuts him off at the toll line. He does scream, in fact he releases a flood of expletives that would make a sailor blush. Then he ups the ante by stepping on the gas and cutting off the other driver, putting himself and his passengers at risk.

Mary is about to fly to Miami. She is sure that the plane will have a problem and the pilot will be drunk.

Mac is having his brother and sister over for dinner. His anxiety level is rising by the second. It's just a casual dinner but, in the house in which they grew up, dinners ended up in screaming matches more often than not.

One of the earliest developmental tasks for children is to learn to self-soothe. Children learn this through repeated experiences of being soothed by a parent. A calm voice, a gentle touch, little needs being met in little ways and big needs being met in big ways teach children that the world is a safe place and they can find what they need in it to keep themselves comfortable. Parents who are fraught with anxiety themselves or lost in an addiction are not able to soothe themselves, much less their children. In fact, addiction often starts off as an attempt to self-soothe, to reduce anxiety.

Trauma and addiction impair our ability to relieve ourselves of our own anxiety. Emotional constriction and numbness keep us from our full expression of feeling that would relieve us of the pent-up emotion that fuels anxiety. They block access to our internal world so we don't know what's going on inside of us, which is anxiety-making. Hypervigilance leaves us anxiously waiting "for the other shoe to drop." An inability to *modulate our emotions* and fear of being *emotionally triggered* generate anxiety. Mistrust of others and a lack of ability to take in support isolate us in our anxious state.

The combination of an impaired ability to self-soothe, along with the symptoms of trauma that engender anxiety, are a potent cocktail for creating it. Anxiety is a normal part of being a person, but adult children of trauma can experience more than normal amounts of it that can also lead to panic disorders.

3. Depression

"Living in a Dark Hole"

Trauma early in life can set us up for depression later in life. "Stress-related events may kick off 50 percent of all depression and early life stress can prime people for later depression. Regarding depression as 'just' a chemical imbalance widely misconstrues the disorder. It is not possible to explain either the disease or its treatment based solely on levels of neurotransmitters," says Yale

University neurobiologist Ronald Dorman, Ph.D. (Marano 1999). Chronic depression with feelings of despair (Van der Kolk et al. 1996) can be a direct outgrowth of trauma. Changes in biochemistry, learned helplessness, emotional constriction, numbness, and a loss of trust and faith all contribute to despair. Trauma also can make feelings frozen and unavailable, which undermines the grief work that would help someone get over depression.

During depression the amygdala, which is the center of negative emotions in the brain and informs the brain of threat, runs unchecked—in other words, everything feels threatening—while the center of memory, the hippocampus, loses nerve-to-nerve links. Brain imaging research shows that both of these centers of the brain are altered in size and shape in victims of trauma such as sexual abuse or the experiences of being a prisoner of war. Currently, research both in animals and in people shows that stress or trauma early in life permanently sensitizes neurons and receptors throughout the central nervous system so that they perpetually overrespond to stress.

"Scientists now know that many people have a family history of chemical imbalance that contributes toward depression. But this is equally key," says Susan Skog in her book *Depression: What Your Body's Trying to Tell You*. Researchers also have discovered that many people with a genetic predisposition don't become depressed. "Low serotonin apparently is more a vulnerability factor, causing depression only when other conditions exist" (Norden 1995).

No one really knows to what degree nature and nurture each have a role in depression. But it is clear that trauma sets up a down cycle in the circuitry, making a person more sensitive to stimuli from the environment that another person might pass by, ignore or not hook into.

4. Emotional Constriction

"I Just Feel Shut Down—Do We Really Need to Talk About This?"

Numbness, according to Jonathan Bowlby, British psychoanalyst and seminal researcher on attachment and loss, is the first stage a person goes through upon suffering a loss or separation. Hiroshima victims, according to R. J. Lifton in his research (1964), experienced a persistent state of numbness that was "so powerful that it became a permanent part of their personalities."

A derivative of trauma, emotional constriction frustrates survivors' attempts to reach out to other people, share their stories and do the grief work that is so vital to healing. It may express itself on the small but not insignificant level of feeling unable to share how you feel with your spouse, or the profound level of an inability to experience, name and share emotion or describe an emotional state with any detail.

5. Disorganized Inner World (Disorganized Object Relations)

"I'm Confused; Things Don't Make Sense"

We internalize aspects of those around us and our environment, and they become an internal representation of self. For children who grow up with addiction and trauma, what they internalize can be fraught with inconsistency. In the case of an addicted parent, for example, the child is forced to try to integrate the discontinuous experience of both a good and caring parent with an abusive or neglectful one. The same is true for the atmosphere or environment. Addicts, co-addicts and ACOAs live in alternating realities. There is the family organization when addiction is active and the family organization in sobriety. Each world has its own feeling atmosphere, rules and regulations, morality, thinking, feeling and behavior. These two alternating realities are what the child is forced to try to integrate into one acceptable working model of family. (We will illustrate this with the diagnostic instruments of the social atom in chapter 9.)

Because of his parents' inconsistent behavior, for example, Bret has trouble holding on to his internalized sense of a "good father." He can't go to football practice and take his father with him as a sustaining internal element. It's hard to hold on to him, because of his father's wide swings in behavior. Instead, Bret's inner experience becomes a preoccupation with thoughts like, "What's my father going to be like when I get home? Who's going to be there when I walk through the door? Will I be criticized or praised, yelled at or greeted like a hero?"

Another complicated internal working model of self that grows out of living in an alcoholic family might be those dark places Bret went to within himself that became a part of his identity. As an adult entering therapy, Bret finds he is blocked in both his career and personal relationships. He sees himself as someone who has darkness inside of him that he can't break out of and stay out of long enough to get a life going. Besides, living in this place has certain advantages for Bret. He doesn't have to deal with aspects of his life while in this state, he gets a certain type of attention that he likes, so he now doesn't want to let go of it. *The dark side of his addicted home has become the dark side of him.* In order to recover, Bret will need to let people into this place and share it with others, to "talk from it." Then he needs to learn to go into it and out of it at will—to go there and not get stuck there—and slowly to integrate it into his working model of self.

6. Traumatic Bonding

"I Keep Choosing the 'Wrong' People"

A traumatic bond, according to Jon G. Allen, Ph.D., of the Menninger clinic, has two conditions: there must be an imbalance of power and the victim must be isolated from other forms of support. "Such persons may not have solid working models for benign relationships. When they are treated with kindness, compassion and respect, they feel anxious and guilty. Unlike those who have been well cared for, they have no working model to encompass such benign experiences" (Allen 1996, Dayton 1997).

The pull toward reenacting painful life circumstances can be understood as, at least in part, growing out of this type of relationship bond. The sexually abused child may become the adult who engages in promiscuous behavior or is attracted to partners with sexual addiction issues. The intensity of the bond pulls us toward those very experiences that we found traumatic. We may have idealized our abuser in order to preserve some connection with a protective presence, and we carry that idealization as part of our traumatic bond that blinds us to the dangers of getting into similar situations. It is familiar; it is what we know. ACOAs often engage in relationships characterized by intense connection alternating with a sense of disconnect.

Traumatic bonds can drive us toward exactly what we wish to avoid. For example, Jackie fears but is attracted to angry men because they mirror her past relationships, and she may actually push a man to get angry in a convoluted attempt at self-protection. Her anxiety at waiting for the blast triggers fear from her childhood of living in a rage-filled house. The waiting gets too painful and warms up intrusive memories that threaten to bubble to the surface. "It becomes actually less scary," she reports, "to just get it over with." In this and other ways, we re-create and reenact aspects of a traumatic bond.

7. Cycles of Reenactment

"I've Been Here Before"

Classic examples of a reenactment dynamic are the abused daughter who marries an abusive husband or the child of an alcoholic marrying an alcoholic spouse. The very situations that caused deep pain get played out again and again. A couple of factors operate here in addition to the pull of the traumatic bond that we spoke of earlier. First is familiarity. We tend to be drawn toward what we know. The information that is stored in our brains on what relationships feel like is the template from which we operate. We choose what we knew; we do what we did. Another force at work is our unconscious attempt to finally "get it right," to master situations that have brought us to our knees emotionally and left us feeling helpless and inept.

It is precisely because this wish or need is unconscious that it exerts such a pressure toward reenacting the very circumstances that have repeatedly hurt us. Were it conscious, we would have some element of choice, we would see it coming and know that we have been down that road before. We would be able to learn from our previous experience because the information about how a situation made us feel would not be suppressed through our defensive system. When we don't let ourselves know how we feel because knowing would be too painful, we don't learn from our own experience.

Our own cycles of reenactments in relationships "send up a red flag marking the spot of where our inner work lies" (Dayton 1997). We learn where we have been traumatized through examining our own dysfunctional patterns of reenactment.

8. Loss of Ability to Modulate Emotions
"Living in a Black-and-White World"

When Dave and Ellen, spouses who are both ACOAs, have a fight, they attack, withdraw or shut down (fight, flight, freeze). Their trauma-based reactions to being hurt keep them from seeing middle-ground solutions. These intense reactions prevent them from talking things out without getting triggered into anger, withdrawal or shutdown.

Cycles of excitation and disappointment, or intense emotion alternating with shutdown or withdrawal, undermine the trauma survivor's ability to live in an emotionally well-modulated state. Trauma victims are emotionally and psychologically wired for intensity. When things get too hot, they shut down. Both sides of this inner world are mirrored by the cycle of addiction, highs versus lows or starving versus purging.

In relationships, this may also manifest as either fusion or withdrawal, overcloseness or overdistance. Or, another couple, for example, might have an anger pattern of letting anger build up until they can't stand it anymore, then they blast or rage.

In thinking, this setup translates into seeing the world as black and white, wherein solutions to problems seem black and white. People who have this setup see it manifest in all sorts of ways. They tend to get stuck in one side or the other of an argument or an ideology. They get opinionated or defensive easily. They can't modulate their reactions. Quick fixes that bring temporary quiet to a feeling world that threatens to burst are seen as a way out. And so it goes—geographic moves, panaceas that promise all, seminars that are supposed to change your life completely and various other snake oils become the addict's or ACOA's "solution." But the inner world of a trauma victim is far too long in the making to be undone in a week. It takes time, therapy and practice to learn to modulate emotion.

9. Emotional Triggering

"I Feel Like a Grenade Just Went Off Inside of Me"

Survivors of trauma tend to respond to current life situations with the intensity of emotion related to their original trauma. It is as if they were experiencing the original situation all over again. They are physiologically and psychologically wired for overreaction. When triggered, they may either "blow up" inside or "blow up" in someone else's face.

As we saw in our previous example with Dave and Ellen, ACOAs, addicts and spouses often feel as if they "walk on eggshells" because they fear explosion. The explosion that they fear ostensibly is coming from the outside, but in truth it occurs on the inside as well. The classic trigger reaction might be the war veteran who "hits the deck" at a loud sound because it takes him back in his unconscious to the sound of gunfire. The sounds of war reverberate in his head for one quick instant, triggering a reaction of terror and an instant need for self-protection. The other classic trigger, as with Dave and Ellen, are the feelings of vulnerability and dependence that are part of an intimate relationship. These feelings trigger in couples early defensive reactions and fears of another rupture in a relationship bond.

Yelling, schedules not being met, the sounds of hitting, or a needy, crying child can catapult such survivors into states where they feel deeply triggered. On the outside they may seem anything from impassive to rageful. On the inside they are reexperiencing the feelings associated with their trauma experiences. This is why a fight between Dave and Ellen can take days to resolve. It's not only a fight between the two of them, but an internal battle with the painful baggage of an unresolved past that gets projected onto the screen of their relationship.

10. Distorted Reasoning

"Stinkin' Thinkin'"

Rebecca had an alcoholic, sexually addicted father. His reasoning was distorted by a drug. "If my wife were nicer to me, I wouldn't drink. If I were wealthy, I would have everything I want, I would be calm and I wouldn't need alcohol. Sex with prostitutes just relaxes me, I deserve it after a hard day's work. If no one knows about it, I'm not hurting anybody. Sexual liaisons that don't involve inter-course aren't 'sex.' Anyway, if my wife treated me the way she should, I wouldn't need this. Actually, I deserve it. I'm doing my family a favor. No one knows, no one suffers. I keep myself happy—everybody's happy." This is distorted reasoning, designed to keep an addiction or dysfunctional pattern of behavior in place and make it seem okay. Rebecca ingested this reasoning from her father. Later, in her own marriage she reasoned that, "I'm only having sex with this guy in order to be more present for my husband. Actually, I'm really detached—this isn't love, I'm not betraying anyone, these are just two bodies meeting their biological needs."

Rebecca's distorted thinking has led her in and out of two marriages, in each case blaming the marital dysfunction on her husbands without ever taking a deeper and disillusioning look at her own history and behavior.

Another distorted conclusion a child growing up in a pain-filled home might come up with is, "If I hide my feelings, my life and relationships will work better." Or, "The world is out to get me so why should I play it straight." Though this may have been the right conclusion to draw at the moment of abuse, it does not apply to all of life or all relationships. It grows out of a combination of the way a person on a drug thinks and the sense that a traumatized child or adult tried to make out of circumstances that make no sense.

11. Loss of Trust and Faith

"Nothing Will Ever Work Out for Me"

With all of the symptoms we are discussing—traumatic bonding, painful patterns of reenactment, distorted thinking and relationship ruptures—it is no wonder that victims of trauma, ACOAs and addicts experience a loss of trust and faith. The defenses that trauma victims have been forced to develop in order to preserve some sense of equilibrium have cost them dearly in losses of authentic connection with themselves and other people.

Naturally, with all of these developmental and relationship deficits, with this loss of a sense of a peaceful and orderly life, with this constant piecing together of the shards of a shattered world, victims of trauma experience a loss of trust and faith.

12. Hypervigilance

"Waiting for the Other Shoe to Drop"

Trauma victims tend to live their lives waiting for the "other shoe to drop." If they are feeling that life is great, rather than relax and enjoy it they may be haunted by feelings of fear or anxiety. After all, they were caught unaware before, thinking all was well and then having their world fall apart. They may scan their environment, trying to anticipate anything that might blow up so that they can protect themselves. Often this leads them to ignite the very set of circumstances they fear happening. For example, fearing an emotional blowup with her father, Sally behaved in such a way as to provoke it. "The waiting is more painful than when it happens. It's like I know it's going to happen so I want to get it over with."

A certain level of shock seems to store itself in the body. Trauma victims may have an exaggerated startle response, flinching at loud noises or startling awake when touched in the night.

Hypervigilance can interfere with long-term committed relationships because trauma survivors may be unconsciously waiting for things to fall apart. They cannot relax, trust and enjoy the good times, using them to store up strength and good feeling to help them weather the tough times. Instead, even the good times are tainted with trauma-related feelings, and small upsets can become larger than they are and more depleting than they need to be.

13. Loss of Ability to Take In Support

"Nothing Will Permeate My Emotional Wall—Good or Bad"

Because of their emotional constriction, loss of trust and faith in relationships and hyperviligance, it is no wonder that trauma victims may lose their ability to take in support from others. They have learned a terrible lesson: "I can shockingly and painfully be let down by those upon whom I depend, and it can happen over and over again or suddenly without warning or time to prepare." To complicate matters even more, trauma victims have often lost access to those very people upon whom they would have relied for support, and so they learn to go it alone, to rely on no one. This can happen for a couple of reasons: one, the support person is preoccupied with his or her own emotional pain; or two, the designated support person is the perpetrator.

ACOAs are particularly vulnerable to this. ACOAs may lose one parent to addiction and the other to constant preoccupation with the addict's behavior. They may have been forced to take responsibility for themselves or siblings prematurely. The parents are not doing their jobs. Like a volleyball team with players who aren't paying attention, positions are left open, and the team soon falls into chaos as other players leave their positions to keep the ball from hitting the ground.

Messages are constantly changing in addicted homes. One day you will be praised for the same behavior that got you into trouble two days before. One week your family is close and acts like a family, another week you live in chaos. One minute your parents are on duty taking care of your needs, giving you love and discipline, the next minute you wonder if they know you're alive.

Because of the constant cycles of excitation and disappointment that arise in an addictive home where messages are constantly changing, children learn not to let anything feel too good, to mistrust support, to avoid making connections that could lead to further hurt and disappointment.

14. Fused Feelings

"My Feelings Are All Wadded Up Together"

As in a burning house, when electrical wires are fused together and become as one in the heat of the flames, trauma victims' feelings, thoughts and behaviors follow a similar pattern of fusion in the heat of emotional pain. "Love and violence, sexuality and aggression can become fused together in the mind of the victim of trauma" (Van der Kolk 1987).

Another common fusion might be sex and shutdown. For Janine, who was sexually abused as a child, the sexual feelings she senses from her husband signal her unconscious to shut her sexual responses down. Often the only defense she had as a child was to numb her body, dissociate or both. Sexual feelings that were stimulated in her made her feel that she was red-hot inside and that her head and body might explode. As a defense against those terrifying feelings, she shut down. Consequently, sex and fear or sex and physical numbness or sex and "disapproving" fused together within her.

Or Allen, who was beaten while his father repeated "I'm

only doing this because I love you," and, "I'm only doing this for your own good," fused the feelings of love and aggression and pain and love. As adults, when one feeling is stimulated the other one comes along with it. Then the behavior pattern can mirror earlier interactions, thereby fueling reenactment dynamics. This leaves these adult children of trauma feeling "crazy," confused and mistrustful of their own insides.

15. Emotional Numbness (Alexithymia)

"My Feelings Have No Words"

Shutdown and emotional numbness are reactions to trauma. *Alexithymia* goes well beyond a momentary shutdown into a permanent state or personality type. Alexithymia, a disorder related to post-traumatic states [see chapter 4], has been described as "the absence of words for feelings" (Sifneos 1973). Alexithymic patients have been described as emotional illiterates; oftentimes they only know what they are feeling through a body sensation such as a pounding head or churning stomach. "Instead of being relayed to the neocortex and finding expression in the symbolic use of words, these emotions found immediate expression through autonomic pathways and were translated into a kind of organ language (somatization)" (*American Journal of Psychiatry* 1984). Alexithymic patients have serious "impairment in their capacity for mourning" (Krystal 1978). They are given to sudden outbursts of anger or rage that disappear and are relinquished as quickly as they come. Both of these characteristics are exacerbated by substance abuse. Without a language for feelings that is connected to an internal world, their capacity for mourning diminishes.

Some of these patients, who are often functioning very successfully in their work, can even seem to be super-adjusted to reality. "Getting past the superficial impression of superb functioning, one discovers a sterility and monotony of ideas and severe impoverishment of their imagination. The characteristic cognitive style . . . 'operative thinking' takes over at the expense of the symbolic or imaginative type. . . . The patient's language is poor; flat and banal, glued to the present and only producing facts stated chronologically" (McDougall 1989).

16. Loss of Spontaneity

"My Life Doesn't Feel Alive"

Emotional constriction, psychological and emotional preoccupations, "the loss of the ability to fantasize" (Van der Kolk 1987), all contribute to the trauma victim's loss of spontaneity. Along with this comes a reduction in ability to play. Spontaneity is defined as "an adequate response to a situation" (J. L. Moreno 1964), adequate meaning an appropriate and natural reaction, neither an overreaction nor an underreaction, but one that is tailored to the particular needs, pressures and dictates that arise out of a given circumstance. Moreno felt that mental illness was the inverse of a high level of spontaneity. That is, there is little genuine spontaneity in the personality of one who is mentally ill. There may be acting out or a high level of affect, but this is not spontaneity, according to Moreno (1964). True spontaneity can be quiet if that is what is called for, attentive, leading, following, compromising or aggressive, gentle or tough—depending upon the circumstance. Psychodrama has often been referred to as "spontaneity training," as it helps clients to work through their blocks in spontaneity and restores people to a natural state of aliveness and equilibrium.

17. High-Risk Behaviors

"I Only Feel Really Alive When I'm. . . ."

Trauma victims can feel dead inside. As an attempt to protect themselves from sudden emotional pain (such as witnessing a murder) or cumulative emotional pain (such as continuous child abuse), they shut down or numb their feelings. This can be one of the reasons that survivors of trauma seek out high-risk behaviors, high-risk careers, dangerous use of street drugs, etc. It's sort of an unconscious attempt to jump-start their emotions, to induce engagement with their internal world.

Another manifestation of high-risk behaviors is abusive relationships. Trauma victims have a tendency to re-create intense trauma-related behaviors like shouting or hitting or sexual abuse or acting out in subsequent parent-child relationships. "This pattern results from sensation-seeking, a traumatic derivative that involves the excessive use of motor activity in the absence of a capacity for affect modulation or linguistic problem solving. The recreation of high risk situations is part of the sequence by which abusive behavior is transmitted" (Van der Kolk 1987).

Because trauma renders people emotionally illiterate, they act out pain and anger that they lack the skills to talk out.

18. Survival Guilt

"Why Me? Why Did I Break Free?"

Survival guilt can take a variety of forms, the most obvious being the soldier who came home from war having lived through the death of his comrades. He survived while they did not. He is the one left with the burdensome questions, "Why me? Was I a coward? Was I a better soldier? Were the fates with me and against them? Did I do something right, wrong or doesn't it even matter? Is life just a lottery?"

Children who grow up in homes with addiction and the incumbent forms of abuse that emerge from it—physical, emotional and sexual—can feel a profound sense of survivor's guilt if they get their lives to work reasonably well while siblings and parents are left behind, mired in the effects of disease. The survivors may have trouble enjoying the fruits of their labors without self-sabotaging their own pleasure. They may feel a painful combination of sadness and anger—anger that their family members continually repeat self-destructive behavior patterns, often refusing to engage in therapy or to own their piece in the unhappiness; sadness from watching someone they love slowly and excruciatingly self-destruct.

The addict who conquers his disease can be plagued with survival guilt for those drinking buddies or heroin companions who remain locked in their disease while he moves on to a sober and productive life. One of my clients, Rick, recently relapsed after several years of sobriety. His wife and mother confronted him immediately, and he got help. When we explored the cause of his relapse, Rick realized that he had picked up on the anniversary of his brother's murder. His brother never got sober and wound up killed in a street shooting. Rick's survival guilt over being the brother who embraced sobriety became unbearable after his brother died. Survival guilt can be a powerful reason for relapsing or sabotaging success.

19. Development of Rigid Psychological Defenses

When, as is the case with addiction and trauma, pain is pervasive, persistent and too much to assimilate, normal psychological defenses overperform. With constant assault from the outside, the fortress of psychological defenses strengthens and solidifies. The following are some of the most common defenses that mobilize around trauma and addiction:

Denial: *"Nothing Bad Really Happened."* This is a sort of rewrite of reality to make it more palatable. My husband disappeared from the party and told no one where he was going because "socializing gets to be too much for him, he had a hard day at work and was tired," while in truth he was drunk and passed out in the car.

Dissociation: *"I'm Somewhere Safe in a Corner of My Mind."* The little girl who is being sexually abused and temporarily leaves her body—that is, goes to another place psychically—is dissociated. A lesser example might be the spouse of an addict who seems to be off in his or her own world far, far away from what is going on around him or her. The body is there but the mind is not present.

Intellectualization: *"I'd Rather Talk About My Feelings than Feel Them."* This defense is the one that uses extensive talking, analyzing, talking around and about an issue rather than feeling feelings of vulnerability, fear, helplessness and so on. When Tony intellectualizes his feelings in group, I look around the room as people begin to fidget in their seats, getting alternately bored and hostile. There is little feeling connected to his talking, and, consequently, he loses his audience. And mysteriously, the feelings he is avoiding leak out into the container of the group and are picked up on by others.

Repression: *"What I Don't 'Know' About Can't Hurt Me."* Much has been written about this common defense. Research has clearly shown that the repression of strong feelings depresses healthy immune system functioning. Think of repression as a sort of pushing down of powerful and painful emotion to a region of the psyche where it is out of reach. Unfortunately, the psychic strength needed to keep it pushed down drains the personality of much vitality physically, mentally and emotionally.

Idealization: *"My (Alcoholic) Daddy Was the Best Daddy in the Whole Wide World."* One example of idealization might be an attempt to preserve a protective part of the parent so that the child feels less at risk. Trauma victims may use the defense of idealization in order to ward off feelings of terror. In later relationships they may idealize people, then hate them when they disappoint them in some way, seeing them alternatively as *all good or all bad,* mean and cruel or perfect and wonderful. This defense is known as **Splitting**. Because the need to hold someone in a place of perfection in order to protect the self arises out of such terror and vulnerability, when it breaks and the idealized object disappoints, the terror that was held at bay through the idealization emerges, leaving the trauma victim feeling frightened and vulnerable. They may *project* these feelings outward. "That person who disappointed me is all bad." The feelings that did not get felt in childhood get projected onto someone else.

Projection: *"If Only You'd Change, I'd Be Fine."* This is what a person does when their feelings get too painful to sit with. They get rid of the feelings by seeing them as being not inside but outside, not about them but about someone else. For example, Fred has a lot of rage toward his alcoholic mother that goes back through his entire life. When he gets a panic call from his mother's spouse that she is sinking yet again, he doesn't know what to do with his conflicting emotion. She's his mother, and he adores her. After all, she was really more loving and interested in him than his cold, disinterested father, and he has good times seeing her when she's sober. On the other hand, he is embarrassed and ashamed of her, hates her when she's drinking and is caught between wanting her to live and waiting for her to die, for her alcoholic death wish to finally play out. All of this churns around inside of him and engages his childhood defense of dissociating so he is out of touch with it. Then his wife, Sophie, walks in the door, tired after work, and makes a comment after dinner, "Can you do the cleanup tonight?" and BAM!—she's the culprit. "She is responsible for the pain I'm feeling." That comment about cleaning up suddenly ignites World War III. The pain stirred up by the phone call gets projected onto Sophie.

Displacement: *"My Son Is Always in Trouble."* This is another variation of projection, in which feelings about one person or situation are displaced onto another. Jean had an alcoholic, physically abusive father whom she also idealized as a child. He never got sober; he died drunk. The fear of failure she felt at never being able to help him gets displaced onto her son, Jeremy. She is constantly plagued by worries that he will not succeed in his life, in grades, friendship and eventually career. It is a terrible burden to Jeremy, who has to constantly ward off his mother's anxiety and all of the feelings that lie beneath it. Jeremy is caught in a bind. He wants to please her—what child doesn't?—but he gets dissonant messages. Conscious: "I can live up to my mother's wishes by succeeding in my life." Unconscious: "I can live up to her wishes by falling apart."

20. Desire to Self-Medicate

"I Feel Okay Again"

Every symptom of trauma we've been discussing can leave a person feeling desperate to restore some sense of equilibrium and inner peace, to self-soothe. Unfortunately, drugs, alcohol, food, sex, spending and a variety of other "isms" are reliable mood alterers. They work. They take away the pain. They soothe our inner world. That is, until we become addicted to them and they destroy it.

TRAUMA SELF-TEST

Rate each item from 1-10, with 1 meaning the item never applies to you and 10 meaning the item is highly applicable.

1. Do you have a hard time envisioning your future?

2. Do you experience flashbacks or nightmares that are reminiscent of your trauma or are otherwise upsetting?

3. Do you experience intrusive thoughts related to your trauma(s)?

4. Do you feel emotionally constricted; is it hard for you to feel freely?

5. Do you have bouts of depression and despair that do not resolve themselves within a reasonable length of time?

6. Are you constantly waiting for the bottom to fall out; do you mistrust calm and orderly living?

7. Do you have trouble trusting in intimate relationships?

8. Do you tend to go from 0 to 10 in your emotional life and have trouble staying on middle ground?

9. Do you feel you re-create the same problems over and over again, getting stuck in the same place?

10. Do you have trouble identifying what you really feel?

11. Do your feelings evidence themselves as body sensations, such as headaches, stomachaches, backaches, instead of as conscious feelings?

12. Do you have larger-than-appropriate emotional reactions when some sort of situation or interaction triggers you?

13. Do you have trouble taking in help and support from others?

©2000 Tian Dayton, *Trauma and Addiction*

TRAUMA SELF-TEST

14. Do you isolate and have trouble being in community?

15. Do you feel guilty when your life improves?

16. Do you self-medicate your feelings or try to alter your mood with drugs, alcohol, food, sex, spending or other "ism"s?

17. Do you engage in high-risk behaviors in order to "feel alive"?

18. Do you experience more anxiety than you feel is normal?

19. Do you find yourself avoiding situations that are reminiscent of your trauma(s)?

Did you answer 5 or greater to more than half of these questions? If so, you may be suffering from some of the effects of post-traumatic stress syndrome.

SIX

Why Am I Stuck in This Loop?

*I was much further out than you thought
and not waving but drowning.*
Stevie Smith
Selected Poems, 1964

*When water covers the head, a hundred
fathoms are as one.*
Persian Proverb

THE BLACK HOLE

Physiological arousal in general can trigger memories related to trauma; conversely, trauma-related memories trigger a state of generalized physiological arousal. The frequent reliving of traumatic events in flashbacks or nightmares probably causes a re-release of stress hormones that further intensifies the strength of the trauma memories. Dr. Jane Stewart of Concordia University in Montreal believes that a hormone called corticotropin releasing factor (C.R.F.), levels of which increase in the brain during stress, actually increases anxiety. This may take place because C.R.F. acts on the amygdala in ways that strengthen emotional memories once they are triggered.

"Such a positive feedback loop could cause sub-clinical PTSD to escalate into clinical PTSD, in which strength of the memories appears to be so deeply engraved that Pitman and Orr have called it the 'black hole' in the mental life of the PTSD patient: it attracts all associations to it and saps current life of its significance" (Van der Kolk 1994).

This, in my experience, is where some patients seem to get "stuck"—in the black hole of their own traumatic associations. As associations intensify, stress increases, along with heightened physiological arousal; and, as stress increases, associations also intensify.

Patients may get frustrated and anxious and sink into early coping strategies, such as those discussed in chapter 5. Hence another generation is put at risk for self-medication. People with this emotional setup often turn toward substances such as drugs, alcohol and food or behaviors such as sex, overspending or compulsive work and so on to "feel better." The wheel of trauma and addiction takes another revolution through a new generation, and it starts all over again until enough people break the chain through long-term recovery.

BLACK HOLE FEEDBACK LOOP

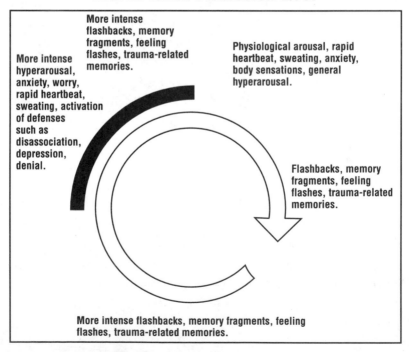

More intense flashbacks, memory fragments, feeling flashes, trauma-related memories.

Stuck in a Feedback Loop with No Way Out: Survival Strategies

In group, I asked members to reflect upon their own feedback loops, to identify triggers and coping strategies. In other words, what situations in their lives trigger them into this feedback loop and what strategies do they use to manage, get away from or control both their hyperarousal and the confusion of memory fragments and flashbacks?

Sacha spoke first. A son of two Holocaust survivors, Sacha's journey took him back to incidents that occurred to him when, as a boy in Russia, he was repeatedly molested by a gardener. "It was the smell of grass being cut. I was sitting in my office in New York when it overpowered me. At first I wanted to stop the man from cutting the grass, I wanted it to STOP. Then, because of what I am learning in group, I breathed and let the memories come. Suddenly, I was with the gardener by my home in Russia, he took me into a barnlike place and fondled me. I hated it, I wanted to get away, I didn't really know what was happening. I wanted someone to stop it from happening." When I asked him what he did when he was in a state of hyperarousal and anxiety today, he said, "I try to get away physically, I leave. Sometimes I have sex in a way that I wish to overpower a woman. She may not even be aware of it, but I want to somehow feel powerful." As Sacha thought of this, tears trickled down his cheeks—the pain of being helpless and wounded was available to him.

Lance broke in, "I don't like doing this. The moment you started describing this I was back in class, afraid to open my mouth, afraid to sound stupid, afraid to be humiliated. The voices get so loud that they are all I hear after awhile. That makes it tough because only

5 percent of me is really in the room listening, so anything I say seems disjointed and out of tune. It's the same in relationships. I want to get close, but the closer I get the more scared and anxious I get. Then this war goes on in my head and pretty soon that's all I'm listening to, and the person I'm with I can't be with." Lance's triggers come up in a group of people where he experiences what's known as "social phobia" or extreme anxiety and fear in encountering groups of people he doesn't know. His fear of humiliation and rejection dates from his alcoholic parents' constant ridicule, beating, neglect and rejection. His strategies, until recently, have been cocaine and alcohol. Now, in early recovery, he is faced with the challenge of tolerating these feelings, which are acute for him, without the help of self-medication. Antidepressants are a possibility, but for now he wants to try it without them and with a great deal of support in the form of group therapy, one-to-one therapy, and Twelve-Step programs.

"My chest is so tight and my heart is just pounding," entered Susan. "My home was terrifying, my mother was so depressed she stayed in bed all the time, she threatened suicide. My uncle was sexually abusing me. I begged my father to take me so I could get away, but he kept telling me I was better off with my mother. I believed him, so I made myself the crazy one. It was just too much to think they were crazy and I couldn't get out. I thought I was the sick one, the crazy one. When I got to be a teenager, I took anything around, I drank, smoked pot, later I had tons of sexual relationships. I don't do that any more, and now I feel like I have no strategies. I guess I withdraw when I get anxious and hyperaroused—I guess I just pull back and sort of stay there—and I don't make trouble, I'm nice. Today I work, I lose myself in work." Still another new member who experiences panic attacks said, "That's where I go—I go to the middle of that circle and I don't know how to get out. Once I'm in it I just keep cycling around like a washing machine and everything else feels far away."

The group continued with story after story of where group members go inside of themselves when their feedback loop gets going. In each of these cases, these children were left to their own devices to figure out how to maintain some sense of equilibrium and control while their minds and bodies were under attack internally with anxiety and fear. Their attempts at self-management often failed and they turned to drugs, alcohol, food, sex, spending, frenetic activity or combinations thereof.

THE TRAUMA TRANSFERENCE

Transference is ubiquitous and ever-present. We constantly transfer the contents of previous role relationships onto relationships in the present. Something that someone does stimulates a set of associations that we attach to our reaction to them. They feel our reactions and react, sometimes accordingly, because our projections stimulate that and we have ever more reason to think our original assessment was right. Separating what is real from what is a transference reaction can be difficult.

In a transference reaction, a set of emotions that were appropriate to an earlier situation, say from childhood, get projected or transferred onto a situation in the present.

Something that the other person is doing is retraumatizing, and that is the trigger. When the transference has trauma attached to its set of associations, it can become fixed and problematic to deal with. The old pain that gets stimulated can make the other person feel frightening to the person experiencing the transference, and that person may act in a way to elicit just the response that scares him or her. Since transference can go in both directions the situation can become awkward and hard to deal with. It can feel as if the present situation is totally responsible for causing these transference feelings.

When people are experiencing transference, their feelings are realer than real to them. They can be totally convinced that there is no historical component to their reaction. They can be, and initially usually are, blind to what is being triggered and how that set of feelings is being layered onto the present.

Moreno (1964) referred to transference as the projection of an old role relationship onto a relationship in the present. The mind seems to have the capacity to store and partially categorize, so that even though feelings were stored in fragments, they coalesce around the person or situation that is triggering them. It feels as if they are appropriately about that situation.

The person caught in the transference may hold on to the meaning that he or she made out of a particular situation from childhood and see it as belonging to the present circumstance. "This word, that look meant just what I think it meant. I am not looking through a distorted lens." In addition, the traumas that these transferences grew out of often occurred in childhood. Hence, the person caught in one might hang on to it with the stubbornness or the tenacity of the two-year-old or the magical thinking or grandiosity of a small child determined that he or she is "right." There may also be a pervasive lack of mature reasoning. Rather, the egocentricity of the young child takes over. "What I see is all there is to see, and I am at the epicenter of all that is going on. The world revolves around me, there can be no other reason for your behavior except as it relates to me."

In Jane's story we will see a therapist, who understands the dynamics of transference, talk about her own transferences onto her husband. She knew that the feelings being triggered in her were excessive, but until it surfaced in group and we could work it through with the help of role-play, the origin of the transference was buried. Remember, because of the defenses we use to protect ourselves during trauma, the information about the trauma situation gets stored without getting processed. Transference can be seen as a sort of misguided attempt to feel and understand those feelings and think those thoughts that are part of our unformulated experience from another time and place.

Jane's Story

Jane brought the following issue into the group. "I've been married over a month now and stuff really gets triggered. Now I understand why it took me so long to do this marriage thing. This sounds weird; I can hardly understand it myself. I mean, my mind understands it, but I still get so triggered. When I come home late at night after working and Jim is already asleep, I go through this combination of rage and feeling of total abandonment. I become a seething bundle of nervous energy. It can take me hours puttering in the kitchen just to calm myself down. In my head, I know he's not doing anything wrong—do I really want him to wait up till midnight for me? No, of course not, but this reaction gets totally out of control."

As we explored further, she recalled that when she would come home as a teenager, both of her alcoholic parents were passed out on couches, beds or the floor. She said at the time she had no feelings about this. It was "just the way it was." But now, faced with the sight of her husband sleeping on a bed, she felt a combination of revulsion and abandonment. This is often the case for trauma victims. Their earlier traumas were survived without feeling, numbed out, put out of consciousness (dissociation) and the victim walked through the situation almost as if it weren't happening. To take it in, in its full horror, would have been too debilitating. To cope meant putting first things first—to simply *get through*. Only later, when the person experiences the safety of distance from the original trauma, can the feelings be felt. But they get attached to the wrong situation and projected onto the wrong person. An act such as sleeping at midnight gets misread, and the trauma survivors move into a psychological nether region, trying to make sense of the overwhelming feelings, body memories, flashbacks and distorted meaning that are a part of their current psychological world but are, in truth, intruders from another time and space. They are lost between two worlds, and the effect can be devastating. They feel crazy, and when they can't stand feeling crazy anymore, they look for someone or some situation to pin the feeling onto.

As we continued to work with Jane, the group began

sharing experiences that they found shameful, many of which were of a sexual nature. Jane re-entered, "I just need to open my mouth. I am so triggered—every part of me is standing on end. My body is so sensitive." Recognizing this to be a physiological response to traumatic memories being stimulated, I encouraged her to continue.

"I feel this revulsion and disgust emerging in me." Jane fumbled for words, which is a natural part of approaching traumatic memory. Feelings that never had words attached to them threaten to erupt. The unspeakable wants to be spoken, but the inner fight against divulging what has so long been hidden is great; these frightening truths are well defended. Attaching words to hidden experiences is tough. Finally, and with great effort, Jane was able to tell us that from the age of six until college she slept in a single bed with her mother. From six to nine this happened a lot, then at nine they got "their own bed." Jane said, "It was like a celebration, a wedding. It was 'our bed.'"

"How did you sleep?" I asked. "Spooning," she said, hanging her head, "and my mother would move her hips, her pelvis, against me and I did too. I didn't know it was sexual. I just wanted to make her happy. I was the good little girl, and she was always so sad. This made us close. She liked it; it felt sweet somehow. Now it seems so sick, but at the time it was all I knew. I didn't know it was wrong. As my mother got drunker, her slip would sometimes ride up and I would feel her bare hips undulating against me or she would occasionally urinate in the bed."

At this point, Jane took several deep breaths and a faint voice from her asthmatic condition was in evidence. "This all feels so shameful. I've never talked about it like this. I mean, I've shared bits and pieces, but I've never strung it together in a story." A story, her story, the one she's never told, the one that kept her out of marriage until the age of forty-nine, the one that made her weave intimacy together with revulsion, shame, sex that wasn't called sex, and caretaking someone else at the expense of herself. Jane had been taught to meet her needs for intimacy by becoming someone else's pawn, which is why in recovery she felt such an intense need to set boundaries where she needed them to be.

Telling her story allowed her to understand why the sight of her new husband asleep at midnight set her internal world into an uncontrollable spin. The hours of fussing in the kitchen were busy activity designed to keep her intrusive memories and flashbacks from overwhelming her. Maybe, if she could get the counter clean enough, she could somehow clean her mind as well.

Living with two addicts, who were medicating their pain rather than processing and understanding it, set Jane up as their unwitting pawn. Her mother acted out her need for intimacy in inappropriate ways. The addict in her mother had taken over and developed a labile life of its own, sexuality run amok with the normal governors of behavior compromised by drugs. Her mother's untreated depression turned into addiction through her own self-medication. Her father, also an addict, "never changed his clothes." When he had to have emergency surgery, they had to "soak his clothes off of him."

This is the living legacy of addiction, the twisting of other people into servants of a Jekyll-and-Hyde–like tyranny—a dark side that forces those around it to live in altered realities and mortifying circumstances. The trauma that the addict is self-medicating does not get cured. Rather, it gets worse and is acted out in strange varieties of abuse which confuse, distort and traumatize those in close relationship. This is why children of alcoholics often become alcoholics themselves. They are medicating their own inner pain that is the result of growing up with addiction. For many, choosing drugs, alcohol, sex and so on is as familiar as the back of their hand. So it goes, hand to hand, generation to generation, until someone breaks the chain.

All of us develop conditioned fear responses that can become part of a transference reaction. We learn to be scared of oncoming traffic or to investigate loud or unusual noises. This is how we stay safe, how we ensure our survival. Trauma exaggerates this fear response. Fear becomes overwhelming and we freeze. Relationship traumas can condition us to fear rather than trust people. Then we're in a real bind. We need intimacy, but intimacy has proven to be a source of great pain. To make matters more complicated, we may have repressed our fear response, so we choose people to be close to who possess qualities that mirror not only our conscious desires but also our unconscious fears. Part of recovering from these traumas is unearthing the story, and another part is reconditioning our fear response. In Jane's story, we saw that the child who reacted with fear at the sight of a drunk, passed-out parent became conditioned to fear her husband lying in bed sleeping. The sight of someone she loved lying down was enough to trigger old fear; she projected or transferred a role relationship from the past onto her relationship in the present.

The magical meaning that children make out of these early relationships and circumstances tends to get lived out in adult relationships. The original meaning attached to a word or event needs to be reexamined. In childhood, we create webs of associated meaning that we carry with us throughout life.

The relationships that most closely mirror this early love relationship are those with life partners and children, where feelings of intimacy, love and dependency tend to re-create various aspects of our original bonds. When, for example, a husband comes home tired and stressed and barks at his wife, who may be equally tired and stressed from her day, it may trigger feelings in her that both relate to his actions and reach farther back into early relationships where, when barked at by parents, she may have felt little and helpless. If she was barked at a lot as a child and has experienced cumulative trauma around that behavior, she may fall back into her earlier responses. Perhaps she will withdraw, cry or attack.

It is no particular stretch to imagine just where all of this will lead between two stressed people. Psychological health doesn't mean that these two people will never get into a conflict. Health means that they will be able to step back, regroup and go through the steps of emotional literacy to find their way out of it. First, they will need to name the emotion: They were both anxious. The husband's barking made the wife feel hurt and helpless. When she was a child, she took her parents' criticism to mean that she was a bad girl, a burden, not worth being thoughtful of. All of this meaning got triggered by her husband's barking, then she felt she had to defend herself. Once she decodes the meaning that she made out of this as a child, she can begin to understand her own reaction and her partner can understand his impact on her. Then she has a choice as to how she wishes to react, and he has a choice as to how to interpret her reaction—choices neither of them had while locked in a seemingly of-the-moment conflict. In fact, to the human psyche, I'm not sure there is such a thing as the simple present, because within us at all times we carry the sum total of all that we have experienced.

Psychodrama is very useful here, as it has a behavioral component through its use of role-play. We can see the story in its concrete form with all of its ramifications. Then, after we work through the issues involved, insight can be accompanied by new behavior. That's why, for example, hearing a lecture or reading a book is not enough to change your life. It may open the door to it, but we have to walk through that door and practice new behavior.

SEVEN

Why Isn't My Life Working the Way I Want It To?

*Grief should be the instructor of
the wise. Sorrow is the knowledge.*

Lord Byron
1817

*Your vision will become clear only
when you can look into your own heart.
Who looks outside, dreams;
who looks inside, awakes.*

Carl Jung

GRIEVING OVER LOSS

People with early childhood wounds have grief work to do. Unfortunately, their defenses against feeling pain associated with trauma interfere with their ability to fully feel their emotions, which is necessary for healthy grieving. Without grieving, pain accumulates until it hurts so much that we look for a way out. One way out is to go through a recovery process that includes grieving and reworking emotional and psychological issues. Another way out is to kill the pain with drugs or alcohol or another means of self-medicating.

When grief work is not attended to, it can lead to primary addiction as well as relapse. It did both in the case of my father. Unresolved grief led him to pick up and caused him to pick up again and again. We didn't know then what we know now about trauma and grief.

My father was an alcoholic, and as a child many questions swirled around my mind. *Why does he shake or walk in that unsteady, determined way like we are riding a boat on a stormy sea? Why does he love me so much one day and hardly notice I'm around the next?*

Why is my family, which once stood out as happy and successful and whom I adored, so very different from before? Why does my mother look so sad and far away and seem only half there when I try to get her attention? Why do my siblings all look like they've shown up for a play that's been canceled? Why am I so confused? I was always guessing—guessing at what had happened that I missed, what had been said that I didn't hear, guessing who might be the person who could make sense of what felt senseless to me.

My father came to the United States from Greece at age sixteen with sixteen dollars in his pocket. His father, by all accounts an alcoholic, had gambled away a considerable inheritance, at which point, through family connections, he was given a parish and a priesthood. He died not long afterward, leaving it to my father to find a way to support his family. My father was sent to seminary to become a priest, but, as he told me, "I kept jumping over the wall. I wanted to go to America and become a businessman." My father, no doubt, suffered much loneliness, fear and anxiety as he worked hard to get the money to bring the rest of his relatives to the United States. All of the trauma he experienced went unattended to, as survival was his primary focus. It resurfaced for him later in life, as it so often does, when he had to cope with the demands of his own wife and children. He married a beautiful woman, succeeded in business and created a family. Then, you might say, he had the luxury to sit back, and that's when this trauma began resurfacing. Though he adored us and we adored him, it became obvious that a part of him was still immersed in deep pain from his past.

My father felt lost, and the man he went to for help

taught him how to drink. It worked for him. It took the edge off his pain—but from that day on, it put the edge on ours. My mother recounts a story about discussing a family friend who was having problems. My father had said, "If only he could learn to drink a little, he could manage it." *Poor Dad. When did you cross that invisible line between when you took the drink and the drink took you?* The Chinese have a saying, "First the man takes the drink, then the drink takes the drink, then the drink takes the man." There it is. The whole disease process in eighteen words. My father never did stay sober.

I will never forget one time my father and I went out together. He had been dry for a couple of months. I felt I had my daddy back, and I was feasting on every precious moment of being with my father while he was sober—the father I had lost a hundred times to binge drinking and who had been the pleasure of my life. I adored it—the days when we would drive somewhere and I didn't fear an accident, when we would make a dinner plan that was still in place by evening or take a walk without fearing embarrassment, when we would talk, talk and talk, sharing deep and shallow thoughts—just be together. I had my daddy back. I had almost come to believe that this time it would last. I wouldn't lose him to drunkenness and swearing and slovenliness again. *This time Daddy would stay with me because he loved me so much he would want to, and my love for him would magically transform him into the daddy I needed him to be.*

However, the addict in him was still too strong; his primary relationship was with alcohol, not with me. The others we were with ordered a drink, and I'm not sure how, but all of a sudden a double Scotch was in his hand, too. My heart fell. I couldn't say anything; besides, I was too numb—I had wanted him so much to stay sober that it took me a while to realize this was really happening. I couldn't change gears fast enough to do anything but sit there. I wanted to be nice—after all, we were out for dinner. Then he saw my face, and the father in him made one last attempt to reach out to me before the addict took over. He held his glass in his hand and said, "Tianna, don't ever go this way. Promise me you will never drink. Look at me, I started and now I can't stop." I felt the weight of twenty years of lost life, his despair, my loss—the truth sat between us for one powerful moment. "I started and now I can't stop." As simple as that. As complicated as years of unnecessary pain and more losses than I could count. *I promise, I promise. I love you, Daddy. Goodbye to my sweet, adoring Papa. Hello to a monster I hardly dare to know.*

The sadness welled up inside of me like a container filling with water. He was leaving again like so many times before. *Thank you, God, for giving him back to me even for two months. I will hang on to them, live on them, somehow make a whole father out of these bits and pieces.*

Since that time, I have come to understand the powerful and destructive impact of unresolved grief. I believe it was part of the reason that my father never was able to stay sober. I believe it is a significant factor for many addicts who relapse after several years of sobriety. When the self-medicating substance is removed, the feelings that have been medicated begin to surface. If the recovering addict does not go through the process of grieving, those deep early wounds continue to fester. And if the people around the addict don't do their grief work, they have trouble integrating a newly or now-sober person into a world that has been organized around addiction. Eventually, for many people, "recovery," that has gone no deeper than removing the self-medication, simply becomes too painful and in search of relief they return to their addiction, they relapse. Family members, too, need to go through their own recovery process in order to get healthy and work through their trauma-related symptoms.

I have learned to identify the many manifestations of grief that my alcoholic family carried in this invisible container we called "us." Being able to name and understand this mass of tangled contradictory feelings I carried around for so many years gave me a way to look at it with some objectivity and to allow myself to move through a clearly defined process to get through it. It gave me hope and a way to act on that hope toward resolution. The whole thing seemed less overwhelming in this context. Once I saw the many manifestations of unresolved grief and how they infiltrate an otherwise satisfactory life, I was willing to take a closer look, to add myself to an invisible list of people who carry a "sense of loss" somehow related to this disease. Depression, caretaking, anxiety, compulsive thinking and behavior, self-destructive behavior and self-mutilation, sudden angry outbursts—all are symptoms of unresolved grief. What a relief! It had a name, a sequence; other people had thought about this, too.

Since my early twenties, I have had a title in my mind for a book: *A Sense of Loss.* I wanted to write a book that described a feeling I carried within me even though my life was fine. Then I heard Ronald Reagan address the

Coalition for Alcoholism. I'll never forget it. The president of the United States said, "My father was an alcoholic," and though clearly he had no complaints about his more than successful life, he went on to say, "And to this day I still wonder how my life might have been different if he hadn't been a drinker." President Reagan echoed my experience: a sense of loss which had wrapped itself so completely around the heart of a son that no amount of success, accomplishment or fame could cancel it out of memory.

The Stages of Grief

The stages of grief, developed by Jonathan Bowlby, M.D., are as follows:

1. Numbness
2. Yearning and Searching
3. Disorganization, Anger and Despair
4. Reorganization

These stages can be passed through again and again or leapfrogged, but they provide an overall framework for moving from hurting to healing. Though the passage is stormy and painful, it is also illuminating and alive. Finally feeling pain that has lain numb and forgotten, hidden inside a self that misunderstands it or pretends it isn't there, has its own reward—and the reward is getting your life back.

The initial stage of *numbing* is a shock response, what happened seems unbelievable and unreal and so we don't really take it in for a period of time. In the case of childhood loss, much of how children will eventually come to accept a loss is influenced by how the adults in their lives handle this stage. If they are told that their anger is bad, to go to their rooms and to shut down the power of the feelings, their wound will go inside where it cannot get the care and attention that it needs to heal. As shock and numbness wear off, slowly the truth seeps in, and we find ourselves lost and wishing for things to be the way they were.

In the stage of *yearning and searching* we deeply miss what we have lost. There is ". . . a loss of the inner world of the sufferer into turmoil. The assumptions and expectations which depended on the presence of the loved one are now thrown into question. Where can the bereaved person hope to find comfort in the face of his inner turmoil and confusion . . . ?" (Klein 1940). The quandary that mourners face now is that the very person they might have gone to for hope and comfort in the face of a major loss is now unavailable to them. One of the key features here is ". . . identification with the lost object [person]" (Klein 1940). That is, we still identify with the person we lost as being an active part of our lives and identity, and we don't know what to do with the void. Eventually, the memory of the person is reinstated in the inner world in the course of a healthy grieving so that he or she forms a part of the composite internal representation of our internal reality.

Disorganization, anger and despair come next. Life doesn't feel the way it used to feel, the order is changed, things don't operate as they did. The yearner feels angry at what is missing, life feels unfair and the yearner despairs that it will never feel good again. "During the phase of *disorganization*, the bereaved person is constantly questioning and questing, but reality passes its verdict—that the object [or person] no longer exists—

upon each single one of the memory's hopes" (Klein 1940). This is the beginning of *reorganization*. Just as the infant, through the mother's tolerance and capacity to process conflict and negative affect, learns that the lost breast will reappear, that his anger toward her has not destroyed his mother's love, so the bereaved person begins once more to build up his inner world. In the process of restoring the disorganized inner world or disorganized object relations, "Every advance in the process of mourning results in a deepening in the individual's relation to his inner objects, in the happiness of regaining them after they were felt to be lost. This is similar to the way in which the young child step-by-step builds up his relationship to external objects, for he gains trust not only from pleasant experiences but also in the way he overcomes frustrations and unpleasant experiences, nevertheless, retaining his good objects" (Holmes 1993).

Fully passing through the stages of grief, loss and mourning not only strengthens the ego and the inner self, but it increases one's trust in life's ability to repair and renew itself. These stages apply to the loss of a loved one. The same basic principles can be seen as pertaining to the loss of any outer object or experience, whether it be a person, a stage in life, a cherished activity or a situation to which one has become attached. Mourning has, at the end of it, great optimism. It is through allowing this process to run its full course that we can continue to engage and re-engage in life as it presents itself to us in a variety of forms over and over again. In our culture, we expect people to get over major life losses in a matter of months. This impatience reflects a misunderstanding of how our primary relationships function. Not only are the people themselves important, but they actually become a part of our sense of self and how we organize our lives. Those closest to us become what we call self-objects— organized into our concept of self and life. This is, in part, why losing them is so destabilizing—we feel we have lost a part of ourselves, and all of our life needs reorganization both inside and out. As our life expectancies extend and we live longer lives, understanding and opening ourselves up to the mourning and grieving process becomes more and more essential, as there will naturally be more loss and more gain through added years of living.

This is one of the ways that, as author and theologian Matthew Fox puts it, we "grow soul."

THE HIGH COST OF ISOLATION

Those who do not acknowledge their losses and grieve them bear their pain in isolation, or, as we say in Twelve-Step programs, "white-knuckle it." When we do not share our loss and reach out for support, we lock ourselves behind walls of loneliness. These walls that are intended to protect us from further pain only make us prisoners of what we cannot, or will not, feel. And the toll they take on our mental and emotional health is tremendously high.

"Communication is vitally linked to our bodies and is probably the single most important force that influences our health or lack of health," says James J. Lynch in *The Broken Heart, the Psychobiology of Human Contact.*

The rhythm of the heartbeat of a coronary patient can be altered through human touch. This holds true for those in coma states, as well as those who are fully conscious. Among women, 34 percent more widows die of heart disease than married women; 46 percent more die of cancer of the cervix; 55 percent more die because of cirrhosis of the liver. More than four times as many widows die in motor vehicle accidents. Death by accidental fire or explosion is six times more frequent for widows than for married women. Divorced women have even worse odds . . . 25 percent more divorced women die of cirrhosis of the liver than do widows. Cancer of the cervix kills 28 percent more (divorced women than widows) and divorced women commit suicide 43 percent more frequently than widows (Lynch 1992).

In males between the ages of fifty-five and sixty-four, divorced men die of heart disease at a rate twice that of married men.

Another very revealing study found that in the years from 1959 to 1961, Nevada had the highest death rates in the United States. Nevada also had the second-highest income level and an average number of physicians and hospitals. In 1960, 20 percent of men in Nevada between fifty-five and sixty-four were either single, widowed, divorced or not living with their spouses. Diseases such as cirrhosis of the liver or suicides certainly are related to trauma and addiction, and the others may be open for interpretation.

Interestingly, findings researched in Alameda, California, in a long-term study about the causes of death found those with strong relationship ties lived longer, and this held true in spite of weight, lifestyle or smoking. Relationship emerged as the single strongest predictor of long life.

Generations ago young males died from infectious diseases. "Today, three of every four deaths among American males between the ages of fifteen and twenty-five are caused by accidents, suicide or homicide" (Lynch 1997). Men with higher levels of support from their families and friends and with more opportunities for social interaction were significantly less likely to exhibit mental and physical health problems as a result of plant closings and downsizing than those who perceived themselves as having less social support (Williams and Williams 1993). "Among women who experienced substantial stressful life events and who had few psychosocial assets, including little perceived social support, 91 percent had complications in pregnancy, compared with only 33 percent of those who experienced stressful events but had strong psychosocial assets" (Williams and Williams 1993).

I cite these statistics to make this point. Loneliness and isolation are some of the most significant diseases we face. Feeling isolated and disconnected from others, being unable to reach out and get support and comfort, feeling locked inside and unable to express emotion or sustain relationships are signs of trauma. This is the empty hole that the addict is trying to fill, the pain he is attempting to medicate, the loneliness she is trying to assuage. People need people at both the deepest and most superficial levels, and we learn our most lasting and profound lessons on how to be and live in relationships first from our families, and second from our relatives and communities.

Sharing the Trauma Story

Therapy offers a clinical container in which pain-filled relationship dynamics can surface and be examined in their concrete form. Distortions and conflicts can be resolved with the help of a professional and feedback from the group. New behaviors can be learned and practiced so that clients can experience more comfortable relationships in their own lives. In other words, both the intrapersonal and interpersonal can grow.

When trauma- and grief-related feelings—such as sadness and rage—get triggered within clients during the healing process, the clients can feel bewildered and threatened. Because those feelings were not fully processed and integrated, they exist within the psyche in a somewhat dissociated state, and when they are felt in the here and now, traumatized persons don't know what to do with them—just as they didn't know what to do with them at the time of the traumatic event. Along with the traumatic memories come the old fear felt at the time of the trauma and the sense that they once again can barely survive the feeling.

When a traumatic or grief memory gets triggered in life, the feelings can become frightening or painful. When they get triggered in therapy, where they can be felt consciously rather than acted out unconsciously, though they may still feel overwhelming, they can be seen and understood in a new light; they can be *reframed*. For this, the therapeutic relationship needs to be cohesive and supportive enough to hold the deep feelings that will arise. Simply feeling the feelings, with the associated thoughts and perceptions, in a supportive and safe context will be healing for the client. Distorted conclusions and perceptions can be understood as attempts made to explain the unexplainable or to justify what should not have been happening—and then they can be worked through. The personal meaning we made at the time can be reexamined through today's eyes.

Many distortions that we live by as unalterable fact are simply our minds' attempts to describe confusing and overwhelming circumstances that we have been unable to understand, feel and integrate. They live within us in a sort of flash-frozen state, and our minds record descriptions or stories to go with them, to try to make sense of them, to try to fit them into some sort of context. When the distortions are examined during therapy, they can be redescribed. For example, a child who felt unworthy of parental nurturing and attention can, as an adult, re-experience the hurt and isolation that he repressed while young. His perception that he was simply not worth the bother can be rightly attributed to a parent's preoccupation with disease rather than to his unworthiness. The hurt, anger and pain can be felt from a place of relative safety, and the person can come to feel compassion for himself rather than loathing. He did nothing, after all, except need a person who could not nurture him, probably because they themselves were so undernourished at the time.

Growing up in the care of addicts puts children at serious risk. A parent who is a slave to addiction may also be medicating his or her own PTSD symptoms. The behavior of addicts makes the people around them feel crazy. When addicts are in an altered state they can behave in many of the same ways as people who are seriously mentally ill. They are out of touch with reality, in another world. They act weird and scary, and the fact that you may be a dependent child or a spouse may hold little meaning for them when they are possessed by mood-altering chemicals. Drugs and alcohol distort reality, both for the user and the person relating to the user. They isolate, each in a world that does not correlate with the normal course of events. They reinterpret reality through a distorted lens.

Anytime one is placed outside of or isolated from normal functioning, the effects can be traumatic, which is why terms like "witness" and "reality check" are such a frequent part of the vernacular in Twelve-Step and recovery programs. "ACOAs don't know what normal is" (Woititz 1980). Talk therapy, group therapy, psychodrama and Twelve-Step programs provide an opportunity to share one's story, have it witnessed, see it in a new light (through a different lens), and find meaning, purpose and personal growth in and through pain. Traumatic experiences can be brought to the surface, re-felt, reunderstood, reinterpreted to the self and then reintegrated into the unconscious with the pain and distorted perceptions to a large extent removed, so that the baseline of learning is significantly altered.

Issues are considered resolved, according to Bessel Van der Kolk (1987), when the survivor is able at will to direct his or her mind toward or away from the trauma. If force is used in this process, there is real potential for re-traumatization. The process of healing in itself is frightening enough. What is crucial is not only what a therapist or group sees, but what clients are able to see within their own minds as a result of moving through these stages, that is, what the mind sees when it reflects back upon itself with this new understanding. This is why safety and trust are so important: They help clients tolerate the pain and anxiety of walking into their own dark sides in order to eventually walk out again with new pieces of the self reexamined, reunderstood and reintegrated into the whole.

The Stages of Healing Trauma

Based on my years of clinical work with clients, I observe that we seem to go through the following four stages while healing trauma. Each person, as you will note, passes through them a little differently. They are simply a map to use as a general guide that the individual can adapt as necessary.

1. *Telling the story and bearing witness to the trauma.* (Sharing feelings related to the trauma.)
2. *Accepting support.* (Taking in caring and support from others.)
3. *Linking current behavior with the original wound or trauma. Separating the past from the present.* (Understanding the meaning we have made out of the trauma and continue to live by. Identifying ways in which our trauma history has been negatively impacting our present.)
4. *Creating a new narrative. Reinvesting freed energy into constructive living.* (The new narrative places the trauma story back into the "remembered" context of life with new understanding and insight. Reinvestment may include setting new life goals, risking entering intimate relationships, or developing creative and nourishing activities and hobbies.)

These stages are all part of telling the trauma story and making sense of it. Stages may overlap, be leapfrogged or happen over and over again as we peel away, like layers of an onion, the layers of pain with all of the thinking, feeling, behavior, meaning and development that is woven into each layer.

My feeling is that the human psyche is programmed for healing in much the same way that our body is; that is, if you set a broken bone, it heals on its own; if you suture a cut, the flesh knits by itself. The various tools of recovery—such as psychodrama, journaling, Twelve-Step programs and therapy—are ways of cleaning traumatic emotions and memories so they can heal.

In the following chapters, you will read stories of healing that illustrate some of these tools. The stories come from both my clients and my students at New York University. The students have integrated the trauma theory we worked with in class in such a way that it comes alive. They have generously given their permission for me to share their stories with you so that the theory we have been discussing so far can come to life for you as clearly as it did for them. All names have been changed to preserve anonymity. I have selected these stories because they so beautifully illustrate what we have been learning in this book. I found them deeply moving; I trust that you will, too.

EIGHT

Letter Writing as a Healing Tool: John's Story

Those who are absent, by its means
become present,
it [letter] is the consolation of life.

Voltaire
"Post" Philosophical Dictionary, 1764

In his story, John identifies his theme: "I Just Wanna Tell SOMEBODY." He illustrates the personal cost he paid for years of inhibition and the relief and growth that came from breaking his silence. Sexual abuse is a classic scenario in which the shame of the perpetrator is visited upon the victim. So often sexual abuse is an abuse of power, and victims are sworn to secrecy by their perpetrators. Victims experience a profound loss of trust in authority figures and may find themselves twisting into unhealthy psychological positions in order to maintain connection to them. They may use denial, rewriting the story so that it's "not so bad." They may idealize the aggressor, therefore exaggerating in their minds the abuser's positive qualities and love for them while minimizing or even "forgetting" the abuse. They may actually move closer to their aggressors in an attempt to stay safe, which can set up a lifelong attachment style or traumatic bond. They may alternate between cycles of fusing with a person, then distancing through anger or cool withdrawal in attempts to get a sense of space. They may have trouble maintaining a sense of self within the relationship. After all, their will was ignored and their boundaries trampled on; they were forced to say "yes" when they felt "no." Or they may play out the shame of unhealthy sexual liaisons by putting themselves in compromising situations or becoming perpetrators themselves: again, the traumatic bond in action.

Here we will see John's story unfold. He has integrated trauma theory into his narrative, showing us how he used it to piece together the mystery of his own life. We see how one trauma that goes unspoken sets the victim up for other traumas. The door that would have stood as protection has been jimmied open, and anyone can enter. John writes a letter in which he allows himself full expression of all of his feelings. *The letter is not for sending; it is used instead as a safe and therapeutic release of pent-up emotion.* It is a healing tool that allows John to release pent-up feelings at a safe distance. In this way he confronts his perpetrator without what might be the retraumatizing experience of doing that in person. He removes the thorn from his own heart so that it can begin to heal, so that he can breathe again, so that he can stop "waiting to exhale." After writing this, John analyzes his own process and puts it into a healing context.

A Young Boy's Encounter with Sexual Abuse

Telling the Story

Although the fortress of protection I constructed to ward off the intensity of my emotional world was highly impenetrable, my repressed traumatic memories seeped out nonetheless over time. When I was a junior in high school, I directed my first play. Out of the many scripts in my drama club's library, I chose one entitled *I Just Wanna Tell SOMEBODY*, by Harold J. Haynes (1987). The play was about child abuse in America, and I remember thinking, "What a great opportunity for actors . . . finally a play with substance," and, "This is an important issue that my community disregards." My attachment to producing this script was intense and, in hindsight, *I just wanted to tell somebody*. In the words of the play's chorus (a jury of ghost-children who died from abuse):

> We've got to tell somebody—we've got to let them know or else this pain we're feeling will never, ever go. We've got to tell somebody—we've got to make them see that child abuse is killing kids like you and me.

However, at age seventeen, *I could not tell*. Instead, I directed over twenty actors in a production of my hell, keeping a safe distance while subconsciously attempting to acknowledge my trauma.

While it is common for trauma victims to self-medicate with alcohol and/or drugs (Dayton 1994 and 1997; Van der Kolk 1987), my parents' values and my martial arts training kept me from that path; yet an addiction that manifested early in my adolescence was a combination of overcommitting and overachieving. I filled my schedule to its limit with academics and extracurricular activities (in which I usually held an office of some sort). Within this behavior, I hid from my issues while avoiding dating as well as any real emotional connection with my family "out of fear of a renewed violation of the attachment bond"

(Van der Kolk 1987). As a way of protecting me from my own trauma, this addiction served a dual purpose. It kept me distracted from memories I was not capable of facing, and it permitted me to re-create a high-stress social environment to match the intensity of my inner emotional world (Dayton 1997).

My first conscious acknowledgment of being sexually molested came in a flashback. As researcher Daniel Akron noted, memories "remain locked in the brain, waiting for a trigger to bring them to the surface" (Dayton 1997). In my case, one morning at college I woke from sleep because I had begun urinating. I leaped out of bed and directed my flow into a nearby garbage can. During this moment I "flashed back" to a time when I was five and afraid to use the bathroom in my home. Thus, I started urinating behind furniture and in the garbage can of my childhood bedroom. I did this for a period of days until my father discovered it and spanked me. At the age of twenty-three, as I finished urinating in my dorm room's garbage can, I kept replaying the scene, wondering why I was afraid to use the bathroom as a child. After many replays, my body began to quake (and remember). I was flooded with stomach cramps and lightheadedness along with a brief string of images and vivid sensations (memory clips) of the first instance of abuse at the hands of my kindergarten teacher in the school bathroom. Accompanying this psychosomatic flood was the intense wish to die. In a state of panic, I picked up the telephone and placed a call, marking my entrance into personal therapy.

In the treatment that followed, there were many instances of acknowledging the shame, fear and rage; the loss of childhood; the violation of trust; the confusion in my sexuality; and the pain of my isolation (because of the silence I maintained for eighteen years). During my experience in counseling, a second memory returned of a later abuse (a friend's older brother who would molest both his younger brother and me on the living room floor when I would spend the night). This went on for a period of six months when I was between the ages of eight and ten. These violations were more confusing than the earlier graphic instance as they contained pleasurable moments.

Recently (yet three years after the trauma entered my conscious awareness), my psychodrama class utilized a letter-writing exercise. I wrote one letter to my abusers. Reading it is the deepest acknowledgment of my loss. The text shows how "experiential therapy allows the traumatized inner child to literally come back from the dead and learn to feel, talk and be alive again. It creates a space where the unspeakable can be spoken" (Dayton 1994). In addition, prior to writing my letter, an intimate friend hurt me deeply. Our connection had grown in and around the process of healing and, of my friends, I was the most vulnerable with him. When he violated my trust, I was stunned. There was no foreshadowing to his harsh actions. I went numb (the first stage of grieving and mourning) and then began "yearning for the lost object (person, situation)" (Dayton 1997). Initially, I was longing for my friend, yet the process quickly gave way to a deeper yearning for the injured child within me. Just as I was unable to block an attack from an intimate friend, I could not have blocked my abusers when I was a child. When I realized this, I also realized that my response to the current situation was grounded in "the pain, anger and fear associated with the early trauma" (Dayton 1994).

While I began crying for the present as I wrote my letter, sobs came from my past.

Kenny Dawson,

I have a story for you. And wherever you are, heaven or hell, I hope the powers that be let you tune in. In 1978, you were my teacher. Perhaps you remember "Johnny Wilson"—you always called me Jonathan. I didn't like that. I don't like you. Several years back my mom mentioned that you had died. I don't recall how she said you died, but I do recall hoping that it was painful. I hoped that you suffered a lot, because you fucked with me, and your fucked-up desires stole innocence and happiness from my childhood. You were a teacher, you fuck. You were a teacher. You said that I would be taken away from my parents if I told. Monsters exist. Your threat stayed with me for eighteen years. Eighteen years of silence, surrounded by family and friends and unable to ask for help. Three years after you fucked with me, my friend's older brother did the same. You set me up. I knew what would happen if I told anybody, so I was silent. You had me trained. You set me up. I was a little kid and I wanted to die. As a teenager the seeds you planted grew into vines that strangled me and fucked with my sexuality. My adolescence was a cycle of defense mechanisms. I remember being so angry at God for letting me live, because I was given the chance to die in 1985. I needed surgery. The doctors told my parents I wouldn't live. My dad was honest with me about my chances. He said, "I'll see you when you wake up and, if not, I'll see you on the other side." And I lived through that. They said I wouldn't, and I lived through surgery. I got a second chance at life, and I was so angry at God for it because I didn't want to live. I was a teenager and asking God why he let me live only to experience hell, to be strangled and trapped in that vine. That's what you did to me, Kenny. You made aspects of my youth into a hell.

In 1996, I broke through my fear. I had found the vine, but I needed help finding the roots, so I started therapy. I told my dad that I was molested. I told him the whole story, Kenny. His face did something I had never seen. It changed, and his eyes changed and he said, "I now know I can kill!" And in that moment, my years of silence hurt most, because more than anything, Johnny really wanted him to kill you, and I regretted my silence because I would not have been taken away from my parents. He would have killed you. And after I told him, he kept staring at me, but it was more like staring into twenty-three years of me. It was the look of a father at the entire life of his son. When I told him that you were dead, he said he would piss on your grave. So would I. And I told my mom, too. She cried and held me, and I cried. In that hug between mother and son, the eighteen years vanished. You are a monster. Your actions and your threats were evil. My mom would have held me, and my dad would have killed you: that's what would have happened if the six-year-old spoke. It took a while, but I found the roots of the vine and I pulled them out. And you are dead. And my mom held me. My dad is dead now, too, and I bet he's looking for you, Kenny Dawson. I am glad that I am alive. I thank God for my life. I wrote God a letter, too. In it I said that I was in the enactment phase of my life and thanked him for helping me get through the twenty-three-year-long warm-up. That's what it feels like, and my achievements have everything to do with God, me and my family and nothing to do with you.

When I completed writing this, I signed it with my full name in ink and my childhood name "Johnny W." in green crayon. It encapsulates my acknowledgment of my trauma in which "the young and vulnerable part of us can feel dropped by life . . . or even by God" (Dayton 1997). Furthermore, it frees a multitude of repressed pain. Last, the creation and sharing of this letter highlights the third stage of grief, "disorganization, anger and despair" and the final stage, "reorganization/integration" (Bowlby 1973).

Telling the Story and Bearing Witness to the Pain

My process of telling the story and sitting with the pain began in 1996. Starting from the office of my therapist, I was able to expand and gain support from my girlfriend and my sister. Not only was I dealing with the early trauma, my sexual preference was an issue as I wrestled between loving my girlfriend and being attracted to men. Almost a year later (after my girlfriend left me), I wrote a letter of magnitude to my father explaining the abuse, my years of silence and my homosexuality. Months after that, I gave this letter to my mom and she held me while we cried (as told in the story above), and I was safe to bear witness to my pain.

My experiences, coming "out of the closet" and coming out of my silences, were all positive with the exception of one. My performance coach in college coaxed her students to be vulnerable in the process of actor training. I trusted her and shared my history. Near the end of the semester, in a disagreement, the professor harshly cited my childhood trauma as the seed of my argument with and attitude toward her. This event was retraumatizing, and her words penetrated a freshly opened wound, attaching her baggage to my trauma. Hence, the abuse that I experienced from teachers initially squelched my willingness to trust my professors; and sadly, I am now aware that this fear extended to my father, who taught college composition. For the three years that I attended the community college where he taught, I purposely avoided taking his courses. In retrospect, part of that was my desire not to see him in that role.

Aside from sharing with family and friends, I learned how to love again in a relationship with a man. He, too, knew my history and struggles. Our relationship spanned a fourteen-month period, which included: the unpleasant ramifications from my experience with the performance coach, a three-month struggle where my father was diagnosed with and died from cancer, my grief process following that loss and, ultimately, my move. While the move ended our relationship as lovers, this man never stopped loving me, a blessing that allowed our connection to transition to friendship in spite of the losses. My relationship with him taught me that I was capable of loving and (more difficult than that) of being loved. This is a paramount discovery in the process of healing from trauma.

While sharing on an individual basis is necessary, "trauma survivors need relationships and groups in which to reawaken the self that went under for protection" (Dayton 1997). Within my psychodrama, I have shared about my early traumas when triggered by the stories of my colleagues. Yet, I have avoided assuming the role of protagonist in an enactment about my sexual abuse, as that does not feel safe. However, in the more distanced medium of letter writing, I was able to tell the story.

Accepting Support

After I shared my story, I accepted a hug from someone who in that moment took on a father-like role. Another student asked, "can my abused child hug your abused child?" and we embraced. Similarly, as the group members shared with me about their reactions to my piece, the most profound comment came: "In a room filled with women, it is so refreshing to be reminded of what it means to be a man." My post-traumatic interpretation of the abuse and my struggle with sexuality (Catholic Church and homophobic society) gave me the message that I was a freak, something less than a man. That piece of sharing validated the man within me and marked a moment of great catharsis and healing. When my past was brought to the here and now, the sharing from the group adjusted the traumatic template on my brain two decades prior.

Linking Current Behavior with the Original Wound

Aside from my addiction to overcommitment, caretaking was a post-traumatic behavior that evolved from my cycle. In the process, I came into contact with many abused and neglected children. During this time I was intensely drawn to help (save, rescue) these "at-risk" kids. Interwoven with my wish to help was my projected need to be saved from my unresolved pain (Dayton 1997). By moving into therapy, I began to shift my rescuing energies to myself, a process which allows me to offer more to others. With the creation of my "trauma time line" (a time line that displays the traumas and losses of my life [Dayton 1997 or Dayton 1994] see appendix), I noticed a key pattern which, to this day, is unsettling and a focus of my personal therapy. As Freud noted, "The patient cannot remember the whole of what is repressed in him and what he cannot remember is precisely the essential part of it. . . . He is obligated to *repeat* the repressed material as a contemporary experience, instead of remembering it as something that belongs to the past" (Van der Kolk 1987). In my case, when the question, "Can you identify areas where traumatic childhood dynamics were reenacted or re-created in later years?" was posed (Dayton 1997), I considered, for the first time, that my homosexual activity (random, unprotected sex) was, in part, an attempt of repressed material to surface. This was very ungrounding, as my "coming out" phase was tumultuous and something I considered settled two years ago. By no means am I inferring a causal link between sexual abuse and homosexuality; however, I am considering the trauma as a significant contributing factor in the reinforcement of my homosexual role. Dayton's statements (1997) such as, "We choose the very situation that we may consciously wish to avoid because, unconsciously, it is deeply familiar," and, "The problems we continually repeat that get us into trouble send up a red flag, marking the spot of earlier trauma," support my thought.

Separating the Past from the Present and Creating a New Narrative

The therapy described and done in this narrative is part of my process of separating the past from the present, as is my current psychotherapy. The process is gradual, yet I find myself becoming aware; and through this, I am authoring my new narrative, an experience of editing and translating volumes upon volumes of previous psychological text: the "Encyclopedia Wilson." Healing is said to have occurred, "when survivors can direct their attention toward the trauma or away from it at will" (Van der Kolk 1987). However, so much of my personality development has been intertwined with my trauma (and its post-traumatic effects on my perception of sexuality, society and spirituality) that the process of divorcing the two is complex. "People who have been traumatized develop an attachment to intense, emotional states. They have, in a sense, a traumatic bond with agitated feeling states. Living without that emotional intensity can feel scary, as if their lives will feel empty and meaningless if they are not engaged in internal conflicts" (Dayton 1997). The process of therapy is one of counterbalance; thus, as old systems are adjusted or removed, the new narratives must be allowed time to fill the space. Returning to the image of my fortress of protection which later became my prison or tomb, I say that although I lost my blueprints long ago, I am still the expert craftsman child who has the ability to disassemble and rebuild his interpretations of his early trauma. Much to my benefit and to the benefit of people in my social atom, I am no longer alone on my path.

NINE

Two Different Worlds:
The Social Atom as a Healing Tool

Whatever games are played with us,
we must play no games with ourselves,
but deal in our privacy with the
last honesty and truth.

Ralph Waldo Emerson
"Illusions"

Survivors of trauma, addicts and people from addicted homes live psychologically and emotionally in two different worlds. For the person who has experienced a sudden loss, there is *life before the trauma* and *life after the trauma*. After a trauma, a person's sense of a predictable and orderly world can feel shattered. Their inner world can be consumed with thoughts and feelings related to the trauma that might manifest as fears, phobias, anxieties or somatic disturbances such as an exaggerated startle response, migraines, stomach or back problems and other stress-related disorders. Life after the trauma can feel different. Bad things can and do happen. Suddenly, the world may feel like a potentially threatening place, and relationships with people can be anxiety-provoking—relationships are neither perfect nor permanent.

For the ACOA and co-addict, there are two distinct realities, *the wet one*, the one while the addict is using, and *the dry one*, the one while the addict sobers up. Each world has its own method of operation and its own mode of functioning. Rules for each are different, as is morality. Relationships and relating styles are unique to each world—dynamics that are present in one world do not necessarily carry over to the other. Consequently, there is a shift in object relations or the inner world that we spoke about in our chapter on characteristics. The inner object world becomes disorganized through trauma. But in the case of addictions, that shift may occur several times within a period of a few weeks or months. Because the environment changes, the child internalizes two homes. We will illustrate how that works in our social atom graphics on the following pages. In control studies, tasks learned while under the influence of alcohol were best remembered when again under the influence of alcohol. The alcohol, in other words, acts as a stimulus for particular memories. There is the sober world and the nonsober world, and thinking, feeling and behavior alter for each.

Carolyn, in my class at New York University, did a psychodrama of a never-talked-about incident in her life that she imagined had been "over" long ago. When she was three, her baby sister suffered a crib death. Not only did Carolyn lose her sister, but she was the one who discovered her lying lifeless in her crib. In her psychodrama she began to weep and stomp her feet. "Wake up, Jennie, wake up!" Carolyn had had a lifelong tendency to become immediately fused with a person, idealizing them, then to withdraw and become angry and disappointed when she perceived that they "abandoned" her in some way, as well as a degree of social anxiety and fear around connecting with people. She had never connected these patterns to her early trauma of losing her sister in such a sudden and tragic way.

I asked Carolyn if she could draw two social atoms, one representing her family of origin before the trauma and one representing them after it. A social atom is a diagnostic tool of psychodrama that can represent an inner map of relationships at any point in one's life. Developed by J. L. Moreno, the social atom influenced the later development of the genogram by the family systems field. Circles are used to represent females and triangles to represent males. I asked her first to locate herself in whatever size or place on the paper that felt right to her. Next, I asked her to locate her family-of-origin relationships in whatever relative size or distance that felt as if it reflected the nature of the relationship (i.e., large and distant, small and close, etc.). This is what Carolyn produced:

ATOM I: BEFORE TRAUMA

Next, I asked her to draw an atom of life after the trauma in order to see if it had changed.

ATOM II: AFTER TRAUMA
SUDDEN DEATH

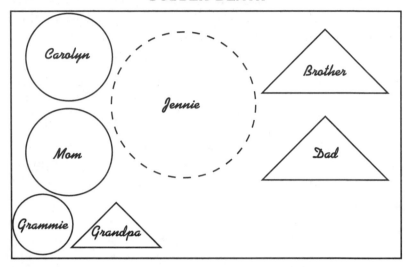

Clearly, the first notable change is that the size of the symbols was greatly enlarged on the second atom. The implosion of powerful emotion that occurs in trauma can make one's internal world feel hyperextended. It is as if the inner and outer worlds of a person are no longer in pleasant balance; rather, a victim of trauma like Carolyn can feel as if she is rattling around in her own inner cavern far away from the world that surrounds her. Second, her sister, though deceased, occupied a central and large role in the family organization, creating distance among family members. Jenny was the proverbial "elephant in the living room." Although she was not openly discussed, her presence loomed large in the family. The third notable feature is that some of the relationships changed in placement. Her dad and brother grew far apart from her, her mother and her maternal grandparents. The family came to be divided into "two sides." We see clearly how alliances shift and object relatedness changes through trauma. Carolyn's father began to drink heavily after the loss of his daughter Jennie, making the loss of one child turn into the loss of both that child and a parent, which led to more distance and loss among the rest of the family.

Carolyn's third atom represented the way that *she wished it could have been,* a corrective experience. She represented her baby sister through a broken line, which is used to represent death in social atoms. "Jennie is with us in our family but not as if she's still alive, if you know what I mean." The family is "equal in status, close but not overlapped, everyone gets along with everyone, it's comfortable. Jennie is still with us but she doesn't take up a space that keeps the rest of us apart, she's with all of us, she's in our hearts but we're the family that's living and we're not locked in the past. She's in heaven."

ATOM III: HOW I'D LIKE IT

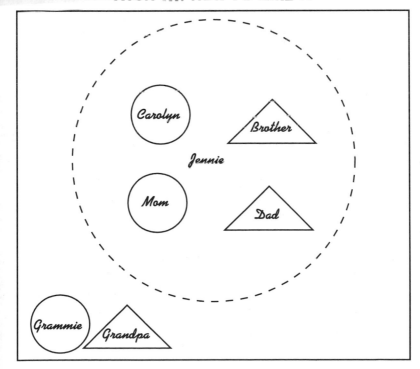

Carolyn felt relieved. "I never thought of it this way before. It makes so many things make sense. I just want to sit with this for a while. That's enough for now, I feel a little lightheaded, but it's a good lightheaded. I didn't know I would be able to go this far."

Carolyn's social atom speaks to the alterations in life and self that occur before and after a trauma, *two different worlds.*

RICH

In Rich's atom we see what happened to his world after his parents' divorce. Rich had one brother, a biological mother and a father who had adopted him at birth. He never knew his biological father, who never married his mother. His brother was the natural child of both parents. After the divorce, his mother took Rich to another state to live and his brother remained with his father. "My whole world fell apart, everything changed. I lost my father, I considered him my real father and I adored him. I lost growing up with my only brother, and I became my mother's sort of only son, husband, I don't know what. I hated having no male role model, I felt I had to give up my childhood and become a man and take care of her at nine years old. I was so lonely."

ATOM I: WITH FAMILY

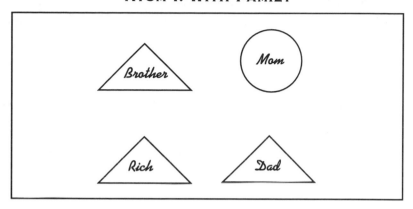

ATOM II: PARENTAL DIVORCE

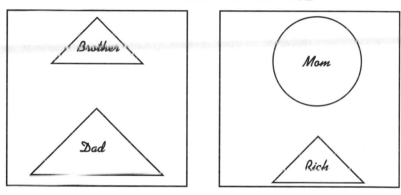

The grief Rich expressed at losing his family was deeply moving. "My heart felt 'torn in two.' I could never speak of it because it upset my mom, there was nothing I could do about it, and boys weren't supposed to cry anyway. Everything that my life could have been has been affected by this. I drank and drugged to fill the loneliness; and now that I'm sober, I know I have to feel this stuff so I don't pick up and relapse, but it hurts so much." Rich's mother used sex and drugs to medicate her pain. With the loss of his family, a mother who was often high, and a constant stream of men going in and out of his life, Rich felt displaced, but no comfort was available to him so that he could heal. Rather, he lived with further conflict and the people he would have gone to for comfort were no longer available to him. Unresolved trauma begets more trauma. Drugs and alcohol seemed, at the time, like a way out, a solution to his pain. Until they stole his life.

PATRICIA

Still another version is the two different worlds of the ACOA, revealing themselves in Patricia's social atoms of her world when her father was drinking and her world when her father was sober. They depict the two realities that virtually all ACOAs internalize as they grow up.

ATOM I: SOBER ATOM

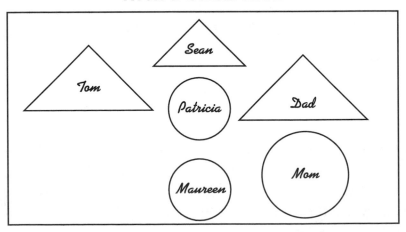

ATOM II: NONSOBER ATOM

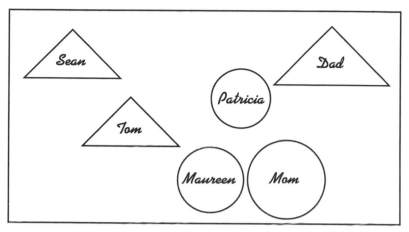

As we see in Patricia's atoms, the object relations shift significantly when Dad is using. Mom and Dad grow distant; Maureen aligns with Mom; Patricia loses her place with Mom, who is now preoccupied with Dad's drinking and is unavailable except to Maureen, who becomes her comfort. Sean withdraws for protection, staying out of the house as much as possible, and Tom gets lost in the middle. To complicate matters further, because no one talks about the "elephant in the living room," namely Dad's drinking, the nonsober world becomes a shadowy and murky place. Everyone lives it, but it tends to be denied and repressed, thus leaving family members feeling "crazy" and "guessing at what normal is" (Woititz 1980). The hallmark of the ACOAs' world is inconsistency. There is the "looking good family" or the family presented to the outside world and the "shadow family" or the family dynamics when under the influence. The shadow world vibrates beneath the thin membrane of the addicted family system, and all of the emotion, thinking and behavior associated with it threatens to erupt at any time. Until this world is made conscious and seen for what it is, it lurks in the unspoken atmosphere of the family as a secondary reality with its own code of ethics, morality and behavior. There is constant shifting between the two worlds. Consequently, it is difficult to sort out and understand what a normal life feels like and how it operates in a coherent, consistent manner.

RANDY

Our last social atom is that of the addict himself. Here we use two examples. In each you will see how the relationships of addicts shift according to their relationship with their substance. When the use of the substance is their primary preoccupation, there is little room for anyone or anything else. The first atom represents Randy's family relationships before he started using drugs and alcohol.

ATOM I: SOBER ATOM

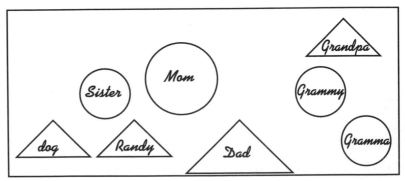

Randy is a fairly typical teenager. He has some learning issues and has not really developed strong extracurricular interests such as sports, theatre, etc. He has friends, but of late has begun to hang around with a different group. His grades are dropping, he has less time for family and his attitude is slipping toward belligerence.

ATOM II: USING ATOM

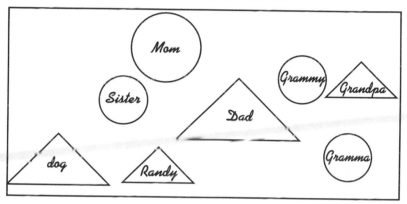

When Randy is using drugs, drinking and smoking pot, he is more distant and isolated from the world of his family. Surrounding Randy we could also imagine added the coteric of drug-using friends with whom he hangs out. His bond with them is strong, as they often share the same drug-induced state of mind. This kind of high on a regular basis leads Randy away from meeting and fulfilling the developmental needs and obligations of a teenage boy, further isolating him in an underworld that ultimately will lead to self-destruction.

The social atom is a powerful tool for illuminating the nature of our relationships. It is a relationship map, a diagram of our internal world or object relations. Much information surfaces in this seemingly simple exercise. It is a

way for the client to gain personal insight or for a therapist to better understand the client's relationship network. (For more on social atoms see *The Drama Within,*
Tian Dayton, Health Communications, Inc., 1994.)

TEN

Journaling as a Healing Tool

The most beautiful things are those that madness prompts and reason writes.

André Gide
Journals, 1894

Celeste and Alysia unravel the complexities of their inner worlds through the use of journaling. Journaling can be an effective way for trauma survivors to piece together fragments of memory and put them into sequence. In the following narratives, both women weave trauma theory in and out of their writing as a way of understanding what happened to them and why it affected their lives as it did. They identify reenactment dynamics that followed them into adulthood and eventually place the full trauma narrative into the context of their lives. Like putting the pieces of a puzzle together, they find themselves in the missing content and put it where it belongs, so they can lay claim to their unformulated experience and see it whole and within a clear line of vision.

CELESTE'S STORY

Celeste, a psychodrama student of mine from New York University, has embarked upon the disequilibrating task of journaling her trauma story. Her internal responses to committing these painful memories to paper are italicized. She experiences an uncomfortable mix of body sensations and psychological and emotional reactions as her memories come forth. She writes with touching clarity and quiet heroism as she pieces together haunting memories. She is an example of how a victim becomes a victor through love, commitment and a willingness to tell her truth.

MY MOTHER'S SUICIDE

My ambivalence surrounding my mother's ultimate abandonment—her suicide—and her lifelong series of abandonments is a current struggle for me. I have two younger brothers, Richard and Raymond. I'm not sure if Richard ever tells people that our mother killed herself. My guess is he is so far from any pain or feeling he has about her, that it wouldn't matter if he did say it; it doesn't touch him emotionally. Raymond, my youngest brother, never tells people. He lets people assume she died of cancer and just doesn't clarify. I have always thought I was more in touch with the pain I feel over her loss. I thought this because I was able to say that my mother died as a result of suicide. I have recently, however, become aware of how similar to my brothers I am in my inability to handle certain aspects surrounding our mother's ordeal. *I am aware, as I write this, of feelings of anxiety, accelerated heart rate and slight panic. I am feeling sadness increasing as I describe these sensations. I also feel a bit dissociated. I am afraid to talk about the details surrounding her death. I almost never tell the story or, if I do, I tell the* Reader's Digest *version.*

Telling the Story

Acknowledging and bearing witness to the pain

My mother and her husband were arrested for growing marijuana. They had a large growing operation in Montana, in a warehouse. Her husband (of ten years) had been in jail twice before for similar offenses. My mother had no criminal record. She was forty-six years old and had a Ph.D. in clinical psychology. There was a trial and she was convicted; of what, I don't know or can't remember. *Numbing out again, feeling sad and dissociated.* The months around the trial were very stressful. She was totally out of control. I was living in New York at the time and would spend a lot of time on the phone with her, mostly listening to her rant over details concerning the trial, her lawyer and the district attorney. They had no money, their house and property were confiscated and, of course, so was the marijuana—their source of income. She would ask to borrow money, and although I was an undergraduate working full-time to support myself, I felt guilty and bad for her and gave her loans off my credit card.

She went to jail for ten days after her conviction, before the in-laws posted bail. Her sentencing hearing was to take place in a few months. During this time, when she was in jail, she called me and wrote to me. It was during one of these phone calls that I first remember her talking about taking her own life, although I'm not sure about this. *I feel very confused about whether or not I didn't always know, somehow, that she thought about this.* She always said she would never go to jail, be locked up or not be in control. This was core to her personality so, in a way, it was not a surprising thing to hear her say. I was, however, very upset. I made her promise not to do anything; to take one day at a time; to call me and write often during those ten days. I promised to send her a ticket to New York. She was in jail during Mother's Day and my graduation from NYU. This trip seemed to keep her going. I can't write about my last visit with my mom. *I can't even write that without crying. The pain of this memory is overwhelming to me. I feel such sadness. Just crying and pain in my throat.*

Two months later, she and her husband left town. They had planned not to await sentencing and to skip bail. She was facing jail time and had already made it quite clear she had no intention of going to prison again for any length of time. *Doing a lot of avoiding now. Getting up, leaving the room, talking to my friend. I don't want to continue working on this, feeling overwhelmed.* My mother and her husband were driving in Missouri. Where they were going is unclear to me. I think at the time the details of her plan were not important, and no one was privileged to their thinking. They had created a world all their own. No one was allowed to influence them or offer them any help or advice unless it was what they wanted. *This is another area where I become confused.* They were parked somewhere and someone called the police to report a suspicious car. The police came and they were arrested. I am not sure what they were arrested for, but I'm sure there were drugs in the car. Maybe the drugs, the illegal car they were driving, suspicious behavior, who knows.

That night my mother wrote my brothers and me a letter, she wrote another letter just raving to the authorities over the injustice in the judicial system and she hung herself in her jail cell. *Had to write that quick. I am aware of my inability to look back over my words and reread what I just wrote. I never say that, how she did it. It is too terrible. I feel tears welling up inside of me and very sad. I wish it wasn't so gruesome, how she did it. Then maybe I wouldn't feel so haunted by it. I find this image in my mind and it disturbs me greatly. I have fear of coming across the image in film, on television and in photographs. You would be surprised to realize how prevalent the word and the image are. I try to avoid it whenever I can, both in my mind and in the outside to shut it out.*

I feel, at times, that all my adaptation and coping around this story is a good thing: my inability to remember details of the story, how I protect myself from disturbing thoughts and images of my mom's death, as well as my resistance to describing the way she killed herself. It is all too much and I feel I would just explode if the whole weight of it were to hit me. But recently I am coming to realize that these same adaptations have also kept me away from working through and incorporating this story into my life.

Share the Feelings, Accept Support

Last year I decided to stop seeing my therapist and see a drama therapist. I had been seeing Julie for about a year and a half. Other than my desire to have a different type of therapy, there was nothing wrong with our therapeutic relationship. We were working well together, and I liked her a great deal. I felt she liked me, that I mattered to her even outside of our therapeutic agreement and that she cared about me. I started seeing her in 1995, just before my thirtieth birthday. This was a very difficult time for me. My daughter was a year and a half old. I was fast approaching thirty with little sense of myself outside of my role as mother and homemaker. I cut my (long) hair short, decided to go back to school, and started therapy. It was the first time back in therapy in about ten years. Looking back (or around, as I still feel very much involved in this process), it feels transformational, like a metamorphosis, an awakening as if from a very deep sleep. I felt quite validated last week in class when you said, "People sometimes drop out of therapy after the death of someone close to them." Going into therapy in the years after my mother's death was one of the last things I would have thought of. Getting married and having a child seemed the healthiest things to do at the time. Although, looking back, I could have used some help, those choices were the best I could make. Anyway, Julie and I never talked much about my mom's death. I rarely brought it up, and she never pushed me on it. We dealt mostly with issues in my marriage and returning to school.

With my current therapist I am sharing more details about my mother and my childhood. He has helped me to acknowledge that my mother was mentally ill, not only at the time of her death but probably during my childhood, perhaps before. This is a difficult and painful realization. It means rescripting a great deal of what I had previously thought to be true.

I have just spent three weeks looking through boxes and drawers to find the letters my mother wrote me while she was in jail and the suicide letters she wrote before she died. I found them and last week I gave them to my therapist to read. I was only able to partly reread these four letters. I became very sad at the sight of her handwriting and the tone of desperation in her voice. *Crying, feeling sad and anxious.* We talked about the letters and what she may have been thinking and feeling. It was very difficult for me to look at the paper. I trust my therapist with this history and know it is a positive move to gain another perspective on this story through the information in those pages. I feel as if I have unearthed some of this pain and loss, and with support I will gain new strength and insight from this journey.

During our class, it was freeing to let out some of the pain I hold inside with the group. I would have wanted to do a psychodrama, but I know I am not ready. I still have a lot of fear of being overwhelmed by my pain. *Feel sad, tears and a tightness in my chest.* During a psychodrama warm-up with Manny and Andrea last week, Manny asked the group to each pick someone to play individual members of their families. When we were asked to choose our mothers, I became overwhelmed, frozen, terrified. I was unable to choose anyone who could play my mother. She is not here—not in the room and not in this world. She is gone. She will never come back. *Crying.* I wound up a psychodramatic star (the person chosen by the group to do a psychodrama) and felt not only sadness over the loss of my own mother but also the responsibility to mother those who had chosen me or their mothers, or mother's mothers. . . . I was asked to share some of what I was feeling at the time. Those who picked me spoke about their dramas with their mothers. I was able to hear how my drama was in keeping through the generations with other people's dramas with their mothers—and to hear about my mother's mother and her struggle. It felt good to know I was a part of the collective story, connected to so many people. Sociometry truly is the power behind this work.

Link Current Behavior with Original Trauma

I currently have no explanation as to how it is I know how to mother Sara. I just know I am a wonderful mother, and we are so lucky to have each other. She is my health. In my ability to mother her and her growth within the relationship, I am re-mothered. Nursing Sara has been the most wonderful part of my life. I can't believe how much I have loved all the hours she has spent in my arms nursing. *Crying, sad and missing her so much.* To have the power to soothe her when she was crying or sick or just needing to suck is the most amazing feeling. I feel we have given each other a wonderful gift and that we will both be made all the better from this relationship. I know my bond with her and my desire to mother her in every way I can is a way of rescripting the loss of my own mother.

I lost my mother slowly and many times during my childhood. *Sad and feeling alone, like a frightened child.* She was not a bad person, just not a very good mother. Continually, she abandoned my brothers and me during our childhood. She did this when she actually would send us to other people to take care of us for long periods of time; and when she just made unsafe choices about who would take care of me for the night or by leaving me alone with no one to watch me at all. Ultimately, she went off altogether to marry her husband. I was sixteen at the time and about to start my senior year of high school. My brothers lived with my father, but he wouldn't let me live with him. I got an apartment and a job and finished high school.

My childhood traumas are my guide and my map in my ability to mother Sara. *It is the direction I will not travel.* My need to have had all that I did not have growing up is what I give to her. Only time will tell. I know as she gets older, I will need to continually seek out role models in parenting, as I was not able to see a lot of good examples growing up.

There are many such connections to make between my current life and my past traumas. In every way I am a product of my upbringing. Another connection would be my need to be seen. As my mother was an ineffective mirror or double, I know very little about what love is. My mother said she loved me all the time, and I am sure she did, but it looked pretty bad. I am left unsure about what love is and what it is supposed to look like in my relationships with men. I was neglected by my mother many times, and I feel I continually am making choices trying to fill the lack I'm left with.

Separate the Past from the Present

I want Sara to grow and leave me in her own good time, unlike in my childhood. I was forced to take care of myself before the normal course of my maturation. I wish, for my daughter, the strength and self-confidence to accomplish all she desires in life. It is my goal to empower her to do so by loving guidance and respectful role modeling. All of this is what I strive to be and hope I am able to accomplish. Yet, I know I must be careful not to overcompensate and frighten her. Sara and Sam left last Thursday for a trip to San Diego. I could not go, and since San Diego is my hometown, she went with him to be taken care of by my family. This was the first time she and I have been separated for such an extended period of time. As I know, all mothers worry about their children when they are not close by, but I think more so for me because of the feelings of separation that were brought up. Having Sara close to me reminds me that I am connected to her. I had a great deal of anxiety the night before they left; I couldn't sleep. Around 1:00 A.M. she woke crying from a dream. I brought her into bed with me so I could feel and see her close all night long. Under normal circumstances, she would have stayed in her own room. I knew at the time I was overreacting to the upcoming trip. I was awake most of the night looking at her and feeling panicked about her leaving. I had stopped having normal fears about our separation. Would she miss me, would she be able to sleep without nursing; all the regular stuff. By this time, during the middle of the night, I was studying every line of her face, afraid, God forbid, something terribly unspeakable would happen to harm her in some way. Knowing I would not survive without my beautiful child. *Feeling sad, afraid and superstitious writing these thoughts.* My mother's suicide was the most horrible thing I could have ever imagined. Knowing that the threat of the unspeakable exists (as all survivors of trauma do), keeps me aware and fearful that it could happen again. *Hypervigilance.* Cognitively, I know these fears are irrational, but in the face of being separated from the person I love most in this world, Sara, I become overwhelmed by them.

Create a New Narrative, Reinvest Freed Energy

(Note: Celeste's entire story may be considered part of the trauma narrative. Here she is reframing her experiences.)

I think I was lucky that my mother prepared me, in a way, for her leaving. She taught me early on not to count on her and to be strong and take care of myself. Without that early preparation, my story, and who I am today, would perhaps be different. My mother's life was tragically flawed. Each step of the way, the choices she made were building to a climactic end. I was just caught up in her drama. I grew strong and adaptive in my struggle to survive. These adaptations are a great strength. My ability to survive and become who I am was a gift from my childhood. It is this gift that will make me a good therapist. My drama will allow me to facilitate others in their healing as it has served me.

THE TRAUMA NARRATIVE

Alysia's Story

The pen is the tongue of the hand.

Henry Ward Beecher
Proverbs from Plymouth Pulpit

In Alysia's trauma narrative, we see the disjointed nature of trauma memories: how they surface in the form of memory fragments and physiological arousal. Evident in her memoir is the murky and confused thinking, alternating with insight and clarity, that can characterize the inner world of the sexual abuse survivor. Later in the story, we see the magical meaning she made out of her abuse; her childlike attempt to make sense out of what feels senseless, to make herself feel cared for in the absence of parental protection. Her parents, both addicts, were not in a position to protect her from harm. She speaks of her confused writing of the words "mother" and "father" that depict her authentic feelings breaking through her emotional defenses. We witness how early sexual abuse acted as a gateway or setup for later sexual abuse. Finally, we see Alysia, like Celeste, moving from victim to victor, gaining a sense of mastery over her traumatic experiences.

Alysia begins her story in the third person in order to give herself the emotional distance that she needs to feel safe. This also speaks to the dissociation that so often accompanies childhood sexual abuse. Children, in order to get through a terrifying experience that they cannot get themselves out of, may psychically leave their bodies and recall their abuse as if it happened to another little child or as if they are watching themselves from outside of their bodies. Slowly, Alysia moves into her own skin and occupies her own memories. She lets us in on her internal response while journaling this story through parenthetical breaks that describe her inner world. The strange recollections of disjointed sights and sounds, along with her responses of shutting down, numbing and dissociating, illustrate how traumatic memory gets stored and recollected.

Trauma Memory Number One— Fragments of Truth

Telling the story, witnessing, opening to support

There is, inside of Alysia, the repressed memory of a four-year-old child who went on a camping trip with her father, grandmother, grandfather, an aunt, an uncle and a cousin who was seven years her senior. *(This image becomes much more vivid as Alysia begins to type this story and her fingers slow in speed.)* The "children" were sent to bed inside a pop-up camper while the adults sat outside enjoying the campfire, talking and drinking. It was dark inside the camper as they walked in and made their way to their separate sleeping bags. They got into their sleeping bags *(Alysia could see the images now of a dark blue and a dark green—the dark blue had a red lining, maybe that was hers?)*. Her cousin was saying something to her in a whisper and she thought she remembered his saying how cold he was. Then he unzipped her sleeping bag *(she could hear the sound of the zipper now)*. He got on top of her and placed his hand over her mouth . . . the memory stops there! She doesn't remember what she felt physically or emotionally. She can recall a vague image of his mother, but she cannot decipher if she was present before or after this scene occurred. . . . Everything is a blur and the time frames seem to be distorted.

Memory Number Two

The next memory and the closest one to this incident *(my typing speed has increased dramatically)* is of me riding in my father's white Ford truck with my mother on the way to my grandmother's house, and as we ascend the corner of my house I begin to cry. My mother asks me why I am crying and I tell her it is because I do not want to go to my grandmother's house! She asks why, because I always enjoyed going to her house and what has changed? At that point I told her in a four-year-old's description, "Scott hurts me." This abuse continued until I reached the age of seven and was able to forcibly say "No" to him.

Events That Triggered Return of Memories

These memories remained totally stagnant in my memory until I reached the age of twenty-three. I was planning to attend UNC in the fall and attempting to reach my goals of becoming a student when my father flew down with his "new wife" to Florida for a visit. During this visit, my grandmother, stepmother, father and I went to visit my aunt and uncle for the weekend. (These are Scott's parents.) At this point in my life, I had practically given up drugs and alcohol but still dabbled occasionally. Scott asked me if I still got high. I said, "I quit." He said, "Come on, I have a joint. Let's smoke it. You don't want to hang out with 'them,' do you?" He was right, the "adults" were ignoring us, as usual. So I said okay.

He told me we would have to walk out to his camper because the stuff was there and we couldn't smoke near the house. So I followed him out to the camper. Once inside the camper he rolled a joint as I sat nervously at his side. Then he lit it and reached over me to turn out the light. I asked him what he was doing and he just put his arm around my shoulder and said he was making it more comfortable as he slipped his arm around me. Suddenly, I felt my body freeze and tighten as I realized what he was actually up to. I remember how numb I became as he started to fondle my breast and kiss my neck in the dark while whispering words that I'll not repeat but described what he would like to do to me and how much he'd missed me. He wanted me to go to the "bed" where we could be more comfortable. At this point I remember the fear and the desire I had to run out the door, but the feelings were of being frozen in time and unable to move. Somehow I was able to pull myself together and say, "I'm leaving now."

I feel like I have a bit of the chameleon inside of me who has always been there to help me to "change colors" so to speak. I suddenly shifted from a child/victim to someone empowered and was strong enough to tell him just how fucking sick I thought he was and how he hadn't changed one bit since we were kids. "You're still a fucking pervert!" I said. Then he insisted upon walking me up toward the house. I declined and said that I could find my way myself, but he insisted that he would have to unlock the gate (my aunt and uncle own a ranchlike piece of land with horses). He followed me up to the house to wish me goodnight and give me an apology for his behavior. I accepted the apology and told him that I forgave him. Then he said, "You can't blame me for trying, can you?" He asked for a hug goodnight, and I recall my barriers went down and I felt very powerful in the role of the 'Seducer' (at this point I was still in remission from the head trauma from my car accident and felt very unattractive). I remember feeling very powerful that after all these years he was still fantasizing about me. He attempted to kiss me again, and I felt myself become very angry and I shoved him away violently. I went into the house and slept in the same room where he had violated me for years on and off. Needless to say, I didn't have a very good rest that night. The next day we pretended as if nothing had happened and, because of my own personal "shame," I never told my family on my dad's side about the current or prior incidents.

Trying to Make Sense of What Feels Senseless

Linking, separating past from present

After returning to my mother's home, I unloaded what had happened and asked her what I had told her as a child and why no one had ever stopped these incidents from occurring. She told me that she had told my father and, because of the fact that it was his side of the family and that her ties to them were shaky anyway, she suggested that it would be best if my father was the one to tell them. I still don't know what, if anything at all, my father said to them. If he said anything, it wasn't enough because I was still left alone with Scott for years after that first experience. Needless to say, I hold a lot of bitterness towards my father's side of the family. I made sense of those occurrences by rationalizing them with the distorted perception of a child trying to make sense of a crazy situation. I remember thinking that my grandmother, my aunt and uncle (Scott's parents) must have wanted things the way they were. I remember thinking, even after I had matured and was an adult, "that my dad's family planned for Scott and I to be together because our family has English descent—and, after all, it used to be quite common for the royal English to marry their first cousins in order to keep the bloodline richer with royal blood."

Weak Support System

Amother *(ironically, I typed "Amother" instead of "Another," thus suddenly realizing that both of these sexual assaults had taken place when I was far away from my specific caregiver—my mother. As I'm typing this I begin to break into tears as I realize the connection between my most recent traumatic experiences having taken place in New York, in which case I have been, once again, isolated from my mother—in regards to distance as well as communication via telephone. She has no phone with which I can reach her. Thus, it is no wonder that my attachment bond has been very distorted.)*

Memory Number Three

Once again, another childhood trauma in which my memories are much clearer took place at the age of nine. The memory is as such: I was spending the summer with my father in Colorado. This was the first summer that I actually spent away from my mother. My parents had permanently separated when I was five years old, but my dad stayed within the area until I was eight, so I saw him up until that point every weekend, or anytime for that matter. Anyway, the story is as such. The perpetrator, who I will call Dan, was my father's best friend since high school and a constant drinking companion of my father's. He was also at one time married to my favorite aunt—on my mother's side, of course. One night the three of us went to a local small-town bar. It was often the case that I would frequent such establishments with my dad, and the bartender would always give me my favorite drinks, a Roy

Rogers and a Shirley Temple. *(At this point I am crying again. I had no idea how intense writing this would be for me.)* I enjoyed the company of adults who often fawned over me and gave me a lot of attention.

My father *(I had to retype the word again because I have oftentimes misspelled the word "father" by spelling the word "farther"*... *a subconscious description of the trauma of being separated by great distance from a man who was too far away physically, mentally and emotionally to provide me with the nurturance and protection that I so desperately needed as a child*... *as well as an adult. I'll continue this story without further interruptions.)* My father was incredibly drunk on this evening and one of his and Dan's friends was driving us all home. Dan got dropped off first, and he suggested that I stay the night with him because he and his two-year-old daughter were driving up to visit some mutual friends of mine and his in the morning. I remember being annoyed at my father for being drunk and viewing Dan as a better caretaker, since he did not appear to be quite so drunk himself. And I was tempted further by the opportunity to go on a road trip, since I have always loved the adventure of traveling. So I chose to get out of the car and stay the night with Dan. But I did not choose, nor did I desire, the events that subsequently followed as a result of my being alone with this man.

I walked in and put on a blue nightgown *(I have no recollection of how my nightgown was present in this house*... *but it was).* I then walked toward his sleeping daughter's room in order to get into bed with her. At that point Dan stopped me by saying, "Don't sleep in there, you'll wake her up. There's room in here in my bed and you can sleep here." (At this age I was familiar with the word *molestation*, because my best friend Mandy had shared an incident in which something had happened to her by an older man and we had discussed such issues.) I remember how nervous and afraid I was getting into his bed. Yet I felt choiceless in the matter and submitted. I remember getting into the bed and curling into a ball as close near to the edge of the bed as I could get. We were watching *Star Trek* on a black-and-white TV when I eventually fell asleep.

When I awoke, Dan was French-kissing me on the mouth and rubbing my body parts. He was on top of me and I felt nothing but the numbness of my vagina/torso area. As an attempt to protect myself, I pretended that I was asleep the whole time . . . until he eventually rolled over and appeared to be asleep. After lying lifeless in the bed for some time, I eventually got up quietly and was headed for the door when Dan asked, "Where are you going?" I quickly made the excuse that I had to go to the bathroom and he said, "Okay, Babe." *(This was my childhood nickname, one which I hate to be called by for reasons that should appear to be obvious to the reader.)* I was still wearing my long, light-blue nightgown with pretty laces around the neck. I paused in front of the bathroom door, then continued through the trailer and past his daughter's room. I paused briefly as I saw that she was sound asleep. I remember the guilt I felt for leaving her in that house. I quietly reached the door, which provided an exit away and out of this nightmare.

I opened the front door quietly and stepped out onto the gravel barefoot and began running as fast as I could. *(This image suddenly caused a flood of emotion and*

tears as I see a scared and beautiful young girl run-
ning across the rocks and unable to feel the pain they
should have caused her feet. This image is like a scene
in a movie.) I recall the fear I felt that Dan would get into
his car and come looking for me, finding me before I had
a chance to reach safe ground. I chose to run through the
fields and risk the chance of snakes, to walk silently down
dark alleys and neighborhoods until I had no choice but to
brave the highway. Once on the highway, I was hypervigilant as to any car that would approach, fearing it would be
him in search of me and to punish me for running away.
Each time a car would approach, I would jump in the
ditch beside the road and hide. Eventually, I reached my
father's house (around 5:00 A.M.) and found the door
locked. I began beating on the door, crying and longing for
safety. My dad's Doberman pinscher was barking angrily,
and eventually my dad's girlfriend came to the door and
asked me what I was doing here in the middle of the night
and what had happened to me. I told her that Dan had
tried to molest me and I sneaked out and ran away. She
let me in and asked me why I was so dirty and bleeding (I
had fallen on the road and skinned my knees; that is what
I remember, anyway).

My father was passed out and so his girlfriend ran me
some bath water and told me to take a bath. I remember
the incredible sense of shame that I felt as she told me to
take off my gown. This was the beginning of my low self-
esteem and guilt in displaying body parts. I developed a
fixation towards wearing sweaters and pants in the sum-
mertime even when it reached the upper nineties. I recall
the shame and resistance towards wearing swimsuits to
the lake, beach or pools. I eventually got into the water

and Cheryl (Dad's girlfriend) sat beside the tub questioning me as to what had taken place. After I told her what Dan had done, I recall her asking a question that filled me with guilt and shame. She asked, "What about Stephanie?" Dan's daughter. Cheryl went on to tell me that she is only two years old and how bad it would be if Dan were to mess with her. I felt incredible shame at the thought that I had abandoned a child who I was often the caretaker of—I had begun to baby-sit Stephanie at a young age.

After my bath, I put on another nightgown and was attempting to reach my bedroom when Cheryl said, "You'll have to sleep in your father's room because I am sleeping in your bed." Apparently, they had had a fight because she did not approve of my father's drunkenness. I felt that I was unable to sleep in another bed with a man and told her that I did not want to sleep in there. She then filled me with more guilt by asking whether or not my father had ever touched me. (The answer to the question is a definite No!) I told her, "No," but that I would feel much better to sleep *alone*. Thus, she gave me my room back, and she went to sleep on the couch.

The next morning, Dan came by to see me. He pretended to be very concerned and asked my father what had happened, that he was drunk and passed out and when he awoke I was gone. My father later told me that Dan had been crying and even though Cheryl had told my father what had happened, my dad felt confused in regard to how to respond to this man. I remember my father telling me, "I didn't know if I should hit him or hug him." My father told Dan he could not talk to me and that I was asleep and would not be going anywhere with him on that day. When I awoke, Cheryl told me that I needed to tell my father in my own words what had happened. I remember feeling very ashamed to tell my father about it and trying to choose my words delicately.

After I explained what happened, they asked me what I wanted to have done about this situation. "Do you want to have him arrested and have to go to court? Do you know what that would do to his family?" The feelings of shame and guilt were immense and my choices were limited. Hence, Dan got away with the pain he caused me while I suffered the consequences that a traumatic event like this one causes the victim to endure for decades, and it has definitely impaired my abilities to have any type of normal, healthy relationship with men. Within the following days to come, I saw Dan at the same bar that we had previously attended. When I saw that he was there, I ignored and avoided him. He called out, "Babe!" I ignored him. He called out my name again in a more forceful tone, I looked up and he said, "Come here, I want to talk to you." I was alone and sitting at the bar. I walked over to see what he wanted. He then apologized for the other night and I said, "Okay, I forgive you."

Putting It All Together
Linking, separating past from present, new narrative

These are the traumatic events of my life. Now they are strung together in a story, my story. Such memories include: Scott and me age four in the pop-up trailer; spending the night with a girlfriend and having her "mother" touch me in inappropriate ways; nine years old waking up with a grown man who had once been my uncle by marriage "touching me"; ten years old being fondled by a schoolteacher and by a man who had stopped by to visit my mother; age fifteen, my stepfather's attempt at seducing me. The hands are very powerful images in my mind and represent a large source of traumatic exposure—because in each of these experiences my body shut down and became numb, my mind dissociated, and my childlike interpretation rationalized and attempted to make sense out of these situations and the reasons that nobody came to her rescue to attempt to protect her. Oftentimes children of sexual abuse disassociate and "see" themselves in the third person. Looking at the memories only offered pain at fully recognizing their effects on my subconscious and the ways in which they have altered my behaviors, reactions and personality—most significantly, the way in which they have dominated my life.

Art has the ability to concretize inner experience, to give shape to that which floats around the psyche in a shapeless state. It portrays inner experience not only as it is seen in the world, but as it is seen in the mind's eye, combining word and symbol so they make sense to the heart. (Dayton 1997)

Throughout my life, I was unable to get in touch with the feelings or a concrete memory of the violations. From all the research I've done on trauma, I've realized that my brain is attempting to protect me by "blocking out the painful memories." Yet as one who has learned that in order to help others one must first help oneself, "Physician Heal Thyself," I desire the unveiling of these occurrences so that my self will become "stronger and healthier for having been tilled and fertilized" (Dayton 1997).

The trauma of childhood sexual abuse is complicated to resolve for several reasons. Many abused children don't remember it clearly as their minds actively blocked the abuse at the time it occurred. Dissociation is a very common psychological defense used by children. They disappear, psychically leave or even have an out-of-body experience and "watch" from somewhere else in the room. Another common defense is physical numbness. Because small children can't get away from their abusers, they numb their bodies in an attempt to ward off their overwhelming feelings of terror. There they are lying back while being overpowered by someone three times their size, probably someone who is supposedly in charge of their well-being, someone they trust. This someone is manipulating the child's genitals in such a way as to send shooting sexual sensation throughout her body, hot, intense sensation that she does not understand the origins of. This can be terrifying. Then there is the violation of trust. A person she has looked up to, depended upon, loved—or all three—is using her to gratify puerile needs for sex and emotional needs for intimacy at her expense. And what if this is her father or uncle or mother? She loses more relationships. The secrecy creates distance and mistrust with the other parent who now is a rival. If the other parent is her mother and she goes to her and her mother does nothing, the heartbreak and sense of abandonment are even more paralyzing. On the other hand, if her mother does something, she risks losing her father. And what of the relationships of other siblings? Is Daddy "playing" with them, too? She cannot ask because it's a secret—she loses a sense of camaraderie and ease. Play can become less spontaneous as her young mind is preoccupied with weighty and frightening matters.

With so many potential disasters looming over her tiny head if she reaches out for help or discloses the truth, our little girl has no alternative but to depend upon the childlike defenses at her disposal in order to survive intact. That is, in order to preserve her sense of normalcy and sanity and in order not to lose connection with the people she needs to continue to raise her, to provide food, shelter and nurturance. Dissociation and physical numbing are at the ready hand of the child—her mind knows how to do this instinctively. Idealization is another alternative for the abused child who desperately needs to preserve some part of the parent as a protector. In the magical thinking of childhood, the abusing parent can be the parent the child mysteriously transforms into her protector. Alysia told herself that her dad's family "planned for her and Scott to be together because they were both of English parentage." We see in this the desperate attempt of a child to preserve a sense of order and dignity—to make sense of the senseless—to make it all somehow okay.

Sexual abuse is common and unfortunate. It leaves its victims with complicated symptoms and painful issues that take years to work through. When the victim is a child, subsequent development is adversely affected, as we have seen in these stories.

In each story we see how addiction creates trauma (these was parental addiction in each case) and how trauma creates addiction. (Both Celeste and Alysia were at risk for self-medication.) They chose instead to break the chain of addiction and trauma through deep, painstaking work that gave them back their souls. The healed became the healers—they changed the legacy.

ELEVEN

Photographs as a Healing Tool:
Eva's Story

One picture is worth a thousand words.
Misattributed "Chinese Proverb"

This is Eva's story. In it you will see how early childhood trauma, secrets and a sense of betrayal led her to self-medicate with whatever she had easy access to: first credit cards, then alcohol, pot and sex. What had hurt her most in her childhood was what she later reenacted as a young adult. This is how trauma passes from one generation into another until someone decides to break the chain of reenactment.

I asked Eva to choose a photograph that held special meaning for her, that she was somehow drawn to, that spoke to her in some way. She chose a picture of a family vacation that felt like a metaphor of her experience within her family.

Eva's story shows us how family secrets affect children. What we think is a secret is not. Instead, it sets the child on a sort of search that has resonance throughout his or her life. Children sense what is unspoken, and they get all the more curious about decoding it. When something is too upsetting to be spoken out loud, our solution may be to join or collude with the destructive behavior in a misguided attempt at protecting ourselves against the pain of confrontation. When we're attached to someone that we fear losing to destructive behavior, we may join the very behavior that so pains us in a convoluted effort to stay close, to preserve our sense of connection with them. In Eva's case, this secrecy, collusion and identification with the perpetrator led to her own acting out in dangerous, self-destructive ways with sex, alcohol and drugs. Again, we see how unresolved trauma begets more trauma. Her sexual behavior was a classic trauma reenactment; she repeated in her own adult life what had given her the greatest pain as a child.

Eva has used an old photograph that consolidated all of the fragmented segments of her story for her. Working with photographs is a very effective way of getting in touch with memories. "One picture is worth a thousand words," and those words come rushing to the surface as we stare at a scene from another time and place that encapsulates great meaning for us.

A Conspiracy of Silence: Eva's Story

Describing the Picture

Telling the story, bearing witness, the beginning of accepting support

I was born on July 16, 1976, at two o'clock in the afternoon. When I let out my first cry, it was already full of anger, resentment and lust. I have never had a good relationship with my family, particularly my father. My battle with him began before I was born.

I found a picture; it is old and faded. I can't see colors because the sun and time tainted it and the picture is all red. I remember hearing the garbled story behind it. Mom never wanted to tell me of the times before I was born except for a few distinct memories that were depicted in old pictures like this one. My father was never very good at taking pictures since he didn't have an auto-focus camera, and he always forgot to take pictures with his glasses on. After finding out many things about my family's past, I realized that there were many things my father wasn't very good at.

This particular picture had the story of the time we went to Niagara Falls. We were standing on the rocks near a bridge that nobody seems to remember the name of. My uncle was taking the picture, and I'm sure he was laughing because my father was standing on the tallest rock being the arrogant, proud father that he liked to portray. He was and still is stuck in a state of cultural shock, because when he decided to become an American he thought that everyone believed that you should live your life through your children. He later realized that this was a misconception, but old habits die hard. Standing proudly above his family, he had a smile filled with pride, while my mother stood below with my brothers on either side. Sam, on her right, looks happy and wears the proud look that my father had because he is the firstborn. Jimmy, on her left, looks like he doesn't have a clue, as usual. It's not that he is dumb, it's that he doesn't photograph very well.

Sam always tried to be my second father. Always feeling the need to do the right thing even it if meant keeping the silent history of our family. He inherited the looks of my mother's side but the temperament of my father. This temperament is not a pleasant one to behold or experience. It is one that consists of a quick temper and a fierce bite that is worse than his overbearing and anger-ridden bark. If you are clever and a good talker, like myself, then he becomes a fun, slightly protective, handsome and lovable older brother. There is an eleven-year age difference between Sam and me. Sometimes people would say, "You look awfully young to have a daughter already." We would look at each other, roll our eyes and break into laughter.

I love my brother, and I hate that he lives so far away with his new wife and a life of his own. It doesn't seem to include me anymore. When I look at pictures like this, I can't help but wonder how this little boy with Dumbo ears and a bowl cut developed into my handsome, successful older brother.

Jimmy, on the other hand, I never could get that close to. When he was younger, I would help him practice his wrestling moves—whether I was a willing participant or not is still under debate. He was a brother who loved to playfully bully his sister who is eight years his junior. He was always the gawky kid who had a lot of friends, but none of them were girlfriends. Sam was a ladies' man, at least until Jimmy learned his charm in college. I always thought that is why they never would visit, because they were too busy with all of their girlfriends.

In the picture, Jimmy is wearing a little polyester suit that makes him look so small. He has the characteristic trait of Dumbo ears that all three of us children have. You can tell he takes after my father's looks, but has the docile temperament of my mother. This doesn't mean he doesn't have a temper. I'll vouch he has a temper, but it is slow to ignite and usually very short-lived. That is always a good quality that I like, but his best quality is his ability to make people laugh. He could always deliver a joke, and which side of the family he got it from is still a mystery. My father can never deliver a punch line, and my mother is always laughing too hard at her own jokes to remember the punch line.

My mother doesn't differ much in height in comparison to my brothers even if they were only ten and seven years old when we went to Niagara. Looking at her in this picture makes me realize how beautiful my five-foot, three-inch mother is. She's wearing a polyester suit (which is blue; I know since I now own it) and huge sunglasses. She still looks amazing. Everyone tells me that my mother is so sweet and they all love her, and that's easy to understand, but I can never understand her mind. She doesn't like to tell me things. She says she forgets, but I have never believed her. Her silence sometimes scares me. The past seems so painful for her, unless she's telling a funny story about Jimmy being a problem child. She would say, "There was only one baby-sitter who would baby-sit twice because as soon as your father and I would leave, Jimmy wouldn't stop until we got home." Or, "One time your father told me to take my time in the grocery store while he waited outside with your brothers. Well, when I came back, he yelled at me because Jimmy had made a big . . . mess in the back seat. And it didn't stay in his diaper!!" She was full of anecdotes but would never answer my serious questions.

Now, I have said "we" were at Niagara Falls in the picture, but where am I? I never got to see the Falls or the Statue of Liberty because my mother was pregnant with

me at the time of this traveling. I was the reason my
mother looks fat in this picture. I was spared all the
heartache and fights that preceded my birth, so I thought.

The Secrets

I wish I never knew. I found out by accident. I forced
the secrets of my family's past into words that I used to
make me understand why things were the way they were.
All I felt was frustration and anger. I was only in second
grade when I was forced to learn. Having two brothers
who were so much older than I am forced me to grow up
a little faster. They hated having an annoying kid sister
who couldn't do anything the big boys could. I learned
how to climb trees a little sooner, and I realized that if I
had Barbies, I should expect them to be defaced by my
brothers and their friends. Thus, a tomboy was born, one
who liked to play stickball, climb trees, play with cars and
one who discovered that the best way to learn was not by
always asking, "Why?" The best way is to keep your
mouth shut and your eyes and ears open. That is how I
discovered the secrets.

I was a television baby of the 1980s. I discovered movies,
sitcoms, *Sesame Street* and MTV. I also learned the meaning of sex, drugs, violence, murder, crime and adultery by
the age of six. While sitting in front of the TV watching a
program I can't remember, I heard my father gossiping
with a friend on the phone. I heard the distinct words, "Oh,
I don't like getting into anything serious. Only one-night
stands for me." Did he think I was so young that I wouldn't
understand? I ran to my room crying and refused to go to
dinner, saying that I was just having one of my random crying fits—the type of fit when you start crying for no reason
and you feel too terrible to leave your hiding spot. My

hiding spot was under my bed or in my closet with all my stuffed animals. I lay there under my bed crying until I had nothing left to cry. The man whom I had put on a pedestal had just fallen off and shattered. Later, I was to learn that it was not his first time, nor would it be the last.

My mother's silence fell when I confronted her with my knowledge six years later. I believe that a fetus is affected by what happens to the mother during her pregnancy. I could feel my father betraying her again. I could see it in his face, in his mannerisms. It was as if he had a malevolent glow about him, which would bring tears to my eyes when I would look at him. I was twelve years old when I confronted him. I was twelve years old when I confronted everyone with everything.

I discovered that this picture I hold in my hand was taken during the first of my father's affairs that my mother was to learn of. I, purely by chance I'm told, have that woman's name. I had forgotten or purposely disregarded this piece of information until I started writing this paper. I hate the idea of having any connection to her, even though I know nothing of her.

I was told that everyone knew about his newest mistress even before I told them. They had hired a private detective and knew her name, had photos, the whole bit. I knew all of this information because he had the nerve to introduce me to Janette, that bitch. I remember the anger and tension in my body as he walked up to my table of friends and said, "Hi, girls! Look who I ran into! This is my friend, Janette." I could feel his lies course through his words. I wanted to hit him. I always hit things at this age. I remember punching my cousin for no reason and then breaking into tears because of the shame. I was cold and withdrawn. I wanted to punish him and numb myself.

Acting Out the Pain

I was too young to have access to self-medicating things in a mall, but I did have his credit card and I knew how to use it. I charged over four hundred dollars within minutes of his leaving the table. I bought presents for all my friends. I bought myself a new hat and sweater. I bought my mom an expensive figurine, because I felt she deserved something better than my father. I later went home with my two best friends and confided in them for the first time everything I knew. It felt so good to let it out. I cried as we sat behind my parents' bar in the middle of the night. We tasted every bottle in that fifteen-foot bar, which was enough to get three young girls completely wasted.

Self-Medicating

That was the beginning of my self-medicating. I drank every weekend that I had friends over. I still drink all the time when I want to forget, to feel better, or not to feel at all. I think that is why I started smoking pot. It makes me laugh, feel numb, fall asleep. It is not a regular occurrence, but it is still a prevalent character in my life. It acts as a screen that hides my pain and depression. I have attempted suicide once and seriously contemplated doing it just this past year. If it were not for my close relationships with my friends, I would not be here today. I did not attend my group the following week because I was scared of being chosen to do a psychodrama. I did not want to see how fucked up I really am. I still don't.

The Reenactment
Linking, separating the past from the present

People always think I am the strong one who is the pillar in the midst of a tragedy. I have tried to live up to that role to the point it is hurting me. I don't feel I can let things out from fear that people will lose faith in me and my abilities. I went through a phase where I became the mistress to three different married men, all within a short period of time *(reenactment)*. I wanted to destroy myself so I wouldn't have to face the disappointment of others. I didn't want to fall quickly, so I did it gradually with self-destructive attitudes. Married men loved how aloof I was with the situation. I didn't care that they were married, had kids or were so much older than I am. I didn't care what happened to me. Just so long as I made everyone else happy. I was the center of attention and made everybody feel good. It didn't matter how much I hated seeing myself in the mirror. I could look at myself and just not see what I was.

My relationship to my family has caused me to mistrust my romantic relationships. In 1997, I didn't have any relationships other than sexual ones. I didn't consider myself "easy." I look back now and call myself a whore, because I was. Everyone thought I was so lucky to have so many men after me. Oddly enough, I am still friends with all of them. I thought of myself as sexual energy and nothing more. I didn't have a mind or a heart, just a pussy. I feel disgusted with what I just said. I feel so dirty when I think back to how I would try to hurt myself. Besides all them, I would get drunk every night. Condom wrappers in all different colors would fly about as a glass of numbing liquid was being lifted to my lips. I would dream at night of my infidelities and the debauchery of my life. It would fly around me in beautiful colors, making me want it more yet nauseated at the same time. I grew to hate myself more and more. "Happy fuckin' holidays," I would think to myself.

The Awakening
The new narrative, reinvestment of freed energy

When I awoke New Year's Day of 1998 and went to work with an incredible hangover, I made a resolution to myself: the first I have ever followed. I decided it was time to make a change. A moment that filled me with such a feeling of empowerment, I made it through the day feeling lighter, almost healthier. I decided to be a "good girl." To be a "good girl," I had to find a definition of the meaning.

I am now in a long-term, meaningful relationship with someone who loves me. He takes care of me and is learning to accept my past . . . slowly, *very* slowly. At times it becomes a hardship because I feel like I always have to prove how faithful I am to him. I have decided it comes with the territory of change—no pain, no gain.

I still cringe when I look at my father. I never respond to him when he says, "I love you." I can't lie and say I do, too. My roommate's father died just last week and to see how hurt she was because she did not say good-bye made me ask myself, "Will I be sad or relieved when he is gone?" I don't want to hear my real answer because I feel it would be "relieved." Thinking about it now makes me feel guilty. Why should I feel guilty when he is the one who screwed up my life? I have to get over this to move on. I love my life too much now to throw it away. My "bad" side is ever-present. I can hear it telling me to go have "just *one* drink." I can hear it tell me, "He'll never know if you sleep with Tim one last time. I won't tell." I refuse to do it; my boyfriend means too much to me, not only because I love him but also he symbolizes the changes I've made so far. I am not dependent on him by any means. I mean, he has made me want to change. He has always held me when I would break out into tears, and he asked no questions. He will let me put down the weight of the pillar, never thinking of me as weak or running away from my responsibilities. I am giving myself a chance to heal.

Reflection

It took me two days to write my initial personal story. I found an old picture of my family, which threw me into all the problems I have been dealing with for so many years. I guess that is the whole point of journaling, not to think too much. Let the psyche speak uninhibited. I haven't discussed this issue of my life in so long I thought that I had recovered from it. I realize it is as prevalent today as it was when I was seven years old hearing it for the first time, or when I was twelve and finally told someone about it. I am twenty-two, and betrayal and loss of a loved one is still a huge fear to me. My friends mean the world to me, and to lose one means to lose a foothold for me, the closer I come to falling off this cliff from which I dangle.

I fell asleep after writing the line, "I decided it was time to make a change." I woke up the next day feeling like I had slept for days even though I slept for five hours, and

I wanted to write a letter of empowerment, but I don't think I am ready for that yet. I don't think I could be truly honest. I am not very big on compliments; I take insults much more seriously. Maybe in a month when I pick up with my journaling I will be able to do it. Maybe.

In Eva's story, we see the power of secrecy. Parents so often feel that their secretive behavior does not affect the children. Eva, bearing the name of her father's affair and her mother's heartbreak, reenacted over and over again what had hurt her most during childhood. She became the "affair," engaging in high-risk sexual behavior, thereby "acting out" the pain and shame that her family could not "talk out."

TWELVE

Psychodrama as a Healing Tool

By the group they were wounded,
by the group they shall be healed.

J. L. Moreno

READER/CUSTOMER CARE SURVEY

We care about your opinions! Please take a moment to fill out our online Reader Survey at **http://survey.hcibooks.com**.
As a **"THANK YOU"** you will receive a **VALUABLE INSTANT COUPON** towards future book purchases as well as a **SPECIAL GIFT** available only online! Or, you may mail this card back to us and we will send you a copy of our exciting catalog with your valuable coupon inside.
(PLEASE PRINT IN ALL CAPS)

First Name _____ MI. _____ Last Name _____

Address _____ City _____

State _____ Zip _____ Email _____

1. Gender
☐ Female ☐ Male

2. Age
☐ 8 or younger
☐ 9-12 ☐ 13-16
☐ 17-20 ☐ 21-30
☐ 31+

3. Did you receive this book as a gift?
☐ Yes ☐ No

4. Annual Household Income
☐ under $25,000
☐ $25,000 - $34,999
☐ $35,000 - $49,999
☐ $50,000 - $74,999
☐ over $75,000

5. What are the ages of the children living in your house?
☐ 0 - 14 ☐ 15+

6. Marital Status
☐ Single
☐ Married
☐ Divorced
☐ Widowed

7. How did you find out about the book?
(please choose one)
☐ Recommendation
☐ Store Display
☐ Online
☐ Catalog/Mailing
☐ Interview/Review

8. Where do you usually buy books?
(please choose one)
☐ Bookstore
☐ Online
☐ Book Club/Mail Order
☐ Price Club (Sam's Club, Costco's, etc.)
☐ Retail Store (Target, Wal-Mart, etc.)

9. What subject do you enjoy reading about the most?
(please choose one)
☐ Parenting/Family
☐ Relationships
☐ Recovery/Addictions
☐ Health/Nutrition
☐ Christianity
☐ Spirituality/Inspiration
☐ Business Self-help
☐ Women's Issues
☐ Sports

10. What attracts you most to a book?
(please choose one)
☐ Title
☐ Cover Design
☐ Author
☐ Content

TAPE IN MIDDLE; DO NOT STAPLE

FOLD HERE

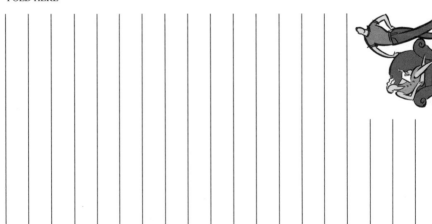

Comments

PARENTIFIED SIBLINGS:
KATE'S STORY

On the following pages we will read Kate's story. It is a narrative of the psychodrama she did after preparing her "trauma time line" (see appendix). The children in Kate's family were assigned roles that were beyond their capacity. Kate became the caretaker of a younger brother who was developmentally delayed—a child who was too much for the parents to cope with became Katie's responsibility. Also, in the absence of genuine nurturing and connection, the children turned to each other for intimacy that became sexual. The pain that could not be brought to their parents got acted out on each other. Relationships across the family were nonmutual.

After Kate's story we will meet Dave, an overeater who wanted to do a psychodrama working with his drug of choice: food. The first story is told through the eyes of the protagonist and the second through the eyes of the director. Kate has given a step-by-step description of the process of being in a psychodrama group and enacting her own drama. She has attached psychodramatic concepts where appropriate. It is a privileged look into the mind of the protagonist.

Through her eyes we see a carefully calibrated method that allows traumatic material to surface and be worked through, then put into context in the protagonist's overall life pattern. Through it the victims of trauma can begin to reexamine the meaning they have made out of circumstances in their lives, reframe their experience and take in support from others. (See the appendix for a more detailed explanation of psychodrama and its terms.)

As the reader, you should be seeing the power of journaling, particularly when used in conjunction with psychodrama and group therapy. What is said in these groups and on these pages is like a draining of toxicity; it is emotional surgery wherein an internal infection that is undermining health in the entire system—physical, emotional and spiritual—can be healed and disowned parts of self can be understood and reintegrated. It is because it is so powerful that containing it in a program of recovery is important. "The pen is mightier than the sword." This, I am convinced, is the kind of pain that gets acted out on the stage of life when it is not courageously and openly addressed through the mental health network. In an increasingly complicated world, we need a more aggressive health-care approach to meet the challenges of a society that is changing at the speed of light. Without it we are left with the residue and wreckage of psychic pain. The violence in our society is fueled by hidden stories such as these. If we are asking our children to assimilate information and social change on a daily basis, then we need to give them the tools with which to do that.

Psychodrama: Enacting a Story of Childhood Abuse: Kate's Talk with Her Brother and Her Ten-Year-Old Self (Katie)

A psychodrama training group of fifteen adults who are graduate students met for three hours once a week. In this example, the leader initiated an *unstructured warm-up*, where group members discussed how they were feeling and what it was like to be back together in psychodrama class. Group members shared where they were at and talked about their hectic lives. As the group warmed up, members began to discuss the assignment that was given the previous week. The group members had been asked to do a Trauma Time Line. At this time, Tian, the *director*, asked if anyone wanted to share it. The group members took turns sharing their timelines and discussed patterns that produced trauma throughout their lives.

These exercises are psychodramatic warm-ups that set a framework for the group. The leader will initiate structured or unstructured warm-ups that facilitate group connectiveness and exploration. Specifically, the warm-up helps clarify the objectives for the group, develop group cohesion and develop a working basis of mutual trust between members. The group begins to trust the leader, the group and the method of psychodrama. Also, the warm-up serves to produce an atmosphere of creative possibility (Blatner et al. 1987).

Warm-Up

As group members shared, there began to be a great deal of emotion in the room. Group members began to share the traumatic events in their lives and expose their *open-tension systems.* "Open tension is a system of unresolved experiences that we carry around in our psyches" (Dayton 1994). These unresolved experiences result in anxiety that may become debilitating. Through this warm-up, a member's *act hunger (the longing to take action toward completion)* begins to be recognized with the group.

On this day, as a member of the group, I had a significant amount of emotion around my early childhood trauma, specifically related to my brother's sexual inappropriateness and my own inappropriateness with my younger brother. I read my trauma story quickly but, given the starkness of the exercise, my defense mechanisms were unable to kick in and resist the emotion surrounding these events. Given I was a new member of the group and not completely connected to its members, I tried to remain cognitive and rational. This was not possible for me, as the sharing of repressed material elicited deep emotion (wounds surfaced). I was "hungry" to work on some of these unresolved feelings left from these early experiences. The director, Tian, the group and I decided (in this case without words) that I would be the *protagonist*, the person whose story would be enacted in the psychodrama. I was already crying and unable to fully discuss the process with the group. I was apprehensive and scared, but Tian assisted me in the beginning process. I felt secure with her by my side.

Enact the Story with Group Witness

Given we decided to enact a psychodrama related to one of my traumas, I would go through the process of *concretization* of my feelings about a particular experience, giving them shape and form. At this time, Tian assisted me in deciding what material would be examined psychodramatically and how that enactment would take place. In this case, I was drawn to talk with my younger brother, Danny, as I wanted to sort out the guilt, shame and hurt I felt in relation to physically hurting him as a child. [AUTHOR'S NOTE: In doing trauma work I rarely reenact the trauma scene, as that is potentially retraumatizing. What we are interested in is the protagonist's "read" on the situation, the meaning they have made out of it and that can be explored in subtler ways. A stand-in can be used to represent the protagonist as an added protection (see appendix).] We were about to pull some of my *surplus reality (unfinished realities, mind, memories, associations, meanings, clarity and distortions)* out of my psyche and place it on the stage where it could be moved through in a safe and clinically appropriate manner. "It is a chance to make real what has felt unreal and to bring to the conscious level what has been swimming around the unconscious in a formless, shapeless state"(Dayton 1994).

At this time, Tian asked me if I wanted someone to play my brother. I said no, as I felt no connection in the room that resembled that of my connection to my brother. I decided to employ the empty-chair technique. I expressed myself directly to Danny in the scene. I asked him for forgiveness, as I used to hit him. Also, I told him how sorry I was for exposing him to sexuality at such a young age. I described how I had shown him how to have sex and pushed him and his girlfriend to simulate sex. I said a lot of things that, for years, I had been too ashamed to remember or acknowledge. The director and the audience entered my surplus reality—that which we carry within our psyches as personal history. I was able to articulate a great deal of shame, guilt and sadness. With the guidance of Tian acting as a *double,* as my inner voice, I began to express the pain and hurt I felt in relation to this experience. She spoke from a more gentle perspective. Her words were less punitive than my own. My superego was beating me up, and Tian tried to balance it. She did this through developing a deep connection with me and speaking from another place inside me, a place inside me that was hurt and bruised. She tried to reframe the story in order for me to recognize a larger context and have a deep understanding of the familial dynamics. She reframed without leaving the enactment.

To enter into dialogue with my brother, Danny, I was introduced to *role reversal,* where I played my brother. This technique allows a protagonist to play a role in the drama in order both to see the self from the outside and to experience the self from the position of the other. As the enactment continued, I spoke from Danny's role. I told Kate how much it hurt to be hit all the time for absolutely no reason. From Danny's place, I talked about how difficult it was to be Kate's younger brother as she made me read all the time and she bossed me around. She made me feel small and insignificant. I (Kate) was able to register more fully and clearly the pain Danny must have experienced.

As I role-reversed [back to Kate] and listened to the double, I began to move into a *psychodramatic trance.* I felt my response systems engage with feelings for Danny.

I felt a multiplicity of feelings in relation to him. I felt like I really was talking with Danny and he was talking with me. He and I were working things out. "When the 'as if' falls away to 'as,' the protagonist may enter a state somewhat akin to a dream state . . . where the subject finds himself . . . in a near-real world" (Fox 1987). It was very scary but we were going there—to the forgotten and unknown places that were full of guilt and pain.

Offer Corrective Experience

At this time, Tian decided that I was taking a lot of responsibility for the chaos in our lives at that time and she wanted Katie (my childhood self) to enter the picture. She asked me if I would like to talk with Katie, and I agreed. She asked me if I would like to choose an *auxiliary ego* to represent her. As the protagonist, I chose a member with whom I had *tele*, ". . . the simplest unit of feeling between two people. It is two-way empathy, a sensing the reality of who someone else is" (Dayton 1994). I felt connected to Danielle even though I didn't know her very well. She reminded me of myself, and also she had seemed supportive ever since I entered the group. Danielle and I role-reversed between Kate and Katie, and I did a lot of shouting back and forth. Kate was really mad at Katie for hurting Danny, and Katie shouted back that she didn't have any other way to assert power and release anger. Katie, too, was angry.

Once, in the role of Katie, I shouted and struck out at Kate (not actually hitting her), but all of a sudden I felt self-conscious. I realized I was extremely angry, and I almost felt out of control. I knew I had to control my rage and protect Danielle and myself. I was afraid of my own rage and, thus, moved into my head (to a cognitive level) and began to lose my psychodramatic trance. All at once I wanted to stop the psychodrama. I felt bad for Danielle as I screamed too loud in her ear. Yet, Danielle didn't respond in an angry way. She didn't scold me for screaming at her. She stayed in the moment as the auxiliary ego. She stayed fully connected and pulled me back in. She echoed the words I had used as Kate, and I came back to the work. She didn't make me feel self-conscious, and neither did Tian or the rest of the group. They supported me throughout the process. *I was not alone in reaching into feelings that had not been allowed to surface before this day.*

As Tian continued to double for me, she helped me see my own wounds and how young and powerless I really had been. She helped me to bring out my inner reality and experience a *catharsis.* "In psychoanalytic theory, catharsis is the release of tension and anxiety resulting from the process of bringing repressed ideas, feelings, wishes and memories of the past into consciousness." Dayton (1994) describes ". . . two essential 'forms' of catharsis: (1) catharsis of separation and clarification, and (2) catharsis of unification and completion; . . . or integration." I experienced catharsis of separation and clarification as I was able to express anger at myself, clarify where that was coming from and understand the experience in a larger context.

Separating the Past from the Present— Linking

Dayton further describes catharsis: ". . . true catharsis actually alters the cell assembly in the brain, changing the person's record of learning" (1994). I am not clear if this has occurred for me, but I do feel differently in relation to hurting my brother. I still have to live with it throughout my life, and I may continue to feel bad about it, but I do not hate myself for it. I understand my actions better now. I am now more willing to recognize the context in which I perpetrated abuse. I was a very young child who was unable to express her negative feelings and anger about her own abuse and neglect. I felt obligated to be used by my older brothers for their sexual curiosity and pleasure. I was unable to discuss this with my parents, as I knew the repercussions would be severe for both my brothers and myself. Instead, I kept a bright smile on my face in return for affection and praise. I am moving toward expanding my story and recognizing the limitations of my parents' and siblings' support. I think my work produced a form of a catharsis, and it has helped me to see that I am eager to continue to work on resolving more of my unresolved feelings towards my siblings and parents.

Catharsis can occur in the protagonist, the auxiliaries and the audience. Given this, the audience and auxiliaries need time to process their reactions and feelings about the enactment. The *sharing phase* of the psychodrama allows the group to process and emote. After my psychodrama, the audience and auxiliary ego, Danielle, shared what came up for them in the enactment as empathetic agents. They discussed their feelings in relation to the scene they witnessed and experienced.

Creating a New Narrative

[AUTHOR'S NOTE: Actually, the entire process can be seen as part of creating a new narrative, but here Kate is grounding it cognitively through reflecting on her process.]

Initially, when the enactment ended, I felt self-conscious and embarrassed. I felt like I had taken a lot of time, and I was worried about their reactions. I was surprised that my work had elicited such emotion in the group. They were significantly affected by my chaotic and confusing work. This was therapeutic for me, as it made me realize that no matter how much I try to deny it, I was hurt as a child, and I need to continue to confront my feelings and memories of those times to better understand and work through them. [AUTHOR'S NOTE: Because of the powerful defenses that are mobilized when we are traumatized, children who are the most deeply hurt may have a very hard time acknowledging it.] They showed me a great deal of support. I knew that I would be able to continue doing this work even though it was difficult.

After the sharing phase, Tian talked with the group and me about the enactment. She helped me, the protagonist, to process the enactment on a cognitive level. She gently provided insight into my reenactment. As Dayton argues, ". . . catharsis should be accompanied by insight in order to ground the learning on a cognitive level, the insight must be accompanied by experience in order to change behavior" (1994). This grounding on a cognitive level occurs during the *processing phase,* the last phase of the psychodrama.

This was an unforgettable experience for me. I spent the next few days in a fog, in hazy numbness. I later began to process it with a friend and then with my therapist. It took me two weeks to bring my trauma chart to my therapist to begin working. Through psychodrama, I was able to gain a new perspective on my feelings about my relationship to my little brother and more insight into my own feelings about him and me. I did not know my own response to myself was loaded with self-blame and rage. I need to continue to do this kind of work, both to have more self-awareness and heal my wounds, but also to be more available and effective with my clients.

FILLING THE VOID WITH FOOD: DAVE'S STORY

Dave began by choosing role-players to represent two members of his Overeaters Anonymous (OA) group and his OA sponsor. He felt frustrated because his friends couldn't meet his needs for open and real conversation. His sponsor, on the other hand, was available to him, interested and open, but that made Dave want to run. "I call him. He's there for me. It feels great. I panic, withdraw and don't call him again for another month until I'm starving." This dynamic of starving and feeding appeared to be a pattern both psychologically and physically.

I asked Dave when he began to overeat. "When I was about ten." Then I asked him if any scene came to mind. "I used to come home every day to an empty house." I requested that he "set the scene." He set up a room with a couch, a chair and a TV. Interestingly, he "forgot" to put in a kitchen—his haven—until I asked him where it was. His mother was in her office upstairs, and the refrigerator was in the kitchen around the corner. As a ten-year-old boy, he would come home from school each day, excited to connect with his mother. As a continuation of his own process of warming up to his own traumatic material, we let him speak aloud the inner monologue or soliloquy he had with himself as he approached his home as a boy.

"Will my mom say hello to me when I come home? I am so excited to see her. Will she be too busy to let me come and talk to her? I want to tell her about my day. I want to see my mom." This began a pattern typical to trauma, repeating cycles of excitement and disappointment. Each day when he came home he said, "Hello." Sometimes he got a hello from his mother; sometimes she was busy. He learned not to say hello a second time because the silence he got in return felt too painful and humiliating. He knew not to ask for her time—she was there, but unavailable. This pattern of relationships without authentic connection started early in life.

Food, however, was always there. And so began Dave's search for something else to fill up on. Food became his comfort and security. He developed a relationship bond with a substance he could count on rather than a person he could not. Setting up the psychodramatic scene, Dave chose someone to represent "Food." His dialogue with "Food" revealed a deep and intimate attachment with a substance: "You were always there for me. When I opened the door I knew I could count on you. We could cozy up together and feel good, you meant so much to me. I really needed you."

When our primary relationships fail to offer the emotional comfort, sustenance and nurturing that number among our fundamental human needs, we look for substitutes. And when our emotional needs for authentic connection are not adequately met at an early age, we don't learn how to modulate our need for closeness through the natural give-and-take of a healthy parent/ child relationship. Because of this unmet need, Dave tended toward all or nothing—overcloseness or withdrawal—because that was how his needs were met earlier. That is, they were unmet, which created a hunger so deep that he would eat anything to fill up—then he went on overload, too much, too fast, so he withdrew to digest and regain equilibrium . . . until the hunger built and he gorged himself again.

Modulation is a skill we learn in healthy relationships, how to take in enough to fill up but not to become over-loaded. Think of the two-year-old who forays from his mother's knee for little bits of freedom, then back for a reassuring pat, cuddle or check-in, safe in the knowledge that his wish to explore the world will not cost him his connection with his mother. These things never really change. We tend to live our lives most happily in this way—small or long excursions from a secure base to which we return for solace and comfort.

Our manner of family attachments early in life stays with us throughout our lives. When our primary care-givers are not available to us on a regular, well-modulated basis, the nature of the attachment formed is shaped by what is available. For a small child, it is traumatizing to have a parent who is unavailable. In his psychodrama, Dave verbalized his inner world [doubled for himself] at coming home to a mother who was there but not there. "Why won't she come and say hello to me? Where is she? Am I so evil that she doesn't want to be with me? Did I do something awful?" So it's not only the fact that Dave's mother was unavailable, but also the personal meaning he made out of her absence. "I must be bad. I did something wrong. She must not love me." Actions speak louder than words. Children (and adults) need to have love shown to them in order to feel valued.

Again, the path out of this buried pattern that Dave continued to act out over and over again was to sit with the feeling and name it, to understand the loneliness and rejection he felt on a daily basis and how he used food to replace love and attention. Then to come to identify the meaning he made out of this mother's seeming disinterest—"I must be evil. I did something awful"—that was triggered every time he experienced even small rejections in his adult relationships. He withdraws from authentic connection in order to protect himself from reexperiencing this pain. After examining this material, Dave was in a position to make choices about steps he needed to take in order to alter this pattern. He decided to share his awareness with his friends, and when he came home as an adult man who still went straight for the refrigerator, he determined to do something else such as call a friend, go to the gym, take a walk or have a piece of fruit rather than ice cream. We let him practice some of these new behaviors through role-play. Working through the buried model scene and making it conscious—feeling it and walking through it—allowed emotional literacy to enter a situation that had no words and no understanding.

Dave is far from being alone in using food to self-medicate. Half of Americans are overweight. Eating disorders in our country are on the rise. On the one hand, eating disorders are seen by professionals as very complicated because they involve a substance, namely food, that needs to be regulated rather than abstained from entirely. This makes recovery hard to define.

As we have discussed earlier, one of the first tasks of development is to learn to self-soothe. The infant incorporates the regulated soothing of the primary caretaker over time into an ability to self-regulate and self-soothe. Through consistent care from the mother, the child learns to tolerate the experience of feeding and weaning. An anxious mother may overfeed a child in an attempt to soothe, which can hardwire into a child's brain the association between self-soothing and overeating. Another caretaker may leave a child hungry for periods of time or in a state of weaning more than the child can tolerate. It is less clear to me what might get hardwired in this case. I imagine that children may attempt to tolerate the state of hunger by turning it into something else in their child minds, by, in a sense, disowning the feeling of hunger and not associating it with food because they are not able to regulate themselves and food is denied to them.

Feeding and weaning are core issues in eating and self-regulation. Overeaters and undereaters have not learned to sufficiently self-regulate. In working with overeaters, my experience as a therapist can be, on the one hand, feeling as if clients wish to incorporate me into them, to fuse or hold me in their inner world as a part of themselves; or, on the other hand, is the wish to distance me, to not let me in even for a second. When I am not available to be incorporated, I often encounter rage from a client. Their anger at not having that feeding experience or that incorporating experience is palpable.

I theorize that this reflects an incomplete integration of their primary caretaker, namely their mother. As was the case with Dave, his mother was not a presence that he could rely on and, eventually, bring into himself for comfort. His attempts to do this were ignored or frustrated, and so he found a substitute comfort—food. It is fast and immediate. In therapy, clients can wish for the same experience with the therapist, a fast and immediate incorporation. What needs to happen is a slow and modulated reincorporation of a good object (the therapist as a substitute for early caretakers) so that the external source of comfort becomes an internal one. Instant gratification, swallowing the therapist whole is not the goal, nor is a distant, cool therapist particularly the ticket. The first case is overgratifying and the second undergratifying. The first teaches no frustration tolerance and the second is too frustrating. Programs such as Overeaters Anonymous (OA) or weight-control programs often include external regulations such as weighing, measuring or calling in food. This speaks to the inability to self-regulate so it is helpful to have external monitors. The child who has been overfed or underfed, not according to their internalized longings but those of the parent, has not learned to tune in to their own feelings of hunger and fullness. They have not learned to regulate their own appetites.

Then there are the other complicating factors: What did food mean in the home in which this child grew up, and how was it used? Did food mean love or reward? Did it mean togetherness? Was it a transitional object connecting the child with primary caretakers, or was it a way of getting close to the self and calming down? How is food used by an adult—as a sedative, as a companion, as an attempt at self-care or as retaliation? All of the particular meanings that food carries are highly personal, and each person needs to analyze them individually.

FOOD HISTORY

What was your early experience of nurturing? Were you held or in a playpen or crib?

_____

_____

_____

Were you nursed or bottle fed? _____

_____

When did you start solid food? _____

_____

Were you fed when hungry or on a strict schedule?

_____

_____

What was your feeding pattern? _____

_____

Did you eat until full? _____

_____

Was overfeeding a primary source of comfort or were you overregulated, left "hungry" until it was "time to eat"?

_____

_____

What were your ways of soothing yourself as a baby, toddler and young child? _____

_____

_____

_____

_____

_____

In your household were you: overfed ☐   underfed ☐
allowed to self-regulate ☐ ?

What was your food sociometry [network of relationship connections]? Who did eating or not eating connect you with? Describe that: _____

_____

_____

_____

_____

_____

_____

_____

How was food used in your home (i.e., for comfort, connection, anxiety reduction, reward, punishment, etc.)? Explain. _____

_____

_____

_____

_____

What meanings did food have in your house? Explain.

_____

_____

_____

_____

How do you use food in your own life? _____

_____

_____

_____

_____

_____

What is your eating pattern today? _____

_____

_____

_____

_____

What meaning does food have in your life today? _____

_____

_____

_____

_____

Do you have trouble saying **no** to yourself or **yes** to yourself when it comes to food? _____

_____

_____

_____

_____

What negative impact is food having on your life today?

_____

_____

_____

_____

_____

At what moments throughout the day do you tend to overeat? _____

_____

_____

What situations trigger you to overeat?_____

_____

_____

_____

_____

_____

Does food connect you with anyone in particular in your life today? If so, who?_____

_____

_____

Can you identify a particular moment in your life or
situation when you began to overeat? Explain. _____

_____

_____

_____

_____

_____

What would you like your relationship with food to look
like today? _____

_____

_____

_____

_____

_____

Possible additional journaling exercises:

- Write a dialogue between yourself and food.
- Write a journal entry as food.
- If you can identify the moment in your life when
  you began to overeat, reverse roles with yourself at
  that time and begin to journal.
- Write a letter to food (from you).
- Write a letter from food (to you).

THIRTEEN

The Character Component—
Intangible Aspects of Recovery:
Resilience, Mental Set and Integration

*"So live as if you were living already for the
second time and as if you had acted the first
time as wrongly as you are about to act now!"
It seems to me that there is nothing that
would stimulate a man's sense of
responsibilities more than this maxim,
which invites him to imagine first,
that the present is past and, second, that the
past may yet be changed and amended.
Such a precept confronts him with life's
finiteness as well as the finality of what he
makes out of both his life and himself.*
Viktor Frankl

RESILIENCE

People seem not to see that their opinion
of the world is also a confession of character.

Ralph Waldo Emerson
"Worship"
The Conduct of Life (1860)

Why do some people who grow up in alcoholic, traumatizing homes thrive in this world and some fall apart? Why can some get lives and careers going, while others move toward addiction and mental illness? Child development researchers in the 1970s and 1980s, using statistical models drawn from public health data, identified risk factors for problems later in life. They are: poverty, overcrowding, neighborhood and school violence, parental absence, unemployment or instability. The more risk factors present in children's lives, the higher the likelihood, according to research, they would eventually fall into the public health or penal system (Butler 1997). But some children grow up in the middle of all of these and still go on to have successful and productive lives. Studies show that even a bad start is not always a "sentence of doom."

What makes the difference? Researchers say it's the important, if difficult-to-measure, quality of *resilience*.

Resilience researcher Emmy Werner, in her forty-year study of children on the Hawaiian island of Kauai (1989), talks about the following elements as being part of what buffers children so that they can eventually put their lives on a positive trajectory: Resilient children tended to have likable personalities from birth that attracted parents, surrogates and mentors to want to care for them. They were of at least average intelligence, reading at or above grade level. Few resilient children had another child born into the family before they had reached the age of two. Virtually all of them had at least ONE person with whom they had developed a strong bond of attachment as children in their family or extended family network.

Resilience is a survival skill that has primitive roots, as even primates display this quality. Meet Sashimi, a chimpanzee immortalized for study by nature photographer Martyn Colbak in the Discovery Channel video, "Why Dogs Smile and Chimpanzees Cry" (Fleisherfilm Inc. & Devillier Donegan Enterprises, 1999). Sashimi's mother died when he was young, leaving him without care at only a few months old. Normally, he would have died, but he endeared himself to a group of males, both by displaying sociable qualities that got their interest and drew attention to him and through mutual grooming, which comprises most of the primate interaction. Sashimi, through his charming behavior and his ingenious use of popular social skills, got himself adopted by this group of males, who protected and nurtured him. Again, his resilience emerged when he got into a fight with another young monkey whose mother became irate and protective and almost bit Sashimi's finger off. Sashimi could have easily turned tail and run, but witness the strategy implicit in what he did instead. Rather than running off and hiding, he located himself in the exact center of the primate group and cried out in such a plaintive way that soon he had several rescuers interested in helping him. Sashimi's tale speaks to the primitive, survival-based, roots of resilience. Resilient children have learned to make the most out of the hand they have been dealt.

Sophie, a long-time client, feels embarrassed when she admits that she learned to "feast on crumbs," to turn the little she got into nourishment and beauty. But, in truth, this is a powerful part of her resilience—this ability to spin straw into gold, to go into a kitchen that others might see as barren and find nourishment. Sophie had, like other resilient children, a marked ability to actively charm and recruit good surrogates, mentors and adults who would take an interest in her welfare. It always amazed me to see Sophie present everywhere. If there was a conference, she helped out; an interesting lecture in her field and somehow she connected with the presenter. Her ability to find good mentors was a powerful piece of her resilience.

Resilient children report having an inborn feeling that eventually their life will work out (Wolin and Wolin 1993). Although they can identify the illness in their family and distance themselves from it, they do not let it destroy them. While they work through their problems to varying degrees, they do not tend to make working on their painful pasts a lifestyle. They take active responsibility for creating their own successful lives. According to Steven and Sybil Wolin, they display both an ability to maintain a constructive attitude towards themselves and their lives as well as a tendency not to fall into self-destructive patterns of:

- "Dwelling on the past and the damage they had suffered
- blaming their parents for what was less than desirable in themselves
- taking the bait in the 'Victim Trap'"(Wolin and Wolin 1993).

Instead, report the Wolins in *The Resilient Self*, the adult children of alcoholics who were free of drinking problems and leading satisfying lives had:

- found and built on their own strengths
- improved deliberately and methodically on their parents' lifestyles
- married consciously into strong, healthy families
- fought off memories of horrible family get-togethers in order to establish regular mealtime routines, vacations, family celebrations and rituals in their own generation.

Interestingly, the Wolins found that resilient children with alcoholic parents seemed to have located "two hundred or more miles" away from them, which the Wolins have named the "two-hundred-mile rule." This provided ACOAs with enough physical distance to remove themselves from the daily debilitating effects of parental addiction. They could gain some measure of control over their world, still keeping in touch but being buffered from the worst of it. They did not get off scot- and addiction-free— that is, the fallout of living with trauma and addiction continued to affect them—but they were able to keep it from destroying them. The price they paid, according to Emmy Werner (1989), ranged from stress-related illness to "a certain aloofness in their interpersonal relationships," both of which therapy and recovery can help.

The Kauai studies revealed that children from at-risk homes who showed resilience became "adept recruiters of nurturing teachers, coaches and other adult mentors." They "drank up support promiscuously wherever they found it." Indeed, they took the risk of being hurt again, but "they also chose well, thus helping to make their own luck. These children actively recruited informal support networks in their community" (Butler 1997).

The Wolins tell the story of Sandra in order to illustrate how deliberately resilient children sometimes enlist support. Sandra and "Mr. Berkowitz" lived in apartments joined by one thin wall; sounds of fighting and the soundlessness of neglect vibrated between them, so that each probably realized the plight of the other. Sandra knew that Mr. Berkowitz's son disliked him and saw an opportunity, a job opening if you will, for a surrogate child. For several weeks, Sandra positioned herself carefully near Mr. Berkowitz's seat on the stoop while she jumped rope within his certain gaze. Over time the old man accepted her presence, but neither spoke. Each disappeared into their respective apartments during the winter but reappeared in the spring, still never having exchanged a word. One day, Sandra came out without a jump rope and "sat on the top step so I was level with his feet." In a childlike attempt at connection, she ran her fingers around the toe and heel of his unusual molded shoes and began asking questions about them. Soon they got into regular conversations. He told her about his Jewish customs that her family didn't observe, and she often went to synagogue with him where she "loved sitting next to him joining in the prayers."

"In relationships of their own making, resilient survivors earn the opportunity to see images of themselves as loving and lovable. These pictures substitute for the distorted reflections collected at home from troubled parents" (Wolin and Wolin 1993).

Resilient children, the Wolins found, have an "inner locus of control"—an optimistic confidence in their ability to shape events.

The Wolins have developed a "Resilience Mandala" that includes the qualities used and displayed by resilient children. These qualities include:

- Independence
- Creativity
- Relationships
- Insight
- Humor
- Morality
- Initiative

These are the qualities that allow children to show resilience in circumstances of hardship which later can lead to a powerful sense of self that comes from having overcome the odds and succeeded in life in spite of a dubious start.

Resilience Can Be Learned

Resilience can be trained. Focusing on strengths that got you through rather than only on what kept you down, reframing, and using life problems as challenges are all resilience-enhancers, according to research. For little children from at-risk homes, programs such as Head Start that put them in situations where they can actively build and exercise resilient qualities, can make the critical difference in whether the child creates a productive life or falls hard upon the public systems throughout their years.

"What we call resilience is turning out to be an interactive and systemic phenomenon, the product of a complex relationship of inner strengths and outer help throughout a person's life span. Resilience is not only an individual matter, it is the outward and visible sign of a web of relationships and experiences that teach people mastery, doggedness, love, moral courage and hope" (Butler 1997).

As clinicians we need not be the center of our clients' universe. They may benefit from new hobbies, jobs or relationships that can support their process of recovery in ways that we cannot. Psychodrama always "sees" clients as being part of a system, whether they are with us in one-to-one therapy or group. I know that when I treat a client I am affecting and interacting with a system, and that the treatment will work best if I can not only work clinically but can recognize that healing is not confined to a clinic. Along with the client, I look at the roles within the system to ascertain which roles may be underplayed, overplayed, which need to be brought into balance, added, reduced and so on.

Both trauma and addiction can undermine resilience, but this does not have to be the end of the story. If, as clinicians, we are conscious of the strengths that pulled our clients this far as well as the emotional and psychological trauma that is blocking them from going further, we can work with both simultaneously. In the following story we meet Guy, a recovering addict with seven years of sobriety who feels unable to move forward into either a committed relationship or a satisfying career path.

Guy did his psychodrama in a workshop with around thirty people. He said that he would like to forgive his alcoholic father, who had deserted him when Guy was eleven. Though sober now, his father had attended no AA meetings or therapy. He removed the medication and sobered up physically, but emotionally he remained locked away in his own painful world, the door of which was barred to deep emotion. Even though he was now present in Guy's life, he refused to "talk about the past or make amends for the years of loneliness and pain Guy suffered at the loss of the father he trusted and adored."

The group identified with his plight and chose him to work. Guy's father stood on a chair: "You're a shadow hanging over my life. I keep waiting for you to accept me. Every time I make a mistake I see you there, disapproving. I want to connect with you, I want you to say you're sorry for leaving me, for throwing away everything that was important to me." When his father "threw him away," he in turn lost access to the child within himself who knew how to connect, trust and love. And along with it went Guy's strongest quality of resilience—a deep ability to form a loving attachment. That child was blocked, shut down, out of reach.

In his psychodrama Guy released the pent-up anger he had stored *against* his father. This is *abreactive catharsis* or the expression of anger against someone that often precedes the *catharsis of integration* that is the eventual goal. The *catharsis of integration* allows for a *shift in perception* or seeing the same situation through different eyes. Guy felt that until his father apologized, he could not risk feeling love for him again. But that apology was not forthcoming, nor did it look as if it would be. And so we did psychodramatically what could not happen in life. We let Guy spend time with the father he had lost. At first Guy could only speak as if in the past. "We *had* a great thing, I *loved* you so much." But eventually the "as if gave way and became as" and Guy reexperienced the love he had lost. "I love you, we don't need to talk about trust, it's just there, we *have* a great thing."

Eventually, as these feelings of love reignited within him, he realized that though he had lost his father he did not have to lose the eleven years of having him. When he felt the love from those eleven years, then the loss hurt all over again. But without feeling the loss, he could not reconnect with the love. As his psychodrama moved along he said, "I lost you but I didn't lose this, this feeling is mine. I want it for my life, to carry into my relationships." Eventually he said, "I want to thank you for those eleven years. It hurt so much to lose them, but they were beautiful and I'm taking them with me." Part of resilience is the ability to feel, to marshal our forces and what was good and take it with us. In resolving trauma and building a healthy life we need not only to revisit and work through painful circumstances but to reconnect with positive and happy experiences so that we can build on those feelings.

Another way to build resilience is in reframing and re-labeling. "Problems can be depathologized when viewed as normative, expectable, transitional stresses. Symptomatic behavior can be viewed as a survival strategy—an attempt to live with an unbearable situation or to prevent a feared outcome" says Frome Walsh in *Strengthening Family*

Resilience (1998). Without understanding the context from which a problematic behavior arose, clients can feel that they are crazy or bad. "Reframing distress contextually helps clients view themselves, their problems and their strengths in a more positive and hopeful light. A problem presented as "inside" an individual, such as a character trait, may be redefined behaviorally in an interactional context." For example, a label of "histrionic personality" may be recast in terms of a wife's futile attempt to get attention from an unresponsive husband. In a vicious cycle, the more she complains, the more he withdraws; the more he distances, the more upset she becomes. Reframing pathological behaviors in a relational context creates a more compassionate picture of how we became the way we are. In other words, we are who we are in part because of who we've been with. Therefore, understanding difficult behaviors as our best attempt at the time to ward off what felt like disaster makes them feel less pathological and more understandable. It also allows trauma survivors to find the meaning and purpose behind their own actions, which can have the effect of reducing self-recrimination and freeing them to choose new behaviors.

Resilience, then, is building on a model of strength rather than a model of pathology alone. Most of our formalized therapy training focuses on what went wrong rather than what went right or what got us this far. Intuitively, the Twelve-Step programs consciously build resilience. Within the Twelve Steps themselves, spirituality and flexibility are fostered, ruptured relationships are restored through amends and, finally, recovery and health are shared with the community through service. Program slogans such as "easy does it," "how important is it?" "one day at a time," and "keep it simple," foster the kinds of qualities that are a part of resilience. Twelve-Step programs also build the intangible qualities of character, including commitment, responsibility, morality and spirituality, while fostering a new design for living and new relationships through the Twelve Steps and "member-to-member" contact.

MENTAL SET

We who lived in concentration camps can remember the men who walked through the huts comforting others, giving away their last piece of bread. They may have been few in number, but they offer sufficient proof that everything can be taken from a man but one thing: the last of human freedoms—to choose one's attitude in any given set of circumstances.

Viktor Frankl

All of us have days that are discouraging. Instead of feeling "on top of life" we feel that life is "on top of us." Maybe we "got up on the wrong side of the bed." Maybe we're angry at a family member or upset over something that has or has not happened, or maybe we're just in a bad mood. When we have days like this, it is easy to notice all the things that go wrong. We tend to exaggerate small hurts and to put the worst possible spin on every careless or casual remark. If our perception for the day is "everybody is out to get me," we will emphasize everything in our world that supports that view.

Conversely, of course, if we are having a good day and are full of energy, confidence and enthusiasm, we tend to emphasize the positives around us. We are likely to see the world as a friendly, helpful place where we can shrug off difficulties and accomplish things easily. Oftentimes the events that happen in a given day might be very much the same; the magic ingredient may be in our perception. As we discussed previously in studies, tasks learned while under the influence of alcohol were best remembered while again under the influence of alcohol. The body chemicals that are released in particular moods stimulate memories which match those moods.

"Ours is a disease of attitudes" is one of the pieces of folk wisdom that we hear in Twelve-Step rooms. The symptoms of trauma can distort our attitudes toward self, relationships and life, leaving us prisoners of our own negativity. We see the world, as St. Paul said, "through a glass, darkly," a glass that keeps light from shining though. Carl Jung felt that we don't really solve our problems, rather we go "to the mountaintop" (in our minds and hearts), where we learn to see them differently. When asked what his secret to longevity was, George Burns looked up wryly from behind his glasses and said, "It's all in the attitude, kid—you gotta watch that attitude." Viktor Frankl in *Man's Search for Meaning* spoke of his attitude as the one thing that was within his control during his years in a concentration camp.

Our attitude toward life can be our best friend or our worst enemy. Our attitude cannot be handed to us on a silver platter or taken away by force; it is something we slowly build and maintain within ourselves.

There is no replacement for a positive and generous attitude. A good attitude literally draws good circumstances toward us, just as a bad one creates disharmony. Here's how that works.

People who see themselves as lucky will unconsciously scan their environment for information and experiences that support their mental set. They will tend to accentuate, notice, catalogue and capitalize on "evidence" culled from their own lives that corroborates their already established view or what we might call their mission statement for living.

This is what Peter Russell refers to as "brain set" in *The Brain Book* (1979). Conversely, people who have an unlucky mental set, who see themselves as victims of circumstances, will unconsciously scan their environments for proof that their self set is accurate. They will notice, catalogue and spend much psychological and emotional time and energy supporting the idea that they are unlucky victims of circumstance.

Turning self-defeating attitudes into life-enhancing ones is part of the healing of trauma. That's where the Twelve-Step program sayings "act as if" and "fake it till you make it" provide an avenue for changing belief systems when you feel as if you are going against what feels familiar. They encourage you to practice until it feels natural or until you've grown a few extra neural pathways in your brain for new behavior.

Addictive substances and behaviors are instant attitude adjustments that can turn depression into euphoria in a matter of minutes—but it's a chemical adjustment that only works for a while. Tolerance sets in, and sooner or later the addict needs more substance to feel less good.

This is why the Twelve Steps are so important. Addicts are powerless over the addiction that holds their lives hostage. When they can accept this, they can begin to "come to believe that a power greater than themselves can restore them to sanity." This helps the addict or ACOA to take a leap of faith, which is a step toward restoring their lost trust and faith. Then, and only then, says the wisdom of program, are they in a position to "take a fearless moral inventory of the exact nature of their wrongs." That is, they need the inner strength that comes through restored trust, faith and ability to take in support, help and guidance *before* they can take a hard and honest look at themselves.

Eventually, as addicts work through their personal issues, they are in a position to "make amends to those they have harmed" in order to further their own healing, own their own behavior and restore ruptured relationships. As their healing becomes well established, they evolve into having a "spiritual awakening," at which point they give it away—the healed become the healers and "carry the message" through sharing their "experience, strength and hope with others." In other words, they "witness" their journey of healing and recovery, they "testify" as to the power of the program. This allows them to maintain sobriety and to grow personally, emotionally and spiritually, returning them to the community at large and charging them with the responsibility of helping others. A design for living if ever there were one—the way out is the way through.

The "Good-Enough Family": Amputation vs. Integration

Creating Resilience

What is a family? As nature and God designed it, it is a weblike structure of kinship relationships designed to meet our basic needs for food, nurturing, care, touch, sustenance—a place to belong unconditionally, a container to greet our first breath and hold our last sigh. From the beginning of time, the beginning of thought or love or words or caring, the family has been the place of passage, the first container of life for every human being who walks the Earth. The family. A network of relationships that has more power to shape how we talk, think and experience our sense of belonging in this world than any of us begin to know. All theories of personality, pathology, patriotism and love dip into the family at one point or another to answer the questions of who we are and how we got to be that way. The family is both mystery and reality; it houses our bodies and our spirits.

According to the National Institute on Drug Abuse, early onset of drug use in children is not random but "a predictable outcome of a developmental progression that begins in early childhood." Poor parental monitoring and frequent parent-child conflict "are two main predictors" of later teen drug dependence.

In America, we have this misconception that a family ends—that when the job of rearing children is more or less taken care of, the family is more or less over. It's a sort of national denial of the truth that we all know in our hearts—that family is never over, that it carries us through life in one form or another through all our days. The roles change, the nurturers become the nurtured, the care receivers become the caregivers, but because love and care are essentially a mutual experience, sustaining to both parties through the bond of attachment, the system can provide for the kind of support that fosters comfortable relating and healthy development if the system is "good enough."

No one really knows how much impact the family has on teaching us to be the people we will one day become, but few would disagree that the role it plays is significant. What, then, constitutes a family that can usher us adequately into adulthood, that can create an atmosphere that is safe enough to allow us to enter into the process of experimentation that allows us to eventually come to know who we are and what our place is on this earth, in this experience we call life? What is a "good enough" family?

"Good enough" does not mean perfect. It means what it says. The "good enough" family meets the basic needs of all involved so that development can be supported more than it is derailed, nurtured more than it is destroyed.

The subject of family is the issue nearest to all of our hearts, the one we came from, the one we build and the one that will ultimately lay us to our rest. We have addressed the issue of parenting in thousands of books, magazines and talk shows, but less attention has been paid to the concept of "familying." Each person in a family plays a pivotal role, and those roles grow and change over the course of our lives. The parents who care for us as children ultimately become the parents we care for at the close of their lives. Happiness should not begin "when the last child leaves home and the dog dies." It should be and persist all throughout the course of our lives as family members. Contrary to the way we have often thought, parenting does not end—it simply transforms as children go from being youths to adults and, ultimately, to caretakers. At each developmental stage, children will require different things from their parents. As the child changes, the role of parent adapts. Families don't end and should not end. Rather, they adjust to changing roles as needs change throughout life.

Much attention has been paid over the last two decades to dysfunctional families, but we have forgotten to balance in the sociological changes that may be contributing to what we call dysfunction. Distance, for example, has become part of most American families. The family support unit that used to live in geographical proximity has been greatly challenged by our mobile society. All too often this physical distance has given way to emotional distance. In other words, we turn our pain over living apart from our family members into a sort of alienation. We haven't accepted the distance and learned to work with it creatively to stay close.

Immigrants who came to this country often left close family members behind. Pioneers who moved west said good-bye to parents or siblings with the knowledge that they might never meet again. Infrequent letters were almost the only form of contact these families had. Today, we are living in a mobile society, one in which relationships are challenged by distance. However, we are simultaneously living in a global village, constantly being drawn together through technology—planes, trains and automobiles, as well as email, faxes, cellular phones and the cheapest phone rates in history. The Internet lets us communicate almost instantly around the world. Families take it for granted that a daughter studying in London can email her college papers to her father for his comments, that a son in the navy can communicate regularly via email even when he is at sea, or that a high-school sophomore can get help from her father on algebra homework by faxing it to him when he is out of town.

In addition, we can travel in a few hours by air distances that would have taken our great-grandparents weeks or months. Because of this ability to travel, we can have regular family reunions if we choose to. We can organize them in any price range from a camping trip to renting a yacht. A few days spent together on a predictable basis can offer tremendous opportunities for bonding and maintaining close family ties. Staying in touch is easy if we can work through our own resistance as to how it happens. Perhaps Sunday lunch at Grandma's is not the tradition it once was. But email, telephones and airplanes that can let us reunite with our loved ones are today's blessings. They can allow us to explore a world beyond each other and still stay in close touch.

Often we take distance personally and feel hurt by it instead of accepting it as a fact of family life in a mobile society. In fact, absence can make the heart grow fonder if we let it. We can choose consciously to pay attention to distant family members, nurturing and valuing those relationships in all the ways we have available. We can choose to maintain them instead of pushing people away by projecting our pain over the distance onto the relationship. Physical distance need not be turned into emotional distance if we learn to family for the years beyond 2000.

It may feel like a double message to say "family is all-important" while at the same time therapists are saying "parents cause your problems." In the 1980s, we all got too stuck in pathologizing our families of origin, and it may have created an emotional trap. But healing also means working through tough problems that you fear will drive you apart and instead getting to the other side. This can strengthen relationships because they become more authentic—the connection is honest and genuine rather than fraught with the insecurity of unspoken feelings. Finding a way to speak your truth without going after another person in an attacking, blaming way seems to be the task of the new millennium.

We need to look for root causes of emotional problems in order to heal them. A piece of the root is more often than not in the family system, when trauma and addiction have eaten away its infrastructure. For a period of time, as we delve into this pain, we may need to create enough space around ourselves to feel safe enough to do the gut-wrenching work of recovery. But we can find our way toward love and forgiveness if we want to—it will take time and hard work. We can take space and create healthy boundaries without "amputating" family members. Amputating creates a "phantom limb" in my experience—it doesn't really work. This is not to say that we remain close at the expense of our sanity and serenity, only that we follow the path that will ultimately give us the greatest peace of mind.

Remember, family members are a part of us, integrated into our own self-system. It is within ourselves that the healing begins. The mother who has hurt us becomes a part of the way we treat ourselves. The father who had no time for the son becomes the son who cannot connect with men, which eventually may include his own son. Healing begins now, with you. Blaming our parents is only a temporary stop on the path of healing. Traumatized children tend to blame themselves for the trauma. Later, when those children become self-abusive adults, they do need to pass through a period of externalizing their anger. That may involve feeling the anger toward a parent in the here and now that was too threatening to feel as a child. This is a real and important part of the healing process—but it doesn't stop here.

Full healing only really comes through understanding. Our parents have their stories, too. We hurt our children out of ignorance much of the time, selfishness, too, perhaps—and mostly, we hurt our children through reenacting the unresolved pain from our own unfelt, ignored wounds. Or as it was stated by the ancient Greek tragedian Euripides: "The gods visit the sins of the fathers upon the children."

In Greek, the word *sin* translates as "missing the mark." The word is "amarthea," which is also an archery term. Missing the mark, not hitting the target, being off center. We hurt our children in the areas where we ourselves are off center. If we are not willing to grieve our own wounds, the pain lives in the container of the family and gets acted out in a wide variety of ways. The child who spills his milk is punished as if he cursed out his parents. The husband who forgets to take out the garbage becomes a villain plotting against his wife. The wife who forgets to pay attention to her husband becomes an abandoning witch. We read our intimate relationships through the window of our own unconscious. If the window is cloudy or fogged up, then that is how we see. Cleaning our unconscious is cleaning the window so that we can see more clearly.

That is why recovery begins here and now, with you. This is why every person who takes on the challenge of breaking the chain of trauma and addiction cleans up his or her own corner of the world. Each person who accepts this challenge, sincerely and wholeheartedly, turns around the intergenerational cycle of pain. The last sentence of "The sins of the father" is ". . . and it lasts for four generations." This is in the Bible; it's not new. We can either pass our pain down through the generations or pass our healing down. The choice is yours.

FOURTEEN

Treatment

*Living well is
the best revenge.*

Oscar Wilde

Eighteen million Americans abuse alcohol, twenty million more are alcoholics and nine million use illicit drugs" (Pace 1997).

"Every day, the alcoholic adversely affects four people in their immediate environment and sixteen other people outside that immediate environment. Alcohol and drug addiction is a major cause of homelessness, HIV transmission and mental illness" (Kleber 1997).

Alcohol and drug addiction tear at the fabric of family and society, stripping away dignity, love and a will to live. Addiction's primary symptom, denial, creates a roadblock to early and successful treatment. "The victim deludes himself about loss of control and causes of other physical disorders often remain undiagnosed. The denial is reinforced by tremendous social stigma associated with the disease. Not only does the patient deny there is a problem, but so do families, friends and coworkers tend to look the other way when confronted by symptoms. But if denial is not broken down, the addict cannot recover" (Pace 1997).

When addiction arises from trauma, the trauma symptoms need to be treated in addition to the addiction itself. The symptoms of PTSD are pervasive and persistent and may take years to untangle. One of the problems in treating this population is imbedded in the symptoms themselves. That is, addicts, co-addicts and ACOAs tend to want to get better all at once. Denial, low frustration tolerance, poor impulse control, a tendency toward rash action, inability to modulate or tolerate strong emotions and fear of a pain-filled inner world may make them want a "quick fix," to come in sick and leave all better—like getting an appendectomy.

But trauma and addiction hit the core of the personality and distort personality development. Addicts and trauma survivors are learning a new way of living that encompasses profound shifts in their mental/emotional world, their physical world and their spiritual lives. Combined treatment appears to be key in the treatment of the addict, co-addict and ACOA. We are creating, in a sense, a new world order to correct the trauma victim's profound loss of same.

To this end, I will list and discuss treatment options. Those who have stayed with long-term recovery seem to use a combination of most of the treatment options that I am outlining in this chapter. For them, recovery becomes knit into the fabric of their lives during a period of time that can range roughly from five to eight years, and often they may continue Twelve-Step work or pieces of ongoing recovery indefinitely. It takes time to transform internally, to alter behavior and create new lifestyles. The ACOA, adult child of trauma or codependent will follow a similar path of recovery aside from treating the core addiction.

Here are the basic components of a combined recovery approach.

Components of Treatment
- Treatment for the addiction itself
- One-to-one therapy

- Group therapy
- Twelve-Step programs
- Psychodrama
- Medication (prescribed by a doctor)
- Spiritual path (meditation, church, synagogue, temple, Twelve-Step work, etc.)

Treatment for the Addiction

For the addict, treatment will usually include coming off of the addictive substance under medical supervision and attending an inpatient program for ten to twenty-eight days in an addiction treatment facility. Some addicts stop using on their own; most need professional help.

Treatment programs vary according to the facility. Generally, the focus is on removing the substance under medical supervision and establishing a foundation for sobriety. Treatment may include psychological evaluation, group therapy, Twelve-Step meetings, life skills, a portion of time for relatives of the addict to be a part of the process, one-to-one sessions and aftercare planning. This treatment is only the beginning of a long-term recovery process during which the addict will deal with the emotional and psychological issues that he or she was self-medicating, as well as the personal and life damage caused by addiction.

One-to-One Therapy

One-to-one therapy is a generic term that refers to the therapeutic model of one therapist treating one client. There are a myriad of theoretical approaches that can be used, but research shows that core to the success of any approach is the quality of the corrective relationship between client and therapist. As trauma is a rupture in a relationship bond, the relationship bond that grows during therapy acts as a corrective experience for the client. Feelings that submerged through rupture reemerge in the course of therapy, triggered by the intimacy of the relationship. In therapy, they can be felt, articulated, interpreted and understood. Fear of getting close, of abandonment, of being misunderstood, idealization and so on, can be explored. The unconscious can become conscious so that the driving forces behind reenactment dynamics can be teased out.

The relationship acts as a "holding" environment for these powerful feelings so that they can surface, be felt and understood. Parts of the client's or patient's unconscious will inevitably be projected onto the therapist, or a transference may develop over time. This too can be analyzed and worked through in the therapeutic context. This allows the unmet needs, unfulfilled wishes, competitive or jealous emotions, destructive fantasies and feelings, etc., to be worked through in a situation where they will not lead to the same relationship ruptures that were so traumatizing to the patient earlier in life. In this way "the relationship heals."

Group Therapy

Group therapy had its origins with the Viennese psychiatrist Jacob Levy Moreno, who is the father of both group psychotherapy and psychodrama. Moreno was the first person to move from treating people one-to-one to treating them in a group. Moreno saw the group as "society in miniature." One of his early experimentations with group was his work with prostitutes to try to "save them from a life of sin and degradation." As society had already dismissed them as unredeemable sinners, Moreno was free to try unusual approaches. So he put them into groups of eight to twelve women and had them meet three times per week. Initially, they talked about their different lives, their pimps, police and their children (Moreno 1964). Soon, however, they began to share more intimate details of their emotional lives. They mysteriously got "better," through support, emotional expression, identification with others and a restoration of hope. This represented a birth of group therapy.

Group therapy encourages addicts, who may develop some degree of social phobia when they let go of their addiction, and trauma survivors, who have formed thick walls of defense and emotional constriction, to talk to each other and feel in each other's presence.

Relationship dynamics that are part of group therapy inevitably trigger the pain, anger, hurt, idealization, neediness, a desire to hide, dominate, freeze and so on that were part of unresolved ruptures in relationship bonds. In this way, problematic or dysfunctional styles of relating become evident and can be resolved and retrained.

The container of the group acts as a "holding environment" that allows deep emotions to surface and be felt. The psychological and emotional numbness and the emotional constriction that result from trauma slowly dissolve as group members share and witness each other's stories, and take in support from each other. Dissociated memory can surface and be reintegrated. The power of

identification with each other's stories literally pulls forgotten or repressed material from the unconscious into
the conscious. Learning to tolerate intense feelings without shutting down, freezing, bolting, withdrawing or raging allows trauma victims to heal sufficiently so that they
can begin to have healthier interactions in their own lives.

Family Weeks

Several addiction facilities run various forms of family
weeks. Often, while addicts are in primary treatment, members of their families join them for a week of therapy. Or
family programs are available, such as the one at Caron
Foundation, in which addicts who are established in their
sobriety or family members of addicts who are in recovery
from codependency issues can work to resolve the emotional
residue of living with addiction, being addicted or both.

According to Abraham Maslow, peak experiences help
people to become self-actualized. In my opinion, these
treatment weeks are often simulated peak experiences
that put people ahead on the path of recovery and self-
actualization. Employing a psychoeducational approach,
they give family members a cognitive grasp of their own
roles within their addicted family systems and of generational patterns of trauma and addiction. Simultaneously,
they allow feelings that emerge from this awareness to be
processed. The camaraderie and bonding that take place
can open the trauma victim's heart to the possibility of
connection with others, and the profound sense of connection and community instills hope (Yalom 1931) for
those whose trust and faith in self, life and relationships
have been shattered.

Psychodrama

Psychodrama has emerged as a preferred treatment in many inpatient and outpatient settings for traumatized addicts, co-addicts and ACOAs. Psychodrama can adjust to the intensity of the inner worlds of trauma survivors, allowing them to bond with therapists and groups in a way that feels ego syntonic or natural. Therapy that offers too little interaction or does not engage the client emotionally can feel, to the trauma survivor, as if they are not connecting. The therapist can slowly role-train the trauma survivors to modulate their internal worlds. Initially, psychodrama allows intense emotion that has been blocked to surface so that it can be felt, expressed and named. It puts internal meandering into concrete behavior so that survivors who may find it difficult to reflect intellectually on their inner world suddenly see it in concrete form. This is often an "Aha!" experience for survivors whose inner worlds have been mysteries. They can begin to understand how their traumas have affected them, because they see themselves actually behaving, acting and responding *in situ*. Emotional literacy grows slowly over time, as more and more feelings and dynamics are revealed and named.

Because psychodrama is a role-play method, relationship is core to the process. You are always "talking to" someone or to an "aspect of self." This allows the blocked or distorted affect to emerge in the context of a relationship so that it can be examined and reworked. Initially, it is the client's reality, distorted or otherwise, that is the subject of a scene, but gradually distortions can be corrected through self-evaluation and feedback from the therapist and group. The meaning that the survivor made out of a traumatic circumstance reveals itself through action as the client expresses buried feeling.

Because psychodrama is a role-playing method, contents can be examined in a role-specific manner. It is possible to go directly to the wounded area. For example, if Lisa is working on unresolved issues in the father and daughter relationship, the thinking, feeling and behavior specific to the role of daughter will emerge for her in the context of a role-play. This allows a daughter traumatized by her father to access that role for healing, while leaving other roles where she may be thriving intact.

Role reversal, so core to psychodrama, asks that survivors learn to "stand in the shoes" of another. This has many benefits. One, it reduces the egocentricity of the trauma survivors by introducing other points of view. This allows empathy to enter their world as they experience the role of another person through that person's eyes. And it allows clients to see themselves as others see them, so they can both correct their own behavior and develop empathy for themselves. By standing in the shoes of another in role reversal, trauma survivors can learn that the negative behavior directed toward them may not have been their fault, but, at least in part, the product of the other person's problems that got projected onto them. This relieves the trauma victims of the pain of thinking that they were bad, at fault and deficient or somehow deserving of negative treatment.

The locus of control in psychodrama is within the client, as it is the client who defines the direction, nature and intensity of the work. This re-empowers the trauma survivors, allows them to feel safe, restores a sense of autonomy and reduces learned helplessness.

Psychodrama "puts the client in touch with their own internal healer," Zerka Moreno said in a 1989 lecture. As this unfolds, a deepened relationship with self and others, and a restored sense of spirituality are very common treatment outcomes. It allows the victim of trauma to "tell their story and have it witnessed" (Herman 1992) in a safe, clinical atmosphere. (See appendix for more information on psychodrama.)

Medication

The explosion in psychotropic medications over the past decade is greatly affecting the options available to clients looking for treatment. For the client who is dually diagnosed—that is, they are addicts plus have another diagnosis such as borderline, depressive, bipolar, panic disorder or PTSD—medication may be used in addition to the other forms of therapy discussed in this chapter. It is generally held that medication is useful if a person is not calm enough inside to be available for psychological and emotional forms of therapy. In these cases, the goal is to create a "therapeutic window" through which the information gained in therapy can get through to the person and the inner world of the person can become available for therapy.

Twelve-Step Programs

Twelve-Step programs contain many of the necessary treatment elements for trauma and addiction. Evolved through the collective wisdom of those "who know because they've been there," these programs go to the heart of issues that need to be addressed in the resolution of trauma and addiction. The community and member-to-member contact slowly restores trust and faith in relationships. Sharing stories, experience, strength and hope with the witness of the group allows trauma victims to "tell their story and have it witnessed" (Herman 1992). It also slowly allows the victim of trauma to learn to "take in support" and caring from others (Van der Kolk 1987).

"Turning our will and our lives over to God, as we understand him" reflects AA's belief that alcoholism is a "spiritual illness." The spiritual format of Twelve-Step programs restores faith in a Higher Power and encourages the addict, co-addict or ACOA to "surrender" their need to control or "outsmart" a disease over which they have little or no control. The program slogan, "ours is a disease of attitudes," speaks to the distorted and self-defeating beliefs and attitudes that keep a victim of trauma and addiction locked in painful cycles of reenactment. The group and member-to-member contact allow for the formation of new relationship bonds to heal those ruptured by trauma. The Twelve Steps themselves not only encourage surrender, but move on to take a "moral inventory of self" reflecting on the "exact nature of our wrongs," which helps the victim to turn around what can become a protracted victim posture. The action of "making amends to those we have hurt" is a behavioral shift and teaches the victim of trauma to take responsibility, not only for their own wounds but for their ability to wound others, and to do something about restoring relationships that may have been lost. Eventually, having had a "spiritual awakening," the Twelve Steps teach us to "take what we have learned and help others," slowly assisting society to heal and reinvesting freed energy in the ideal of recovery. The "one day at a time" philosophy of Twelve-Step programs helps trauma victims to break the task of living physically and emotionally sober lives into manageable components. Twelve-Step programs offer a "design for living" that helps to restore the trauma victim's ability to conceive of and take steps toward actualizing a positive future.

Meditation

Meditation calms the central nervous system (CNS) and elevates immune functioning. The rhythmic breathing that accompanies meditation, in addition to regulating the CNS, is a self-regulating skill that can be returned to again and again throughout the day to restore equilibrium and calm when anxiety starts to build.

The yogis teach a concept called the "inner witness," akin to the observing ego of psychoanalysis. It is the part of the mind that witnesses or observes our mental processing. Developing the inner witness has several benefits. It allows us to learn to sit with or tolerate strong emotion and intrusive thoughts without getting "involved" with trying to "control" them or "acting out"; we simply witness them impartially, without judgment, as they move through our minds. This reduces impulsivity. Also, because trauma-related memories can bypass the cortex, they are not thought about. Split-off parts of self, split-off affect and memory fragments can be integrated as they emerge in meditation and are observed and thought about by the "inner witness." Accompanying this flood of memory, emotion and physical sensation are varying degrees of intensity. Learning to "sit" in meditation through whatever comes has the effect of slowly moving the inner world toward modulation and equilibrium.

The Road to Recovery

One of the frustrating aspects of treating addiction that arises from trauma is that, once people stop the medicating behavior, they want to be better right away. For years they have seen getting better as laying down the addiction—but in truth, laying down the addiction is what paves the way for the work to begin. Addicts have low frustration tolerance. They have become used to quick and reliable sources of synthetic mood management. When faced with the need to elevate their moods and modulate them on their own, they can feel resentful, frustrated, desperate and alone, which can lead to relapse. When the issues related to the trauma they've been self-medicating reassert themselves, they have to do a great deal of catching up to develop the emotional maturity and ego strength to cope with them. Their addiction has seriously arrested the emotional development that would have taken place had their emotions been available to them. Unfortunately, that has not been the case, and so they are left trying to manage large and complicated problems with limited skills and resources.

During a recent session, a beautiful young woman fiddled with a pillow on my couch, squeezing it, giving it childlike punches. "Why am I not feeling better? My abuse was when I was fourteen, I'm twenty-seven and feel like I've been in therapy for lots of that time." She had just begun to see me and as I explored her history, the reasons for her feeling blocked became very clear. Janice, the epitome of the girl next door, was abused by a clergyman over a period of a year and a half. People found out, then other victims came forward, and the clergyman was incarcerated. She got therapy. But in the intervening years Janice worked as an exotic dancer to put herself through school, and whenever she felt "bad" she went to bars to pick up men and eventually women as well. This is simply recycling the pain rather than resolving it. It is a classic reenactment—recreating the original trauma in a variety of new ways. The abused girl herself becomes sexually addicted, and while her own acting-out behavior is medicating the pain of her abuse, that pain is not available for resolution. Now, at twenty-seven, she was in my office wondering why previous experiences in therapy hadn't worked.

Another client, Lucas, wants his life to turn around now that he is sober from alcohol and wonders why progress is so slow. Though he sobered up, he only took the first step toward healing—he removed the substance he was using for self-medication. All of the emotional and psychological pain he was medicating was still crying out for relief. Meanwhile, he smokes two packs of cigarettes per day and is roughly fifty to sixty pounds overweight. He doesn't like to exercise—who would, given those conditions? But he does want to get better. He goes to meetings, says the right things and is deepening his insight. But insight alone does not cure; it needs to be accompanied by a change in behavior. Insight can and often does lead to a change in behavior, but the power of addiction is so strong that it can roll over our best intentions and cloud what we think is our clearest vision.

Remember, the purpose of addiction related to trauma is to *make feelings and intrusive memories go away.* When this happens there is no way to resolve the trauma, no way to access the emotional and psychological material related to the trauma and integrate it. Trauma needs to be gone over, talked about, synthesized and understood. Until this happens, the emotional and psychological pain will seek some form of comfort and relief, whether it be from drugs, work, alcohol or a hybrid combo like smoking, coffee, frenetic activity, chocolate and excessive masturbation. Anything to stay away from the self—to keep intrusive memories and somatic responses "under control."

We do not, however, wish to give the impression that sharing your feelings is a cure-all. Oftentimes, I see ACOAs, addicts and co-addicts who come out of treatment thinking that if they are "honest and open" about everything they feel and state their needs clearly, that their life will work out and their needs will be met. When their expectations aren't fulfilled they can feel angry and disappointed. But life and relationships are not that simple, all feelings are not appropriate to share and all needs are not necessary to meet.

This is somewhat symptomatic of reworking missed developmental stages, wherein children's egocentricity keeps them from realizing that there are other people in the world whose needs also matter, and may require negotiation and compromise. The urge to apply simplistic solutions to complex situations may have a couple of origins. Many therapists and counselors in the addiction field are, themselves, in recovery from addiction or codependency issues and lack distance from their own trauma-related issues. Their identification with their client may be so strong it colors their therapeutic neutrality. In other words, they give in to their urge to give out quick fixes because they too become overwhelmed by the client's pain. And trauma victims can be extremely demanding clients, which can challenge even the most skillful therapist to remain constructively within therapeutic norms. However, when those norms are adhered to in a dull and conventional manner, the therapist can fail to engage the trauma victim in a profitable therapeutic alliance.

A delicate balance is needed—a mixture of empathy and structure. Without the power of a genuine relationship to ground therapy, trauma victims may feel neglected and invisible all over again. However, when they begin to feel themselves forming a deep attachment to a therapist they may become hypervigilant, constantly scanning their environment, in this case the therapist, for signs of flaws. As their fear of a renewed violation of an attachment bond increases, the hypervigilance does also, and they may direct at the therapist anything from criticism and rage to attempts at humiliation, making even the most practiced therapist have fantasies of retaliation. To complicate matters further, because trauma can have the effect of getting the victim partially stuck in a developmental phase at which the trauma occurred, children who have been traumatized by addiction can hold on to their defensive positions with the stubbornness of a two-year-old defending his toys. Because these defenses have been a part of the self-system for so long, giving them up feels like giving up a piece of self. Trauma victims may fight to keep their defenses with the ferocity of a drowning person because that is what they were—children drowning in chaos, using whatever defensive system they could devise in order to stay afloat: "any port in a storm."

Another common dynamic between therapist and clients may be idealization. Traumatized children may have needed to idealize their parents in order to preserve a sense of a protective presence. If therapists, in their need to feel helpful and appreciated, mistake this as an accurate reflection of their real qualities, they may be in for a painful awakening when the idealization gives way to disillusionment and retaliation, which it may well do. Some clients are able to move from idealization to a more authentic connection relatively methodically, and for others it can drive them to attack and criticism. They may harbor the childlike hope that the therapist can replace what was lost and, with loving attention, make their pain magically disappear. When it doesn't happen, all of their unexpressed hatred toward the parent that was never integrated alongside authentic love can get fired at the therapist. This, along with daily "holding" or witnessing the most pain-filled parts of a person's life, can mean that therapists may experience vicarious traumatization in their work.

It also makes it tempting to run the sort of group that fosters idealization and a sort of inverse traumatic bonding where these powerfully disruptive feelings do not get expressed. In these instances, the therapist may more or less join the client in a we–they posture. In psychodramatic terms, the therapy might be all doubling or acting as a client's inner voice, with little mirroring or pieces of reflection as to how the world might see the client. Such groups can become codependency training, a new way to tell people what to feel and what not to feel, with the meta message being that negative feelings will compromise or destroy the relationship with the therapist. This is, of course, a replay of the earlier parental attachment bond in which authentic emotion was a threat to the relationship. Programs that are of short duration can be part of this period of idealization and the clients leave on a sort of therapy high. Both therapist and client need to understand this dynamic in order to avoid a crash when the client returns home. What we want for our clients is that they learn to create productive and healthy lives. These types of highs can make them feel that their real life is inadequate and they can't get it right.

In addition to what will form the core of therapy, traumatized people from addicted homes will benefit from other learning that will support new ways of living. These might include parenting classes, couples therapy, meditation or spiritual development. Healthy eating and appropriate exercise are a part of recovery that should not be ignored. Everything isn't an emotional or psychological issue, and emotions and mental state are very much affected by food and exercise.

Last, this is a population that needs to learn how to have good, clean fun. Incorporating experiences that offer play, laughter and imaginative interaction enliven the spirit, reengage trauma survivors with the enjoyment of living and restore a sense of wonder.

There was a young man who, as he was
exploring the world, discovered that his feet
were sometimes cut, scraped and bled as a
result of walking on sharp rocks, thistles
and the like. "I have an idea," he said to a
wise man, "I'll cover the entire surface of the
world with leather and then I can walk
without ever getting cut again."
The wise man spoke, "If you cover the world
with leather, it is true you would no longer
cut your feet but nor would you see the beauty
of the earth, flowers, grass and stone.
Why not try this instead—cover your own
feet with leather and walk where you will,
protected among Earth's treasures."

Hindu Tale

FIFTEEN

An Ounce of Prevention:
A Case for Emotional Literacy

With the dawning of this love
and the voice of this calling
we shall not cease from exploration
and the end of all our exploring
will be to arrive where we started
and know the place for the first time
through the unknown, remembered gate.

T. S. Eliot

It is a new road to happiness
if you have strength enough
to castigate a little the various impulses
that sway you in turn.

George Santayana

We readily attend to a wound to the body. We would not ask ourselves to walk through life with an uncast fractured leg—we would see the foolishness of that, understanding that if we did not attend to it we would never again be able to walk or run or dance normally again. Yet we leave wounds to the heart, to our emotional/spiritual selves, regularly unattended, sentencing ourselves to a life where we cannot love, trust or dream because it feels too risky, too dangerous. We do not conceptualize these as wounds, perhaps because we feel in some way at fault—and this makes us feel undeserving of help. However, this is not a good reason not to get help. If we had a deep cut on our hand, chances are we could feel partially responsible for it, but we would nonetheless go to an emergency room and get it sewn up so we could use it again. The knowledge that we need the full use of our hand to be functional would drive us to a doctor no matter how guilty we felt about how we cut it.

We need to understand that we need the full use of our hearts to be complete as well. It is our responsibility to attend to a wound to the heart as carefully and responsibly as we would attend to a wound to any other part of us—not because we deserve to but because we need to, so that we can go on with life fully and frankly and so that we do not ask those who love us to carry the residue of our unhealed pain.

We clearly see that it is irresponsible to refuse care if an ulcer is eating away at our stomach lining, but if an emotional wound is eating away at our inner world, undermining our ability to enjoy life and live fully, we feel we should be able to let it go—to move on and get over it without help.

Most of us recognize that in order to remain physically fit we need to make some adjustments to our daily routines. We need to exercise, eat well and curtail bad habits like excessive drinking and smoking; to give our bodies ample rest and relaxation and find ways of reducing the kind of stress that takes its toll. We embrace this to such an extent in the United States that fitness and health food have become major industries. *Emotional fitness* requires the same ideological approach as physical fitness. In order to maintain emotional fitness, we need to keep ourselves on a daily, healthy regime in which we actively develop and maintain good "emotional tone" in much the same way in which we would keep up good muscle tone.

In the 1960s, John F. Kennedy created a presidential

initiative for physical fitness. Up until then, gyms were only for athletes, and health food was the exclusive realm of eccentrics. Why can't emotional fitness become equally accessible? In truth, we are halfway there with the boom of interest in pop psychology and self-help. Today, we think nothing of investing considerable time, energy and dollars in our physical fitness. We see it as life-enhancing and part of the prevention of disease.

Emotional fitness is no different. Previously we felt that being partners with professionals in our physical health was presumptuous; today it is ordinary. Acquiring emotional skills equivalent to jogging, exercise, massage and healthy lifestyles is an idea whose time has come. The language and theory, in other words the emotional literacy, that those of us who are in the field of psychology use daily are skills that those willing to invest some time, energy and resources can acquire and use throughout life. Emotional fitness can act as a preventative for depression, addiction and anxiety, to name only a few. Emotional fitness can profoundly alter our ability to have and maintain healthy relationships in both partnerships and families.

People in therapy fear they will not survive their own tumultuous feeling states, that they will, somehow, get lost in the intensity and complexity of their own inner world, that feelings will be so strong that they will be reduced to babbling idiots, inarticulate and overwhelmed. One of the ego-strengthening aspects of therapy is simply learning that feeling states can be experienced and described with words. After all, words are just symbols attached to thought and feeling that enable us to communicate what is going on inside of us. They allow us to enter into a community by providing a common language understood by the mass of people.

What if, as a part of our teaching of young people, we illuminated a path not only outside but inside a child? We might start at a very young age to use words to describe feeling states at a simple level, then graduate in complexity as feelings grow more involved and complicated. What if, just as we move from simple arithmetic to division and multiplication, we learned to move from happy, sad, mad, glad, to resentment, hurt, joy and contentment, then toward such advanced concepts as projection, displacement and dissociation, the equivalent of higher math? Any of these more advanced languages used to describe psychological dynamics are well within the reach of the average eleventh grader. High school students are far more interested in decoding their own complex inner world than any other subject. And yet, at this critical moment of emotional curiosity, we feed their hunger with chemistry and math and miss the opportunity to teach them about who they are, what it means to be a person trying to live a life. We send them out into the world ill-equipped, and when they get to college or the work place, they are taught that they should have big heads and small hearts. They are overtrained in some areas and woefully underequipped on the subject of themselves, their siblings, family and friends, self and relationships. We fall silent on this great subject and leave their curiosity to be fed by television, the media and the tremendously powerful pop culture that surround them.

But these high school and college-age students will never be as ripe for learning on the emotional levels as they are at this age, when every part of them is hungry for self-knowledge and shifting and growing into the person they will eventually become. When we send them into the world without a language to describe who they are to someone else, we diminish in importance the most core subject of their worlds—themselves—and we focus all of our attention on letter grades and outward accomplishments as if their inner world were a place to visit only as last resort, between *The Simpsons* and graphic arts. We fail to make the connection that acting-out behavior, out-of-control drinking and drugging are direct results of a troubled inner world trying desperately to assert itself, to be known and seen.

What if we gave these children *a language before the fact?* What if we equipped them with words that could be used to describe their inner states and communicate them to others so that the relief they seek would not need to be had at a high price? There is not a person among us who doesn't know the relief of a heart-to-heart talk or a good cry that opens us up to entering into a calmer, more focused dialogue. Holding feelings in prevents us from knowing them. Then, by the time they come out of us, it's too late for using appropriate, moderate language to describe them. They come out in a torrent and grab at any word they can find, be it accurate or misleading. But when we learn that we need not fear our feelings, that we can sit with them, then describing them becomes much simpler. The ability to use language to describe what is happening inside of us on an emotional level gives us the skills that we need to move forward in our own lives.

Emotional literacy is a learned skill. It can be taught. Each age has its own developmental tasks for acquiring emotional literacy. For the small child it may be, "I am sad. I feel scared. I want to see my mommy," simple descriptions of emotional states. For the adolescent, "I feel left out of a clique. I feel overwhelmed by my parents' high expectations."

For the emerging adult, emotional literacy takes on subtler tones. "I feel defensive when you approach me in that way, and I want to withdraw or shut down." "All of the sexually explicit media I am exposed to makes me shift between wanting to be sexual before I'm ready and wanting to avoid close relationships so I don't have to deal with the question of sex."

Recently, we went through that harrowing passage that parents and children spend so many years working towards—college admissions. The anticipated, agonized-over and dreamed-about days finally arrived with acceptance letters—large, puffy envelopes with words like "congratulations," "yes," and "welcome" popping off the page. As we were standing in the kitchen celebrating, our son Alex said, "Actually, it never really occurred to me that I wouldn't get into college. I know that's probably a defense, but. . . ."

Alex was speaking to a complicated emotional operation. He was having a feeling that was threatening and might have debilitated his ability to maintain his equilibrium through the long process of college visitation and application, so he defended against it by not allowing it to cross his mind. This particular defense was a useful one for a couple of reasons. First, the likelihood of his not getting into any college was very low, so to focus on that thought would have been unrealistic and not worth the energy depletion and loss of inner peace. So the defense allowed him to enjoy high school, remain optimistic and continue to work toward his goal. As soon as the danger was over, as soon as he got into college, he dropped the defense and named it as it fell. He was then able to use the right words to both name his inner experience and describe its function. "It never really occurred to me that I wouldn't get into college" (i.e., I did not let myself entertain this unrealistic or threatening thought), and he named the function, "I suppose that was a defense." This kind of statement requires the skills of emotional literacy.

More than language, emotional literacy is the language of emotional intelligence. We are, because of pop psychology and its constant presence in the media, being swiftly educated to be more emotionally intelligent. However, we need to be taught how to take the essential steps into emotional literacy that build emotional intelligence. As my daughter said recently, "All of my friends have the same thoughts and feelings inside as I do, but they don't have the language. I guess because you and Dad are therapists, I've sort-of learned a language to describe what's going on inside of me from talking to you." That language is *emotional literacy*, and it builds emotional intelligence.

For a long time we have seen emotions as something to control or even hide, something to drown out with alcohol, drugs, food, etc., but as a new century dawns it is increasingly being recognized that emotions are meant to be understood and integrated. We are emotional beings. It is through feeling that we love our children, choose a mate and recognize the power of our passions and dreams. It is emotion that makes an everyday moment transcendent, an ordinary or plain face moving and beautiful.

When we take learning the skills of emotional literacy as seriously as we take learning math, we are recognizing that they are as (if not more) driving a force behind success in love and work as any other.

"An ounce of prevention is worth a pound of cure." Acquiring the skills of emotional literacy is what will allow us to meet the complex challenges that will confront us in the rapidly changing world of our new millennium. While the rule of the last millennium has been "survival of the fittest," in the new millennium let it be "survival of the wisest." There is no wisdom without mastery over the mystery of our internal world, the world that opens the door to understanding others.

Appendix

The Use of Psychodrama in the Treatment of Trauma and Addiction

Trauma memories are stored in parts of the brain that were formed early in man's evolution as fight, flight and freeze responses designed to preserve survival. The cortex, or the part of the brain where we think about and reflect upon what we do, was developed later in human evolution. Because of this we tend to have difficulty in reflecting upon, remembering or placing into context memories related to trauma. This can manifest, in therapy, as what may appear to be resistance. Psychodrama, through role-play, allows for our hungers and open tensions to spontaneously emerge through action. Once behavior is in concrete form it can be reflected upon. Words can be attached to feelings that emerge alongside behavior. The feeling searches for a word to describe and contain it, which is easier than the reverse. Because the mind has learned to block trauma memories, using a word to "search" a feeling does not always work. Even the question "How do you feel about . . .?" can baffle the trauma survivor. "One picture is worth a thousand words." Psychodrama allows a picture to be created that can be witnessed, reflected upon and read by all members of the group. Through role-play the protagonist's issues emerge, and through identification the group members' issues come forward as well. Then they can process what is in front of them.

Psychodrama, a method that uses clinical role-play, was developed in the early part of this century by J. L. Moreno, a Viennese psychiatrist, and further developed by his wife Zerka Moreno. The five elements of psychodrama are: protagonist, director, auxiliary ego (role player), audience (group) and stage. Psychodrama is protagonist-centered; that is, it empowers the protagonist to tell her story as she sees it and have it witnessed by the group. The protagonist selects group members to play the roles of significant people in her life or aspects of herself so that she can examine issues from her life in concrete form. The role of the director is to listen and follow, to allow the protagonist to lead the way in the unfolding and exploration of her personal truth. This is useful in some of the following ways:

1 It empowers the protagonist.
2. It provides a guide to help to "hold" the experience and a group to act as witness, which helps to create a feeling of safety for the protagonist as she revisits painful or confusing emotional material.

3. It places the protagonist in the center of her own experience rather than on the periphery.

4. From this central position, the protagonist can identify where she has lost a sense of personal power so that she can reawaken her ability to take the reins of her own life and make choices as to the most productive and satisfying way to live.

How Can Psychodrama Address Issues of Trauma?

Relationship trauma constitutes a rupture in an affiliative bond. Other types of trauma rupture our sense of a dependable and predictable order in life. They may leave us with deep feelings of despair, helplessness and even terror, because of the malfunctioning of a core relationship or a predictable world order.

Psychodrama places clients at the center of their own drama, their own life story, their own psychological and emotional processes. The psychodramatic stage is given to clients as a vehicle through which they can encounter their inner world in concrete form; they can tell their story and have it witnessed. The director serves as a sort of coproducer, following the lead of the clients (protagonists), allowing them to be in charge of their content of life issues that will be manifested. The group members are available to play roles of actual people from the life of the protagonist so that the conflict or issue can be brought to life and given shape and form, voice and movement. Every aspect of the psychodramatic method is designed to restore a sense of power and control to protagonists as they time travel through their own inner space, bringing to the clinical "stage" for reexamination tragedies too painful to look at and dreams they have not dared to have.

If they need greater distance from traumatic material, protagonists can use stand-ins to represent themselves as they witness the content of their own drama; in this case they can move in and out of the scene through role reversal, or "double" (see glossary) for themselves, thus giving them a safety net if work becomes too intense. They also have the opportunity with the director to freeze the scene so that they can step back and get a deeper look at what might have been going on for them at a given juncture in their lives. This allows protagonists to get perspective on their own "feedback loop," or how they may be reacting in ways that are "trigger" reactions with origins in earlier traumas. The fact that psychodrama is a role-based method allows a client to explore damage that may have occurred in a particular role, say that of son or daughter, while preserving strength and resilience that may still be present in other life roles.

Role-playing can stimulate the surfacing of intense trauma-related memories and emotions that may otherwise remain buried. When handled with care, this can help clients break through the emotional constriction and numbness that so often accompanies trauma, slowly train the trauma victim to tolerate the intensity of their inner world and gradually modulate it.

Built into the method of psychodrama are many therapeutic opportunities that are useful in resolving trauma-related issues.

1. It *reempowers* the client by allowing him to be at the center of his own experience with clinical

supervision and support. It allows him to view this material again in the light of today.

2. It provides a method through which *emotional triggering* can occur in a clinically safe environment so that powerful reactions can be worked through toward resolution. Feelings that were *fused* can be reexamined and untangled.

3. Scenes can be played out in their concrete form where *distorted reasoning* becomes evident as personal meaning that was made at the time of the trauma can be clarified and reframed, and understood in the light of today.

4. Psychodrama allows the protagonist (client) to learn to *take in support* from the group through identification and sharing.

5. It provides a therapeutic alliance with the director, double and group that allows the client to explore repressed and threatening material with support, so that *psychological defenses* that the client used in childhood can be identified and understood.

6. It slowly breaks down *emotional constriction* through spontaneous role-play.

7. It releases and externalizes pain and anger that can cause *depression*.

8. It slowly reduces *anxiety* as protagonists confront and work through situations that they fear.

9. It provides a therapeutic *alternative to self-medicating* emotional pain, allowing pain to be felt in an atmosphere of support and understanding.

10. It *restores relationship bonds* through positive group dynamics and examines the source of *traumatic bonds* and the transference dynamics that are a part of them.

11. It explores *reenactments* of dysfunctional relationship dynamics through role play so that their origins can be understood clearly.

12. It reduces *hypervigilance* by working through the source trauma issues and increasing tolerance for sitting with threatening material within the self and the group and slowly moves toward *modulating emotions*.

13. It elevates the immune system through the release of repressed material and examines *somatized* material through role-play, which can help to clear up psychosomatic symptoms.

14. Having internalized this restorative relationship experience, the client begins to restore a sense of *trust and faith* in self, other, community and spirituality or universal order.

Moreno theorized that the self emerges from the roles that we play (Moreno 1969). As part of the psychodramatic method the protagonist is encouraged to make and remake life choices and expand his or her role repertoire through adding new roles, either within the self or in relation to other people. This can: facilitate the learning of new coping skills such as mastery (role-training); provide a corrective, socially supportive network or a reworking of *object relations* through surrogates (social atom repair); protagonists can learn self-directed problem-solving skills using their own and auxiliaries' resources to help solve issues and experience the self-esteem related to task completion. Psychodrama can also help an individual to form the corrective perception that they have some control over their environment, which counters the trauma victim's sense of *learned helplessness*.

How to Use the Roles and Techniques Within the Method of Psychodrama to Resolve Issues Related to Trauma

A. Roles and Basic Elements

Director: The role of director is to aid the protagonist in actualizing his or her own story so that it can be reconstructed and examined in concrete form. The protagonist is allowed to lead the way in choosing what material to explore with the aid of the director. This creates a therapeutic alliance and restores a feeling of empowerment to the protagonist.

Protagonist: The role of the protagonist is to take a leap of faith in self, director and group and delve into his or her internal world with the intention of resolving inner conflicts.

Auxiliary Ego: The roles of the auxiliary egos are to represent the people in the protagonist's life or aspects of the protagonist's inner world as accurately as possible, using information shared by the protagonist as well as their own experience of what thinking, feeling and behavior appear to be a part of the role they are portraying.

Group: The role of the group is to play auxiliary roles and act as witnesses to the protagonist's life drama, as well as to create a safe container for personal exploration. Group members also identify issues from their own lives that get stimulated as a result of witnessing or participating in the enactment. Through this identification they can identify issues from their own life that may need attention.

Stage: The stage is offered as a concrete situation within which a protagonist's story can be brought to life in time and space. Life happens in situ, and psychodrama allows resolution to occur through simulated role-play that mirrors real life.

B. Techniques

Doubling: The technique of doubling is used to help protagonists to come to the threshold of their own internal experience. It consists of standing behind the protagonist in their own role or in role reversal and speaking their inner life. Doubling gives protagonists a sense of being supported as they face threatening personal material or as they revisit their own traumatic past through role-play. When once they may have felt alone and helpless, they now have a therapeutic ally in the face of a painful situation.

Spiraling: Spiraling is particularly useful in the resolution of reenactment dynamics. It allows protagonists to begin a scene where they experience conflict in the present day. Then they can spiral back to a scene from the past that might be affecting their current thought or behavior; the scene from which the conflict arose is the "seed" of the problem or the "status nascendi." They can work with the past scene toward resolution, then, when the conflict has been fully explored, spiral back to the present day, replaying it with new awareness and practicing new behavior through role training. Through linking present-day problems with their origins in the past, clients are able to have a choice between blindly (unconsciously) reenacting past pain and making new choices as to how to behave.

Stand-in: Protagonists may choose to use stand-ins to represent themselves so that they can view a situation from the outside, gaining both perspective and a greater sense of safety. This can provide some therapeutic distance, so the protagonists feel less threatened approaching traumatic material. This also gives them the opportunity to "double" for themselves or to rework issues by reversing roles in and out of the scene as they feel comfortable. Viewing a conflict from the outside allows protagonists the emotional and psychological distance to "unhook" from their knee-jerk responses and gain insight that might be unavailable to them in the heat of the moment.

Interview: The initial interview is used to gather material that is relevant to the situation being explored. The interview can allow the director to ask questions that encourage the protagonist to respond spontaneously in order to move through resistance and denial and gain access to deeper truth. The protagonist can also be interviewed in role-reversal, i.e., the daughter can reverse roles with her mother and be questioned "as the mother," deepening through her spontaneous response her understanding of her mother's role. This can serve to relieve the protagonist of the burden of feeling that she was the "cause" of a dysfunctional relationship by identifying how the mother's own issues may have affected the situation, as well as promoting empathy for her mother.

Role-reversal: One of the most important techniques of psychodrama, role-reversal allows the protagonist to stand in the shoes of another person. This lets them, first, gain empathy for themselves and the other person, and second, see themselves as they are seen by others. Often survivors of trauma feel at fault, as if bad things happened to them because they are in some way bad themselves. Role reversal enables them to experience the complexities, needs, drives and motivation of another person, perhaps the person who hurt them. This helps the protagonist to depersonalize the abuse, to understand that the abuser may have abused anyone who was in the protagonist's position. It opens the door to understanding the humanity of the other person as well.

The Reconstructive Experiences Built into the Method of Psychodrama

Psychodrama, in addition to offering an arena in which emotional blocks and reenactment dynamics can be examined, can, through reconstructive role-plays, provide the opportunity for protagonists to experience what they feel was missing. Until someone has the actual experience of being held or loved or is able to replay a scene as they wished it had happened in order to recognize what was missing and take this in on an experiential, feeling level, it can be difficult for that person to seek out similar experiences in everyday life. The following techniques allow for this corrective experience to be constructed through role-play.

A. The reformed auxiliary: The reformed auxiliary offers a representation through role-play of the relationship as it is wished for (reformed) by the protagonist. For example, protagonists can choose the father they would have liked to have and interact with that person.

B. The reconstructive scene: Protagonists can construct a scene and experience it, first as it was and then as they wish it had been, thus taking in on an experiential, feeling level how they wish a situation might have occurred in their lives so that a new "template" from which to operate can be formed.

C. Group sharing and identification: After each enactment, group members share with the protagonist ways in which they identified with the protagonist's scene from situations in their own lives. This both allows the protagonist to break the isolation of feeling alone in pain and teaches the protagonist how to take in support from others. It also allows group members to heal through identification or experience a "spectator catharsis."

D. Catharsis:

1. *Abreactive catharsis:* In the abreactive catharsis the protagonist is allowed complete latitude in releasing pain and in giving full expression to feelings of hurt, anger, alienation, love, etc. They can express previously taboo feelings, thoughts and words, so that which was repressed or denied can emerge and find voice and expression, thus giving an infected wound a chance to drain and get air.

2. *Catharsis of integration:* This is the eventual goal of catharsis. It is meant to bring about a shift in perception that will allow clients to view the same situation from a different perspective. This allows them to reintegrate painful emotional experience with new insight and understanding, seeing the "same landscape through different eyes." This is fundamentally reempowering, because it allows clients to come to terms with a painful past rather than amputate the parts of themselves that have gone into hiding. The nature of traumatic memories is that they are split off

from normal memory storage. They often enter partial consciousness through flashbacks and somatic memories. Psychodrama allows for bits of memory to resurface over time. Eventually fuller memory of the traumatic event(s) can be recontextualized and reintegrated into the memory system of the protagonist.

E. Spontaneity: Psychodrama restores spontaneity into the self-system. Indeed, it is a central goal of psychodrama to consciously remove blocks in spontaneity so that the authentic personality can be allowed to emerge. Numbness, emotional constriction and anxiety can all be reduced through the process of role-play. Traumatic memory tends to be stored in the "old brain," which was evolved along with the early defense systems of fight, flight and freeze. When trauma memories are stimulated, the person's response system is limited to earlier functions. Recontextualized memory is processed in the more recently evolved parts of the brain, including the cortex, which is associated with conscious thought. Psychodrama defines spontaneity as an adequate response to a situation, "adequate" being appropriate to the situation as it presents itself, neither too much nor too little but "just right." It frees up the personality and removes blocks to spontaneity so that a person is able to react more fully and appropriately in the here and now.

On the following pages I describe three tools that I have developed to work with trauma and addiction: first, *The Living Genogram*; second, *The Trauma Time Line*; and third, *The Trauma Resolution Model for Creative Arts Therapists*.

THE LIVING GENOGRAM

Substance abuse decreases the ability of a family to provide a healthy environment for its individual members where bonding, growth and development can occur. Relationship traumas tend to get passed down through the generations. Children of alcoholic parents are conservatively estimated at twenty-two million people (Deutsch 1982). It is no new fact that children of alcoholics are at an over five times higher risk for becoming alcoholics themselves and frequently marry alcoholics or ACOAs (adult child of alcoholics).

"The development of the genogram was greatly influenced by Moreno's concept of the Social Atom" (Marineau 1989). The genogram is an instrument from the family systems field that can illuminate patterns such as trauma and addiction that get passed down through generations. It is an invaluable tool for providing family history.

I have adapted the genogram to psychodrama, that is, moved it from the paper to the stage as the "Living Genogram." In this process, the genogram is completed on paper then put into psychodramatic action, allowing not only the history to become conscious, but concretized along with its emotional and psychological content as well. For too long the solution to family addiction was seen as getting the alcoholic to sober up, assuming that this would clear up the problems that extended into the family system. This approach ignored the underlying family pain and pathology that both contributed to and resulted from years of living with addiction.

The Living Genogram is a genogram brought to life through the use of role-play in the same way that a social atom becomes an action sociogram. It combines the family systems tool of the genogram with the psychodramatic method of role-play. It brings what was on paper into space, giving it concrete form and dimension, allowing a client to obtain a three-generational visual picture of the family system that they grew up in. The full genogram need not become an action sociogram in one session. It can act as a treatment map that both brings into focus areas that need work and provides a way of understanding how issues of trauma and addiction have manifested through generations of unhealthy family dynamics.

When clients are permitted through the use of the Living Genogram *to see* the whole picture, they can:

- Sense where their unfinished business lies by observing their feelings as they explore the various relationships in their sculpture.
- Have an opportunity to make a sort of mental time line for where they need to go in their personal work.
- Get a sense for the origin of their transferences, where their feelings of attraction and rejection lie as well as noticing act hungers, and open tensions by actually taking a walk through or revisiting their own pasts.
- Have the opportunity to identify patterns of generational dysfunction. This can help to free the self from the pathological grip of a pain-filled or petrified system. At the same time, through self-defining and separating, the client can view a system now separate with perspective and compassion.

The Living Genogram provides an overall map from which psychodramatic treatment, group and individual therapy can work over time. When the genogram is put into action, it can be done so in its entirety or through vignettes. Possible questions to be explored are:

- Where are some of the triangles in this family system?
- Along what generational lines does family addiction and dysfunction seem to travel, and what does that indicate in terms of risk categories?
- What are the types of addiction in this family?
- What are some of the strengths that continue to show up through the generations?
- How did the gender roles in this family system get played out?
- How does it feel to look at your Living Genogram, to look at your family?
- Where are you most comfortable; most uncomfortable?
- Where do you feel that you have unfinished business?
- What are the sources of current reenactment dynamics?
- Who do you wish to talk to in this genogram?
- Who do you feel you do not wish to talk to? Why?
- Who do you feel connected with?
- Who do you feel disconnected from?
- Rearrange this genogram so that it reflects dyads, triads, clusters, alliances and cut-offs. What do you feel?
- How might the dynamics you observe be playing out in your life today?
- How does the path of addiction run through this family?
- Who do you feel close to, distant from, affectionate toward, antagonistic toward? Where is your positive, negative or neutral tele?
- Rearrange this genogram so that it reflects the way you wish it had been.

The Living Genogram:

- Acts as a segue between the field of psychodrama and the broader mental health field, connecting family systems theory with psychodrama.
- Brings the genogram to the psychodramatic stage where its contents can be made visible through the casting of role players to represent people in the genogram.
- Provides for a visual picture of personal history along with the further option to move that history into a psychodramatic enactment. The client can, if he wishes to, choose someone to play or represent himself, then move in and out of the picture through role reversal. This provides a stand-in (mirror) so that if the protagonist is at risk for becoming flooded or retraumatized, they can locate themselves at a safe distance.
- Allows the client to give concrete form to the family that lives in their imagination or surplus reality and to get a visual picture of the intergenerational family system.
- Provides a venue through which the protagonist can tell their story of trauma through action, have it witnessed, and resolve open tensions and act hungers.

The Living Genogram Narrative

In Russell's genogram which follows, we see how addictive life patterns are being passed down through three generations. Addiction breeds addiction. Doing his genogram helped Russell to get a grasp of how addiction in two generations above him (that we know of) may have set him up for his own addictive problems. Both of Russell's parents, Miranda and James, grew up in alcoholic families. Though Miranda and her sister Melissa avoided drinking, Miranda became an overeater at age eight while Melissa was tacitly assigned the role of "family hero." In essence, her personal likes and dislikes, wishes and desires were placed second to constant and diligent work at "maintaining the family honor." She was a class president, cheerleader, on the debate team and a top student. Though these were indeed estimable accomplishments, she felt that without them she would not be a welcome, valued member of the family. In a sense, her job became to act out the spoken values of the family, and Miranda's and eventually Russell's jobs were to act out the unspoken ones. The unspoken values were emotional silence, stoicism and caretaking.

James, on the other hand, became an alcoholic. He took his first drink at age eleven and he liked it. It calmed his inner world and restored a sense of equilibrium. He carried on the father's name and the father's disease.

Russell's relationship with food began in early childhood. His mother's (Miranda) way of nurturing him was by feeding him constantly. This is how she dealt with her own unresolved issues from childhood, and she and Russell felt close through their mutual preoccupation with food.

When Russell was able to see his family patterns laid out in this manner, he felt less burdened with unspoken family history, and he understood that his addiction problems came from somewhere. This was the beginning of his getting a handle on the patterns of his own disease.

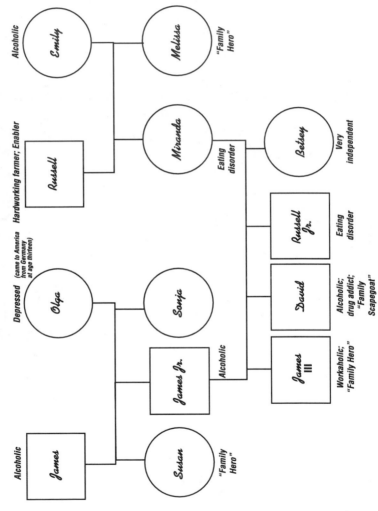

RUSSELL'S GENOGRAM EXAMPLE

Alcoholic — Emily

Melissa — "Family Hero"

Hardworking farmer; Enabler — Russell

Miranda

Eating disorder

Betsey — Very independent

Depressed (came to America from Germany at age thirteen) — Olga

Sonja

Russell Jr. — Eating disorder

David — Alcoholic; drug addict; "Family Scapegoat"

James Jr. — Alcoholic

James III — Workaholic; "Family Hero"

Alcoholic — James

Susan — "Family Hero"

MY GENOGRAM
In the space below, make your own genogram.

MY LIVING GENOGRAM

In the space provided use the instructions for the Social Atom.

First, locate yourself; then locate your other family members from your genogram the way it feels, the way it existed in your surplus reality.

Use the symbols to represent closeness and distance from you. In deference to Moreno's contribution to the genogram, you may wish to use triangles to represent males and circles for females.

The Living Genogram Narrative

In Russell's *living genogram,* or we might say "feeling genogram," we see not just who the relationships are but how he experienced them, how they felt. "I felt small and on the bottom. Mom was closest and most important but also sort of smothering. My Dad was way far away, I wasn't close to him at all or to his parents (my grandparents). My Mom's parents were close to her and I felt close to them too. My brother James was always the perfect one, but I was fat and uncool. David was always in trouble and Betsey just sort of took care of herself. She just kind of had her own life. It makes me feel less crazy to look at it on paper like this. This is how it felt."

RUSSELL'S LIVING GENOGRAM EXAMPLE

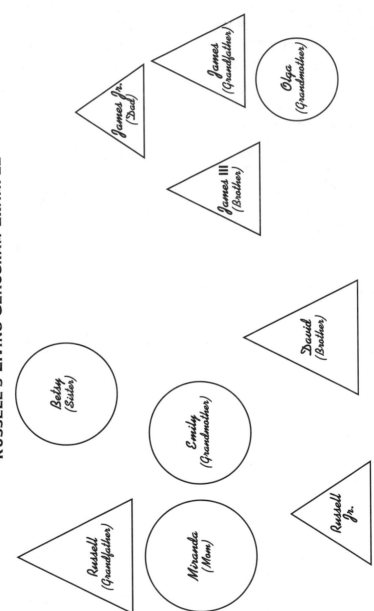

THE TRAUMA TIME LINE

The Trauma Time Line is a paper-and-pencil technique that can be used exclusively as a paper-and-pencil exercise or can also lead to psychodramatic exploration. Clients can identify themes and reenactment dynamics that weave through their time lines and can trace them back to their origins. Patterns of addiction become evident as to where they began and how long-lived they are. Clients are able to identify how traumas may bunch up during a particular period of their lives or, conversely, how certain traumas are cumulative and persisting over long stretches of time.

Part of the task facing any clinician who works with addicts, trauma survivors or family members is to assist in identifying and sharing long-repressed memories and feelings and encouraging the essential grief work. Recovery and healing from both trauma and addiction involves a grief process (Dayton 1997). The losses due to trauma and addiction are multiple and substantial.

The Trauma Time Line helps the client get a handle on how trauma may have affected their overall life pattern and development. This leads to a greater sense of mastery over what can be an overwhelming series of events. The client can identify where there are *open tensions* or *act hungers* throughout the time line. They may identify a *status nascendi* or a time of or before a trauma that changed their lives occurred. The client may also get in touch with periods of happiness or calm in their lives upon which they can build a happy self today. The client can do psychodramatic scenes exploring issues related to any part of the time line to which he or she feels warmed up. The Trauma Time Line is also useful in creating a context so that traumatic events that feel split off can be recontextualized within the client's life span. In this way, working with the Trauma Time Line can be part of the trauma narrative (Herman 1992).

The entire time line can be psychodramatized as a developmental time line across the floor, or parts of it can be enacted in vignettes.

YOUR PERSONAL TIME LINE

Create your own time line by filling in words in the appropriate spaces that express any trauma or loss that you have experienced.

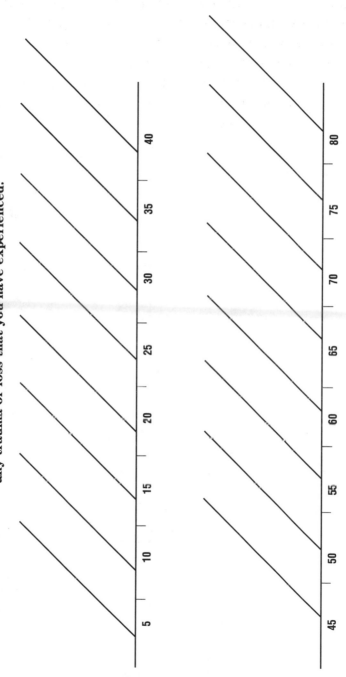

Trauma Time Line —Birth Through 80 Years

Alice's Trauma Time Line (Example)

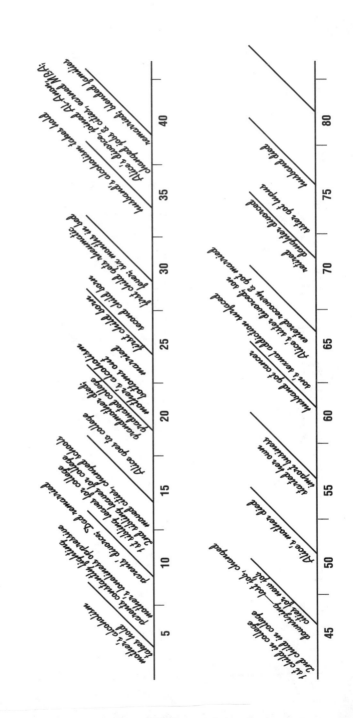

Trauma Time Line Narrative

Alice is a child of an alcoholic. When she was ten, her parents divorced. Her father remarried a woman with two children with whom he involved himself more than his own children. Alice and her two siblings were raised primarily by their alcoholic mother and each other. When her older siblings left for college within two years of each other, Alice felt again abandoned. Her grandmother, who was a powerful surrogate figure and put Alice through college, died before she graduated—another loss containing guilt and sadness that her grandmother could not see her graduate. Sad and alone, Alice fell in love and married someone who felt familiar to her insides, and they had two children. She did not connect the beer in his hand with alcoholism, as that disease had never been openly addressed in her family. Alice eventually joined Al-Anon, left her alcoholic husband, went back to college, remarried and blended her family with her husband's two sons. Much of Alice's life improved through her recovery work. Her awareness of alcohol increased tenfold and she was helpful in steering her children away from it as their father's alcoholism grew worse. However, the underlying trauma in their family system went largely unaddressed. Hence, the children went on to their own trauma re-enactments. The son became a sex addict, and the daughter married a man who was unavailable to her and had multiple affairs.

When Alice saw the trauma of her life laid out on a time line she was able to wrap her mind around her own life and the lives of her children. Themes of trauma and addiction emerged and reenactments became clear. Seeing her life on paper, she began to develop some compassion for herself that helped to lift the shame she had carried most of her life. After a considerable amount of grief work, Alice felt less threatened by hearing her children's pain. Toward the end of her life she was able to use the time line to experience a Life Review (Erikson 1988), through which deep healing took place for herself and her relations.

NOTE: This is a therapist's narrative. Clients can write their own in greater detail after preparing their Trauma Time Line. In this way they can extend their time line into a journaling exercise. They can do this any way they wish to. They can journal in blocks of years, reversing roles with themselves at five, ten, thirty and forty and writing as themselves at that time; as a free-write in the first person; or they can simply write down associations and feelings that come up as they look at their time line. If they feel a need for distance, they can write a story about their lives in the third person. They can also paint a picture or write poetry if they choose.

TRAUMA RESOLUTION MODEL FOR CREATIVE ARTS THERAPIES

The trauma resolution model for creative arts therapists is a grid that any creative arts therapist can fit into her particular discipline as it applies to trauma resolution. The initial model describes how the experiential and arts therapies can offer methods of direct expression, accessing charged emotional material that in a sense bypasses linear thinking. Oftentimes traumatized clients need to experience themselves in a mix of spontaneous outbursts and regressions, to see their own behavior in its concrete form *before* they are able to self-reflect in any meaningful way. Experiential methods can speed up the therapeutic process, which can be either an advantage or a disadvantage depending upon the skill and wisdom of the therapist, the ego-strength of the client and the client's support system.

The model is a guide for the overall sequencing of the experiential approach to healing trauma and resolving the issues associated with it. Experiential therapies offer a variety of ways for clients to come into direct contact with their internal worlds and to concretize them through some form of an expressive arts approach. The distinct advantage of these approaches is their ability to offer alternative ways for clients to connect with and communicate emotions stored in the brain and body that may be difficult to access or talk about in words.

Trauma Model for the Experiential Therapies

1. *Warm up to trauma story.* Use appropriate techniques to warm up the group and help them get in touch with their own story or personal metaphor of their loss or trauma experience.
2. *Enact the story with group witness.* Using whatever experiential therapy is your specialty (i.e., psychodrama, art therapy, drama therapy, music therapy, gestalt therapy), concretize the story experientially with the witness of the group.
3. *Offer corrective experience.* Allow protagonist to recreate a scene as they "wished it had been." This should provide an opportunity to create a corrective "memory" that can be internalized, so that the client

has a blueprint of health to draw from stored within them, and so that the trauma memory is not the only memory.

4. *Separate past from present. Link current behavior or reenactment dynamic to past wound.* Identify the present-day reenactment dynamic that is creating a life problem and link it up to the originating wound, loss or trauma.

5. *Create new narrative/find meaning.* Reintegrate the trauma back into the overall context of life along with newly gained insight and meaning. Begin with the *status nascendi*, or the time of life when the trauma began, and move to the present day. Trauma tends to be "decontextualized" within the self-system. It needs to be reintegrated as part of one's overall life pattern.

TRAUMA RESOLUTION MODEL FOR THE CREATIVE ARTS THERAPIES (DAYTON 1994)

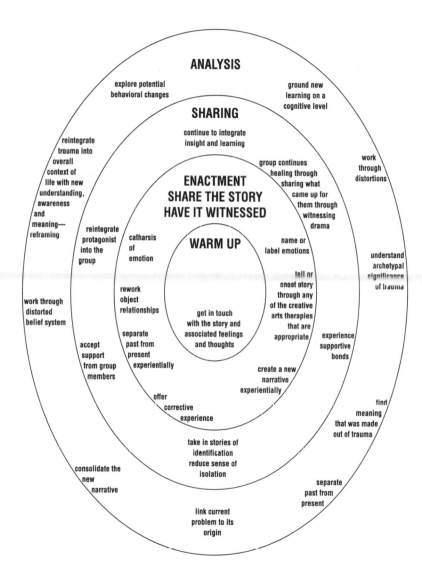

Glossary of Psychodramatic Terms*

act hunger: A deep inner drive that hungers for action and completion, an impulse searching for action.

action sociogram: A social atom put into action.

audience: The members of a psychodramatic group who, while not directly participating in the enactment as auxiliaries, participate internally as spectators who identify with support and *hold* the work.

autodrama: A drama that is enacted without a director; that is, the protagonist chooses the auxiliaries and directs the drama himself.

auxiliary egos: The people playing the characters in a psychodrama other than the protagonist.

*From Tian Dayton, *The Drama Within: Psychodrama and Experiential Therapy,* Health Communications, Inc., 1994.

concretization: The act of giving shape and form to the intrapsychic objects and dynamics of the protagonist.

cultural conserve: According to J. L. Moreno, a once-spontaneous act that has become in some way fixed in the culture, for example, Beethoven's *Fifth Symphony*, or a funeral or a wedding.

de-roling: When auxiliary egos who played roles in the protagonist's drama de-role [e.g., "I am Sondra. I am no longer your mother."].

director: The person directing the psychodramatic action, usually the therapist.

double: The inner voice of the protagonist.

drama game: A structured experiential exercise with a predesigned focus, which can be used as a warm-up or a complete exercise.

enactment: The action phase of psychodrama.

family sculpture: A living picture of a family, in which a protagonist and auxiliary role-players are used.

future projection: A scene that has not actually happened but is anticipated, feared or wished for in the future.

interview: The investigation by a therapist of a protagonist to discover further relevant information about a protagonist or an auxiliary ego.

mirror technique: The employment of a double or stand-in for the protagonist to play him so that he can watch the scene and himself from another perspective, "as if in a mirror" (Moreno 1969).

monodrama: A drama in which there is only one person representing all the parts, along with a director.

multiple auxiliaries: The protagonist may choose to have more than one auxiliary represent a role or a person.

multiple doubles: More than one double may be used for the protagonist or other roles being doubled.

open tensions: Areas within the psyche or self-system that feel unfinished, incomplete or left in a state of anxious closure.

protagonist: The person whose story is being enacted in the psychodrama.

psychodrama: A therapeutic method that uses action and role-playing techniques as therapeutic agents.

reformed auxiliary ego: An auxiliary who, after the conflict or drama has been played out, is offered to the protagonist as the protagonist might wish him to be, that is, in a reformed state.

role analysis: The examination of one role played in life and analyzing it in depth.

role-playing: The acting out of an aspect of the self or of a significant person in one's life within the context of psychodrama.

role reversal: A technique that allows the protagonist to play any role in the drama, in order to see the self from the outside and to experience being in the role of another person; to "stand in the shoes of another."

scene setting: The process that the protagonist goes through in setting the scene for the enactment as he sees it or wishes to have it.

sharing: The portion of psychodrama, after the enactment, in which role-players and auxiliary egos share what comes up for them throughout the enactment.

social atom: The nucleus of people in a person's life that help that person to remain in social balance and connection.

sociometry: The network of connectedness through attractions, repulsions and neutrality that forms the social grid for all social interaction.

soliloquy: The speaking out in the first person of the inner goings-on of the protagonist at any given point in a psychodrama or group process.

spectator catharsis: The catharsis that occurs within an audience or group member as a result of witnessing and identifying with the protagonist's drama.

spectrogram: The allotment of personal values, intensities or definition along a designated line: for example, one-ten, hot-cold or very much–very little.

status nascendi: The point, conflict or situation in one's life out of which a complication grew.

surplus reality: What is carried in the psyche as personal history, which affects the whole of who the person is and how he relates: the intrapsychic personal material that a person carries within the psyche in reference to the self and others pertaining to the self.

tele: The simplest unit of feeling between two people; an unspoken connection, be it positive, negative or neutral.

time regression: Any enactment that represents or concretizes a scene, or a metaphor from the past.

vignette: A small scene enacted with only one or two role-players chosen by the protagonist.

Bibliography

Allen, J., 1996. "The Renfrew Perspective." Summer, 2(2).

American Psychiatric Association. *Diagnostic and Statistical Manual of Mental Disorders,* fourth edition. 1994. Washington, DC: American Psychiatric Association.

Baker-Miller, J., with I. P. Stiver and T. Hooks. 1997. *The Healing Connection.* Boston: Beacon Press.

Blatner, A. 1987. *The Foundation of Psychodrama: History, Theory and Practice.* New York: Springer Publishing Co.

Bowlby, J. 1973. *Attachment and Loss,* Vol. I: *Attachment.* New York: Basic Books, a Division of HarperCollins Publishers.

————. 1973. *Attachment and Loss,* Vol. II: *Separation, Anxiety and Anger.* New York: Basic Books, a Division of HarperCollins Publishers.

————. 1980. *Attachment and Loss*, Vol. III: *Loss, Sadness and Depression*. New York: Basic Books, a Division of HarperCollins Publishers.

Butler, K. 1997. "The Anatomy of Resilience." *Family Therapy Networker*, March/April.

Carnes, P. J. 1997. *The Betrayal Bond*. Deerfield Beach, Fla.: Health Communications, Inc.

Chelston, G., and W. Bonney. *Addiction, Affects and Self-Object Theory*.

Cohen, P. 1999. "The Study of Trauma Graduates at Last." The *New York Times*. (May 8).

Danieli, Y. 1984. "Psychotherapists' Participation in the Conspiracy of Silence About the Holocaust." *Psychoanalytic Psychology*.

Darwin, C. 1969. *The Expression of Emotion in Man and Animals*. Greenwood, Conn.: Greenwood Press.

Dayton, T. 1994. *The Drama Within*. Deerfield Beach, Fla.: Health Communications, Inc.

————. 1997. *Heartwounds*. Deerfield Beach, Fla.: Health Communications, Inc.

De Beauport, E., and A. S. Diaz. 1996. *The Three Faces of Mind*. Wheaton, Ill.: Quest Books, an Imprint of Theosophical Publishing House.

Deutsch, C. 1982. *Broken Bottles, Broken Dreams: Understanding and Helping ACOAs*. New York: New York Teachers College Press.

Eil. 1984. *The Family*. New York: Center for Family Learning.

Erikson, J. M. 1988. *Wisdom and the Senses: The Way to Creativity.* New York: W. W. Norton & Co.

Fitzhenry, R. I. 1993. *The Harper Book of Quotations.* New York: HarperPerennial, a Division of HarperCollins Publishers.

Flannery, R. B. 1986. "The Adult Children of Alcoholics: Are They Trauma Victims with Learned Helplessness?" *Journal of Social Behavior and Personality,* Vol. 1, No. 4.

Fox, J. 1987. *The Essential Moreno.* New York: Springer Publishing Co.

Galsworthy, J. 1996. *Forsyte Saga.* New York: Simon & Schuster.

Gilligan, C. 1993. *In a Different Voice: Psychological Theory & Women's Development.* Cambridge, Mass.: Harvard Univ. Press.

Goleman, D. 1998. *Working with Emotional Intelligence.* New York: Bantam Books.

Grady, D. 1998. "Hardest Habit to Break: Memories of the High." The *New York Times.* (October 27).

Gray, R. M. 1999. *Addictions and the Self: A Self Enhancement Model for Drug Treatment in a Group Setting.* New York: Presentation at NASW and Addiction Conference 1999 at Rutgers University.

Greenspan, S. 1999. *Building Healthy Minds.* New York: Perseus Books.

Grinker, R. R., and J. Speigel. 1985. *Men Under Stress.* New York: Irvington Publishers.

Herman, J. L. 1992. *Trauma and Recovery.* New York: Basic Books, a Division of HarperCollins Publishers.

Hibbard, S. 1987. "The Diagnosis and Treatment of ACOAs as a Specialized Therapeutic Population." *Psychotherapy* (Winter), Vol. 24.

Holmes, J. 1993. *John Bowlby and Attachment Theory.* New York: Routledge.

Horowitz, M. J. 1997. *Stress Response Syndromes.* Northvale, N.J.: Aronson.

Isaacs, K. 1998. *Uses of Emotion.* Westport, Conn.: Praeger Publishers.

Johnson Institute. 1986. *Intervention.* Minneapolis, Minn.

Kalsched, D. 1996. *The Inner World of Trauma.* New York: Routledge.

Kellerman, P. F. 1992. *Focus on Psychodrama.* London: J. Kingsley.

Kleber, R., and D. Brom. 1987. "Psychotherapy and Pathological Grief Controlled Outcome Study." *The Israel Journal of Psychiatry and Related Sciences* 24.

Klein, M. 1940. "Mourning and Its Relation to Manic Depressive States." *The International Journal of Psychoanalysis* 21.

Krystal, H. (Ed.). 1968. *Massive Psychic Trauma.* Madison, Conn.: International Universities Press.

———. 1978. "Trauma and Affects." *The Psychoanalytic Study of the Child* 33.

———. 1984. "Psychoanalytic Views on Human Emotional Damages." *Post-Traumatic Stress Disorder: Psychological and Biological Sequelae.* Washington, D.C.: American Psychiatric Press.

Lacoursiere, R., K. Godfrey, and L. Rubey. 1980. "Traumatic Neurosis in the Etiology of Alcoholism." *American Journal of Psychiatry* 137.

Langone, J. 1985. *The War That Has No Ending.* Discover.

Leshner, A. I. 1998. *Drugs, Minds and Brains.* American Academy of Addiction Psychiatry Ninth Annual Meeting (Winter 1999 Newsletter Insert from the AAAP).

Ledoux, J. 1996. *The Emotional Brain.* New York: Simon & Schuster.

Lifton, R. J. 1964. "On Death and Death Symbolism, the Hiroshima Disaster." *American Psychiatric Journal.*

Lifton, R. 1979. *The Broken Connection.* New York: Simon & Schuster.

Lindemann, E. 1944. "Symptomatology and Management of Acute Grief." *American Psychiatrist.*

Lynch, J. 1985. *The Language of the Heart.* New York: Basic Books, a Division of HarperCollins Publishers.

———. *The Broken Heart, the Psychobiology of Human Contact.* Ornstein & Swencionis.

Marano. 1999. "Depression Beyond Serotonin." *Psychology Today* (March/April).

Marineau, R. F. 1989. *Jacob Levy Moreno 1989–1974:*

Father of Psychodrama, Sociometry and Group Psychotherapy. New York: Tavistock, an Imprint of Routledge.

Marlin, E. 1989. *Genograms: A New Tool for Exploring the Personality, Career and Love Patterns You Inherit.* Chicago: Contemporary Books.

Marty, P., de M'Uzan, M., and David, C. 1963. *L'Investigation Psychosomatique.* Paris: Presses Universitaires de France.

Marty, P. and de M'Uzan, M. 1963. "La Pensée Opératoire." *Revue Française de Psychanalyse* 27.

McDougall, J. 1989. *Theaters of the Body.* New York: W. W. Norton & Co.

McGoldrich, M., and R. Gerson. 1985. *Genograms in Family Assessment.* New York: W. W. Norton & Co.

Middelton-Moz, J. 1993. *After the Tears.* Deerfield Beach, Fla.: Health Communications, Inc.

———. 1999. *Boiling Point.* Deerfield Beach, Fla.: Health Communications, Inc.

Moreno, J. L. 1964. *Psychodrama.* Vol. I. Ambler, Penn.: Beacon House.

———. 1993. *Who Shall Survive.* (Student Edition) Roanoke, Va.: ASGPP, Royal Publishing Co.

Moreno, J. L., and Z. Moreno. 1969. *Psychodrama.* Vol. III. Ambler, Penn.: Beacon House.

Nemiah, J. 1978. "Alexithymia and Psychosomatic Illness." *Journal of Continuing Education in Psychiatry.*

Nemiah, J. and P. Sifneos. 1970. "Affect and Fantasy in Patients with Psychosomatic Disorders." *Modern Trends in Psychosomatic Medicine,* vol. 2. London: Butterworth.

Norden, M. 1995. *Beyond Prozac.* New York: HarperCollins Publishers.

O'Gorman, P. 1994. *Dancing Backwards in High Heels.* Center City, Minn.: Hazelden Educational Materials.

Olsson, P. A. 1989. "Psychodrama and Group Therapy, Approaches to Alexithymia in Group Psychodynamics." *New Paradigms and New Perspective.* D. Halperin, Ed. Chicago: Year Book Medical Publishers.

Olsson P. A., and P. A. Barth. 1983. "New Uses of Psychodrama." *Journal of Operational Psychiatry,* Vol. 14, No. 2.

Ornstein, R., and C. Sweneronis. 1990. *The Healing Brain.* New York: The Guilford Press.

Oschman, J. L., and N. H. Oschman. "Somatic Recall." *Massage Therapy Journal.* Summer 1995.

Pace. 1997. *Psychiatric Times,* (March).

Pendagast, E. G. 1984. *The Family.* New York: Center for Family Learning.

Pennebaker, J. W. 1990. *Opening Up: The Healing Power of Confiding in Others.* New York: The Guilford Press.

Pert, C. 1997. *Molecules of Emotion.* New York: Scribner.

Pert, C., H. Dreher and M. Ruff. 1998. "The Psycho-somatic Network: Foundations of Mind-Body

Medicine." *Alternative Therapies,* (July) Vol. 4, No. 4.

Piaget, J. 1981. "Intelligence and Affectivity: Their Relationship During Child Development." *Annual Reviews.*

Pitman, R. K., et al. 1991. "Psychiatric Complications During Flooding Therapy for Post-Traumatic Stress Disorders." *Journal of Clinical Psychiatry* 52.

Pollock, G. H. 1989. *The Mourning–Liberation Process.* Madison, Conn.: International Universities Press.

Rando, T. A. 1993. *Treatment of Complicated Mourning.* Chicago: Research Press.

Russell, P. 1979. *The Brain Book.* New York: Penguin Books.

Schore, A. N. 1994. *Affect Regulation and the Origin of the Self.* Hillsdale, N.J., and Hove, U.K.: Lawrence Erlbaum Associates Publishers.

Schultz, W., P. Dayan and P. Montague. 1997. "A Neural Substrate of Prediction and Reward." *Science,* Vol. 275, No. 5306.

Seligman, M. 1975. *Helplessness: On Depression, Development, and Death.* San Francisco: Freeman, Cooper & Co.

Shapiro, E. R. 1994. *Grief as a Family Process.* New York: The Guilford Press.

Sifneos, P. 1973. "The Prevalence of Alexithymic Characteristics in Psychosomatic Patients." *Psychotherapy and Psychosomatics* 22.

Sifneos, P. 1975. "Problems of Psychotherapy in Patients

Characteristics and Physical Disease." *Psychotherapy and Psychosomatics* 26.

Skog, S. 1999. *Depression: What Your Body's Trying to Tell You.* New York: Wholecare.

Steiner, C., with P. Perry. 1997. *Achieving Emotional Literacy.* New York: Avon Books.

Tauvon, K. 1998. *The Handbook of Psychodrama.* Principles of Psychodrama. New York: Routledge.

Taylor, G. 1984. "Alexithymia: Concept, Measurement and Implications for Treatment." *American Journal of Psychiatry.* (June) Vol. 14, No. 6.

Van der Kolk, B. 1987. *Psychological Trauma.* Washington, D.C.: American Psychiatric Press, Inc.

———. 1993. "Group Therapy with Traumatic Stress Disorder." *Comprehensive Textbook of Group Psychotherapy.* Kaplan, H., and B. Sadock, Eds. New York: Williams & Wilkins.

———. 1994. *The Body Keeps the Score: Memory and the Evolving Psychobiology of Post-traumatic Stress.* Boston: Harvard Medical School.

Van der Kolk, B., with A. McFarlane and L. Weisauth (Eds.). 1996. *Traumatic Stress: The Effects of Overwhelming Experience on Mind, Body, and Society.* New York: The Guilford Press.

Vaughan, S. C. 1997. *The Talking Cure.* New York: G. P. Putnam's Sons.

Walsh, F. 1998. *Strengthening Family Resilience.* New York: The Guilford Press.

Werner, E. 1989. "Children of the Garden Island." *Scientific American*, April.

————. 1989. "High Risk Children in Young Adulthood: A Longitudinal Study from Birth to 32 Years." *American Journal of Orthopsychiatry* 59.

Williams, R., and V. Williams. 1993. *Anger Kills.* New York: Harper Paperbacks, a Division of HarperCollins Publishers.

Woititz, J. 1980. *Adult Children of Alcoholics.* Deerfield Beach, Fla.: Health Communications, Inc.

Wolin, S. J., and S. Wolin. 1993. *The Resilient Self.* New York: Villard Books, a Division of Random House, Inc.

Yalom, Irvin D. 1970, 1975 and 1985. *The Theory and Practice of Group Psychology.* New York: Basic Books, a Division of HarperCollins Publishers.

Index

A

abreactive catharsis, 296, 351
abuse, 4, 5
acceptance, 71, 204, 227
action memory, 6
addiction. *see also* substance
    abuse
  behavioral, 5
  causes, 8
  characteristics, 7
  dependence stages, 7, 8
  environments. *see*
    environments,
    addictive
  handling trauma, 5
  interference with
    emotional literacy, 43
  leading symptoms, 4
  path to, 5
  personality changes,
    133–134
affective attitudes, 37
age correspondence reaction,
  84–85

alcoholism. *see* substance
  abuse
alexithymia, 111, 132, 149,
  150
Allen, Jon G., 140
amnesia, 120
amygdala, 137, 161
anger, 4
anxiety, 4, 120, 135–136
  disorders, 4
  reduction through
    psychodrama, 345
  triggering, 99
  visceral sensations, 109
atoms, social, 210–220
auxiliary ego, 271
avoidance, 59, 120

B

Baker-Miller, Jean, 60, 61, 71
battle fatigue, 125
bearing witness to pain
  healing process, within,
    202–203

bearing witness to pain *(cont'd)*
  journaling therapy, within,
    225
  narrative, within trauma, 235
Beauport, Elaine de, 112
behaviors
  addictive, 5
  impulsive, 59
  unpredictable, 4
betrayal, 4
bimodal responses to trauma,
  120
black hole, 162, 163, 165
bodymind, 105
bonding, traumatic, 140, 141
boundaries, 70
Bowlby, Jonathan, 118, 138
brain, effect of abuse on, 8
Brain Book, The, 301
Broken Heart, The
    Psychobiology of Human
    Contact, The, 185

C
catharsis, 272, 273, 274, 351
catharsis of integration, 296, 351
cellular memory, 108
childhood trauma. *see also*
    family trauma
  effects on later relationships,
    19
  long-term effects, 12, 13, 14,
    15
  sexual abuse, 246
chronic disconnects, 71, 72–74
chronic phase, 8
codependence, 4
cognitive memory association,
  32
cognitive processing, 35

commitment and trauma
  survivors, 69
communication and trauma
  survivors, 70
concretization, 269, 374
confession, 10
confrontation, effects from, 11,
  14, 15
confusion, 4
constriction, 59, 136, 138
content memory, 6
control attempts, 17, 18
coping strategies, 114–115, 163
corticotropin releasing factor,
  161
CRF. *see* corticotropin releasing
  factor
cycles, reenactment, 141, 142

D
Darwin, Charles, 28, 29
declarative memory failure, 101
defenses, developing
    psychological, 153–156
denial, 1, 153
depression, 4
  endogenous, 4
  psychodrama effect, 345
  reactive, 4
  trauma, 62
  trauma in early life effect,
    136–137
development
  deficits, 4
  neurobiological, 90
  neurochemical, 90
  psychological and emotional,
    89
  tasks, 91
diffusing, 104
disaster syndrome, 132

disconnection, pattern of, 59
disengagement, 59
disorganization, 182, 183, 210
displacement, 155, 156
dissociation, 153, 233, 245
distancer dynamic, 81
distorted reasoning, 144, 145,
   345
Dorman, Ronald, 136–137
doubling technique, 348
dual mental system, 35
dynamics, trauma survivors, 71
dysfunctional defensive
   strategies, development of,
   5
dysfunctional families, 305

E

eating disorders, 4
Ekman, Paul, 31
electrophysical studies, 94
emblems, 31
emotional brain, 111–113
Emotional Brain, The, 28
emotional fitness, 334, 335
emotional literacy
   benefits, 55–56
   childhood, 93–94
   choosing to share with
      others, 46–47
   definition, 42
   demonstration, 50–54
   developmental tasks, 48, 337,
      338
   exploring the meaning and
      function, 45–46
   feeling the power, 43–44
   integration tool, 114
   interference, trauma and
      addiction, 43
   labeling, 44–45

learned process, 54
learned skill, 48, 337
relationships, effect on, 48
role in emotional intelligence,
   339
skills, reapplying, 54
stages, 43–47
emotional memories, 40
emotions
   adaptive behaviors effect, 28
   affective attitudes, 37
   associative process, 32
   cognitive memory association,
      32
   Darwin view, Charles, 28
   denying, 38
   Ekman, Paul, 31
   evolution, 28, 29
   identification of states, 39
   Isaacs, Dr. Kenneth, 32
   learned expressive actions, 28
   Ledoux, Joseph, 28, 29, 31
   literacy, 39
   modulation, 40, 70
   origin, 27
   para emotions, 37
   Plutchick, Robert, 30
   primary emotions, eight, 30
   purpose, 27
   reading, 38
   reference points, creating, 40
   repressing, 38
   storage, 105
   Twelve-Step programs, 36
   understanding our own, 40
enactment, 374
enmeshment, 59, 78
environments
   addictive, 4
   growth-inhibiting, 95

environments *(cont'd)*
   growth-producing, 95
epilepsy research, 33
*Expression of the Emotions in
   Man and Animals,* 28,
   107
expressions in animals and
   humans, facial, 107

F
family, impact of, 303–307
family trauma
   components, 59
   connection difficulties, 60
   depression, 62
   development, child, 60
   disconnected relationships,
      64
   emotional atmosphere, 65–66
   inaccessibility of parents,
      61–62
   isolation, 61
   mutually satisfying
      relationships, 60
   nonmutual relationships, 60
   parentification, 63
   relationships, 60, 69–71
   resolving issues, 64
   resurfacing, 69
   secrecy, 61
   self-in-relation development,
      60
   triggering, 64
   unresolved, 69
family weeks, 318
fear-conditioning experiments,
   29–30
feedback loop, 162
financial burden of addiction,
   societal, 8, 9
flashbacks, 109, 117, 125, 161

Forsyte Saga, 94
Frankl, Viktor, 300
frustration over uncontrollable
   events, 5
fusion, 71, 78, 148, 149

G
genetic predisposition, 127
genogram, living, 353
   adaptation to psychodrama,
      353
   application, 353–354
   benefits, 356
   definition, 353
   exploration questions, 355
   narrative demonstration,
      356–358, 361, 362
Gilligan, Carol, 60
Greenspan, Stanley, 95
grief
   manifestations, 181
   over loss, 177
   resurfacing, 178
   self-medication, 177
   stages, 182–184
   unresolved grief, 177
group therapy, 316–318
growth factors, 105
growth-inhibiting environments,
   95
growth-producing environments,
   95

H
Haley, Sarah, 126
harmful dependence phase, 7
healing process, 188–190
   accepting support, 204
   bearing witness to the pain,
      202
   family impact, 308

journaling. *see* journaling
photographs. *see*
  photographs
stages, 191–192
writing letters, 196–202
Heartwounds, 71
helplessness, learned, 4
Herman, Judith, 103
high-risk activity participation, 5
high-risk behaviors, 151
Hiroshima victims, 138
hyper-reactivity to stimuli, 120
hypervigilance, 41, 71, 80, 136,
  146

I
idealization, 154
identification flipping, 88
illiteracy, emotional, 49, 50–54
illiterate, emotional, 20
illustrators, 31
impulsive behavior, 59
inaccessibility of parents, 61–62
indicators, losing access, 21, 22
infant brain development, 95
infant/mother relationship,
  90–91
information substances, 105
inhibition
  childhood abuse, 14
  confrontation, effects from,
    11, 14, 15
  effects, 10, 11, 15
  influences, 11
inner world, disorganized,
  138–140
intellectualization, 153, 154
interpersonal costs of addiction,
  8
interview technique, 349
intimacy

emotional literacy
  connection, 48–49
  relationship, effects of trauma
    and, 12, 13
  trauma survivors, and, 69
Isaacs, Dr. Kenneth, 32, 35, 37
isolation, 61, 185, 187

J
journaling, 223, 224–233

L
learned helplessness, 4, 134–135
Ledoux, Joseph, 28, 29, 31
ligands, 104–105
limbic brain. *see* emotional brain
linking, 244
  behavior to trauma, 204, 205
  journaling therapy, within,
    230
Littleton, Colorado, 3
Lynch, James J., 185

M
Maslow, Abraham, 318
medication, 321
medication, self, 8, 19, 20, 24,
  156, 177, 345
meditation, 323, 324
memories
  accessing, 39
  action, 6
  content, 6
  editing, 113–115, 119–120
  emotional, 40
  storage, 100, 108, 117, 341
  trauma, 5, 161, 233
  triggering, 101, 102
  types, 6
  unconscious childhood, 83, 84
memory, cellular, 5
memory, somatic, 109

mental functioning concepts,
109–111
mental setting, 299–302
Minnesota Multiphasic
Personality Inventory, 82
mirror technique, 375
modulation, 70, 136, 142–143,
277
modules, 27
mood management, 18
Moreno, J. L., 5, 6, 85, 150, 166,
211, 316, 317, 342, 346
Moreno, Zerka, 6, 321, 342

N
natural disaster victims and
Post-Traumatic Stress
Disorder, 127
nature and nurture relationship,
89–90
neuropeptides, 105, 106
neurotransmitters, 104, 105, 108
nightmares, 109
numbing, 21, 136, 182
emotional, 149, 150
losing access to indicators,
21, 22
phase, 17
psychic, 120–121
suffering, 138
nurture and nature relationship,
89–90

O
object relations, 346
one-to-one therapy, 315–316
onset phase, 7
Opening Up, 10
open-tension system, 268
operational exhaustion, 125
Operation Phoenix, 126

operatory thinking, 110
opiate receptor, 103, 104
Overeaters Anonymous, 275,
280

P
panic, visceral sensations, 109
para emotions, 37
parentification, 63
Pennebaker, James, 10, 44, 112,
113
Pennifield, Wilder, 33
peptides, 105
perceptions, 296, 346
perceptual defenses, 119
perfectionism, 71
personality, preexisting, 128
personality changes, 133–134
Pert, Candace, 6, 103, 105, 108,
112
photographs, 251, 252–262
physiological arousal, 161, 233
Piaget, Jean, 92
Plutchick, Robert, 30
Post-Traumatic Stress Disorder
black hole. see black hole
childhood experiences, 131
declarative memory failure,
101
diagnosis difficulties, 132–133
diagnostic criteria, 22
emotional signals, losing, 121
natural disaster victims, 127
self-medicate, desire to, 131
Vietnam veterans, 125–127,
128, 129
presymptomatic phase, 7
processing phase, 274
processing trauma, 4
projection, 154–155
protest phase, 17

psychic numbing, 120–121
psychodrama, 5, 6, 33, 319–320, 375
  auxiliary ego, 271
  catharsis, 272, 273, 274
  concretization, 269
  demonstration, 267–275
  demonstration, Overeaters Addiction, 275–286
  development, 342
  elements, 342
  healing tool, 265, 266
  open-tension systems, 268
  processing phase, 274
  reality, surplus, 269
  reconstructive experiences, 350–352
  resolving traumatic issues, 344–345
  role reversal, 280
  roles and basic elements, 347, 348
  techniques, 348–350
  trauma, addressing, 343, 344
  treatment uses, 341–342
  unstructured warm-up, 267
psychodramatic trance, 270–271
psychosomatic illness, 109–111
psychosomatic symptoms, 4
psychotherapy, body, 6
psychotic episodes, 4
pursuer dynamic, 81

R
reaction formation, 86
realities, dry one, 209
realities, wet one, 209
reality, surplus, 269
reality check, 190
recall experiences, 106
reconstructive scene, 350, 351

reenactment, 71
  cycles, 141, 142
  dynamics, 41
  exploring through psychodrama, 346
  relationships, within, 74–75
re-experiencing effects, 22, 23
reformed auxiliary technique, 350
reframing, 114, 188, 298
regression, time, 378
relationships' role in predicting longevity, 186
reorganization, 182, 184
repression, 154
resilience, 289, 291
  building, 297–298
  creating, 303
  family, impact of, 303–304
  impact on risk factors, 300
  learnedness, 294, 295
  primate study, 290
  reframing, 298
  resilience mandala, 294
  self-destructive patterns, 292
  undermining, 295
resilience mandala, 294
Resilient Self, The, 292
resolution model, trauma, 368–370, 371
response factors, trauma, 127–128
rigid defense systems, 5
risk factor identification, 289
risk factors for drug abuse, 8
road to recovery, 324–329
role, 85
  analysis, 376
  creation, 86
  observations, 6

role *(cont'd)*
    playing, 85, 319–320, 376
    reversal, 270, 349, 376
    stages, 85–86
    taking, 85
roving ISMs, 9–10
Russell, Peter, 301

s

scene setting, 376
Schmitt, Francis, 105
scientific study of PTSD, 5
searching, 182
secrecy, 61, 126, 252–262
selection processes, memory,
    118
self-destructive patterns, 292
self-emergence, 85
self-image distortions, 4
self-in-relation development, 60
self-soothe, 91, 135, 279
self-test, trauma, 157–158
sensations, visceral, 109
sensation-seeking, 8
separating past from present,
    206
    journaling therapy, within,
        231
    narrative, within trauma, 238,
        244
sexual abuse, resolving
    childhood, 246
sharing, 376
shell-shock, 125
silence, costs of, 10, 11
Skog, Susan, 137
sleep disturbances, 4
social atoms. *see* atoms, social
sociometry, 65, 376
soliloquy, 377
soma sensory level, 101

somatic memory, 109
somatization, 6, 111, 346
spectrogram, 377
Spielrein, Mme., 91
spiraling technique, 348
splitting, 71, 78, 79, 154
spontaneity, 150, 352
stand-in technique, 349
status nascendi, 377
steroids, 105
Stewart, Dr. Jane, 161
Stone Center, 60
substance abuse
    characteristics, 7
    chronic phase, 8
    control attempts, 17, 18
    dependence stages, 7, 8
    doubting reality, 41
    emotional responses, 41
    expenses, emotional, 18
    mood management, 18
    nature, 4
    occurrence statistics, 7
    onset phase, 7
    presymptomatic phase, 7
    risk factors, 8
    statistics, 313
support, loss of ability of
    accepting, 147, 148
survival guilt, 151, 152, 153
survivors, trauma, 209
    adoption of dysfunctional
        relationship styles,
        119–120
    dynamics, 71
    relationships, effect on later,
        69–71
symptoms
    psychosomatic, 4
    trauma, 4

syndromes, clinical, 4
systems
    addictive, 4
    rigid defense, 5

T

talking about trauma, 3, 38, 67
    avoidance and its effects, 41
    effect on symptoms, 38, 39
    healing traumatic emotional
        memories, 40
tension, chronic, 4
transference, 71, 75–77, 165,
    167
    addiction, 9, 10
    definition, 165
    demonstration, 167–171
    experiences, 166
    reaction, 165
    relationships, early, 172
    responses, conditioned fear,
        171
    triggering effect in later
        relationships, 172–173
trauma
    addiction, path to, 5
    childhood. see childhood
        trauma
    dynamics of trauma survivors,
        71
    families, see family trauma
    handling, 5
    interference with emotional
        literacy, 43
    life adaptations after, 23
    memory storage, and, 109
    origins, 3
    personality changes, 133–134
    physical effects, 99, 100
    response factors, 127–128
    self-test, 157–158

somatization association, 6
symptoms, 24
talking. see talking about
    trauma
uncontrollable. see
    uncontrollable trauma
Trauma and Recovery, 103
trauma resolution model. see
    resolution model, trauma
trauma time line, 267, 363
    application, 363, 364
    demonstration, 365–366
    narrative demonstration, 367,
        368
    treatment, 314. see also specific
        forms of treatment
    components, 314–315
    family weeks, 318
    group therapy, 316–318
    medication. see medication
    meditation, 323, 324
    one-to-one therapy, 315–316
    psychodrama. see
        psychodrama
    Twelve-Step programs,
        321–323
triangulation, 86
triggering, 71, 84
    emotional, 143, 144
    healing process, during, 188
    life, during, 188
    narrative, within trauma,
        236–238
    psychodrama, within, 345
trust, losing, 145, 146
Twelve-Step program, 36, 132,
    164, 190, 298, 299, 301,
    302, 321–323
two-hundred-mile rule, 292

U

unconscious childhood memory,
    83, 84
unconscious experiences' role in
    later experiences, 116
uncontrollable trauma,
    psychological response, 17
unstructured warm-up, 267
Use of Emotion, 32

V

Van der Kolk, Bessel, 17, 20, 101
Vaughan, Susan, 34
Vietnam veterans and Post-
    Traumatic Stress Disorder,
    125–127, 128, 129

vignette, 378
visceral sensations, 109
visual images, 109

W

Walsh, Frome, 297
Werner, Emmy, 290, 293
withdrawal, 78
witness, 190
Wolin, Steven, 291, 292, 293,
    294
Wolin, Sybil, 291
writing letter for healing
    process, 196–202

Y

yearning, 182, 183

About the Author ————————————

Tian Dayton, Ph.D., T.E.P., has a doctoral degree in clinical psychology and a master's degree in educational psychology. She is the Director of Program Development and Staff Training at the Caron Foundation in Wernersville, Pennsylvania, and New York City. Dayton is a fellow and certified trainer of the American Society for Psychodrama, Sociometry and Group Psychotherapy, and was a faculty member of New York University from 1991–1999. She offers psychodrama training and is a therapist in private practice in New York City. Dayton is also the author of many books, including *Drama Games; The Drama Within; Daily Affirmations for Parents; Daily Affirmations for Forgiving and Moving On; Keeping Love Alive; The Quiet Voice of the Soul; The Soul's Companion; Heartwounds* and the forthcoming *It's My Life.* She has been a national speaker and guest expert on radio, television and the Internet.

For further information on psychodrama training or therapy, contact:

Tian Dayton
262 Central Park West
Suite 4A
New York, NY 10024

For further information on treatment for trauma and addiction issues, contact:

Caron Family Services
Box A
Galen Hall Road
Wernersville, PA 19565
phone: (800) 678-2332
Web site: *www.caron.org*